STUDIES IN EDUCATION/POLITICS
(VOL. 1)

THE POLITICS
OF EDUCATORS'
WORK AND LIVES

GARLAND REFERENCE LIBRARY
OF SOCIAL SCIENCE
(VOL. 915)

STUDIES IN EDUCATION/POLITICS

GENERAL EDITOR: MARK B. GINSBURG

**THE POLITICS OF EDUCATORS'
WORK AND LIVES**
edited by Mark B. Ginsburg

THE POLITICS
OF EDUCATORS'
WORK AND LIVES

Edited by
Mark B. Ginsburg

GARLAND PUBLISHING, Inc.
New York & London / 1995

Library of Congress Cataloging-in-Publication Data

The politics of educators' work and lives / edited by Mark B.
Ginsburg
     p. cm. — (Garland reference library of social science ; vol.
915. Studies in education/politics ; v. 1)
  Includes bibliographical references and index.
  ISBN 0-8153-1435-3 (hardcover, alk. paper)
  0-8153-1923-1 (pbk.)
  1. Teachers—Political activity. 2. College teachers—Political
activity. 3. Politics and education. I. Ginsburg, Mark B.
II. Series: Garland reference library of social science ; v. 915.
III. Series: Garland reference library of social science. Studies in
education/politics ; vol. 1.
LB2844.1.P6P65 1995
371.1'04—dc20   94-13184

Paperback cover design by Patti Hefner

Printed on acid-free, 250-year-life paper
Manufactured in the United States of America

Dedication

This volume draws on the individual and collective efforts of educators throughout history and around the world. The political dimension of their work and lives has not always been acknowledged or recognized, but whether active or passive in form, whether in classrooms or communities as locales of struggle, whether conservative or change-oriented in purpose, or serving the interests of dominant or subordinate groups, educators' actions have been and will continue to be significant. Thus, we cannot afford to ignore the conditions, processes, and implications of educators' work and lives.

That there is a political dimension to educators' work and lives means that their efforts are not neutral; they are conditioned by and have implications for the distribution of power and material and symbolic resources. This book as a product of educators' work and lives is no exception. Both in its content focus and as an example of scholarly activity of educators, this volume signals how educators are political.

Given the political stance of at least myself as editor of this volume, therefore, I especially want to dedicate this book to past, present, and future educators who in their work and lives have struggled on the side of the exploited, immiserated, oppressed, subjugated, and dehumanized. Presumably, this would include most educators at least in relation to some aspects of their work and lives, though I believe that up to the present only a small number of educators have lived up to this ideal most of the time.

One collective example of such educators is the Boston Women's Teachers' Group, Inc. (P. O. Box 169, West Somerville, Massachusetts, 02144, USA), which publishes the journal *Radical Teacher: A Socialist and Feminist Journal on the Theory and Practice of*

Teaching. Because the members of this group—and the other educators whose voices are amplified through this journal—exemplify one version of this ideal, the volume editor's and authors' royalties obtained from the publication of this volume will be given to the Boston Women's Teachers' Group to facilitate their efforts and to encourage other educators to develop further their involvement in progressive social struggles.

Contents

Series Preface

This series features researched-based monographs and edited volumes that examine from historical and contemporary points of view the political dynamics of education. The series focuses on the dialectical relationship between education and the struggle over the distribution of symbolic and material resources and the use of power to control the means of producing, reproducing, consuming, and accumulating these resources.

Politics of and through education involves the activities of teachers, students, administrators, staff, parents, government officials, and other citizens in classrooms, schools, universities, education systems—and in local, national, and global communities.

Books in this series focus on dynamics in the United States as well as develop comparative and international perspectives with the United States as one of the prominent cases. Particular attention is given to individual and collective political work of educators that reinforces, challenges, or transforms existing class, gender, racial/ethnic, or international relations.

Mark B. Ginsburg

Recapturing the Political Dimension

Maxine Greene

Tony Kushner's *Perestroika*, the second part of his *Angels in America* (that "Gay Fantasia on National Themes"), begins when an old blind man comes on an empty stage. He introduces himself as "the World's Oldest Living Bolshevik" and, as a red banner appears behind him, he asks how the world is going to live without a grand theory. He recalls the comprehensive certainties of an earlier time that were consequences of that theory, and he wonders how human beings can survive. There was, he laments, "the grandeur of the prospect we gazed upon: like standing atop the highest peak in the mighty Caucasus, and viewing in one all-knowing glance the mountainous, granite order of creation." And then he asks what the children of this theory have to offer in its place. "Market incentives? American Cheeseburgers? Watered-down Bukharinite stopgap makeshift Capitalism! NEPmen! Pygmy children of a gigantic race!" (Kushner 1994, p. 14).

Seeing that play not long ago, more nostalgic for ideologies than for angels, I thought about the changes for the better that might reasonably be sought in time to come. I thought about how my sense of a project is linked to a notion of change, a vision of "a better state of things" (Sartre 1956, p. 435). My very notion of teaching is affected by Sartre's suggestion that we only notice what is seriously deficient in our world when we are able to shape a vision of possibility. This always seemed to me fundamental to a political view of things, especially since the noticing depends upon active dialogue among those with diverse vantage points, diverse situations in the world. To speak with people sharing precisely the same perspective is, more often than not, to see a seamless pattern of things, what is taken for granted as "normal." Blind to the gaps, the torn places, the perceiver is not moved to thoughts of something better, something whole. Taking what is regarded as a neutral view, she/he is convinced it is a view of "the way things are." Why question, then? Why learn? Why reach beyond?

It happens that I came to teacher education relatively late in my life, ten years after undergraduate school. My memories of growing up are interlaced with images of the persisting economic depression and of an upsurging fascism in Europe. My father sent me to Europe "on business" when I was a teenager, and I happened to meet people deeply involved with the Spanish Republic suffering the Franco offensive and the civilian bombings that accompanied it. The letters on their posters seemed written on the sky: "Libertad." Later, when I was doing odd (and ardent) jobs for the so-called Loyalist Embassy in Paris, the writing on the sky extended to "Liberté, Egalité, Fraternité." They were the peaks on my Caucasus; but they were peaks still to be climbed. I wanted at that time to spend my whole life provoking others to see what I saw and to grasp "the order of Creation" before it was too late.

World War II began; I graduated, eloped, had a baby, began editing a newspaper for the American Labor Party. Later, I made streetcorner speeches instructing very thin multitudes on the Dumbarton Oaks Conference and the founding of the United Nations, which (as the song said) heralded "a brave new world." But this was before Hiroshima and Nagasaki; and we agonized about how much there still had to be done morally and politically once we began hearing about what happened at Los Alamos, once we saw the pictures of the destruction in Japan.

My sense of outrage has always been in some manner mediated by and intensified by works of art. Even now, I think of Picasso's *Guernica*, of Henry Moore's drawings of people in bomb shelters, of the children's art work at Teresin, of the film *Night and Fog*. And I reread Galway Kinnell's "The Fundamental Project of Technology," telling of the museum at Hiroshima: the

glass dishes changed in color, the empty eye glass frames, a skull
bone fused to the inside of a helmet. Then:

> An old man, possibly a soldier back then, now reduced
> down to one who soon will die, sucks at the cigarette
> dangling from his lip, peers at the uniform, scorched, of
> some tiniest schoolboy, signs out bluish mists of his own
> ashes over a pressed tin lunch box well crushed back then
> when the word *future* first learned, in a white flash, to jerk
> tears. (Kinnell 1985, p. 47)

How could anyone dare to be neutral in the face of something
like that?

A peace movement began to take shape, of course, in the
face of an increasingly demonized Soviet Union and *its* atom
bomb. Many of us believed that mass marches of decent people,
orderly protests, along with individual witnesses would
somehow expose the chauvinism of the "iron curtain" and lead
in time to unilateral disarmament on the part of a guilt-
shadowed United States. We had no way of anticipating the Un-
American Activities Committee, the McCarthy hearings, the
Rosenberg case. We, who remained radical or progressive, were
in some odd fashion innocents. We did not confront the history
of paranoia and persecution in this country, reaching back
through the Roosevelt period to the Palmer Raids after the First
World War, back through the centuries to the Alien and Sedition
Acts. Like the progressives at the beginning of this century, we
believed that intelligence, honest communication, hypothetical
thinking, and (of course) education would counter small-
mindedness, prejudice, and even greed.

It was in 1950 or so that I decided to go to graduate school.
I had written two almost-published novels, one of them on the
pre-Jeffersonian period, the Democratic Societies, and (yes) the
Alien and Sedition Acts; the other on the WPA Arts Projects, on
discriminated-against Black women artists, and on the Spanish
Civil War. I had another child by then; but I felt like a failure
with too much energy bottled up in me, too many
dissatisfactions, too many unfulfilled dreams.

I had heard of, but not known directly, Teachers College
(Columbia University) brand of liberalism, which I associated
with a politically progressive approach to education. The great

names of Teachers College—Counts, Childs, Rugg, Watson, Dewey—were for many of us somehow linked to the high moments of the New Deal. That meant (at least for me) the WPA programs, the post office murals, the youth administration, the Civilian Conservation Corps, the theatre, the Wagner Act, the Tennessee Valley Authority (T.V.A.)—all the benevolent government interventions people said were intended to "prime the pump of capitalism." Whether or not, the memories and associations made me think of public education as one dimension of that New Deal sweep of reform.

New York University (NYU) opened its doors first to me; but I thought I found the same spirit in the courses in history and philosophy of education I took at the start. One notable course was taught by three professors: George Axtelle, Theodore Brameld, and Adolphe Meyer. Although I had minored in philosophy and majored in American history at Barnard College, I knew nothing of John Dewey nor of his contributions to democratic thought and democratic educational theory. Axtelle was an impassioned interpreter of Dewey's works, especially when it came to democratic values and to Dewey's conception of the individual; and, for a brief period, I experienced an almost religious commitment to experimentalism and all that it implied. Brameld, however, had termed himself a "reconstructionist," opposing an overly individualist emphasis and, as well, the preoccupation with process and ongoing growth that marked the Deweyan point of view. For me, the two were engaged in a political contest: Axtelle found his ancestry in Emerson, Thoreau, and William James; Brameld found his in Rousseau, Marx, Freud, Kurt Lewin, and those he called proponents of the "group mind." Axtelle, in Deweyan tones, spoke of democracy as a community always in the making; Brameld called for "cultural blueprints" and a "design for America." I read the history of American education very much in terms of the tension between individualism and a kind of communalism; and I heard echoes of that in the disagreements between Axtelle and Brameld.

Perhaps oddly, they joined forces in opposing what they thought of as "essentialism" in education, or the neo-Thomism of Robert Hutchins, or any point of view oriented to conservation rather than to the direction of change. If asked, they would not have identified themselves as political actors in the contemporary sense of being concerned with power relations. Certainly, neither ever took note of the influence of patriarchy; nor did either one pay serious heed to racism and related forms of domination. I recall publishing an article in *The Educational Forum* six years after I was awarded my doctorate. It was called "The Teacher and the Negro Child: 'Invisibility' in the School" (Greene 1965), and I can only recall extreme disinterest on the part of my mentors at NYU.

Impatient with what I saw as a cool gradualism in Dewey (and an absence of the tragic sense of life), somewhat unnerved by the talk of "group mind" in Brameld's work, I found myself responding very strongly to Jean-Paul Sartre, when I began reading him in a seminar initiated, it so happened, by Brameld. Sartre's conception of freedom and commitment seemed to me to be focal to the political role necessarily played by teachers. His notion of "praxis" and the project still seems to me to have great significance for our efforts to arouse teachers to confront their own political beings. The human being, wrote Sartre (1963, p. 91), is characterized above all by her/his "going beyond a situation, and by what he succeeds in making of what he has been made. This going beyond is what we find at the very root of the human—*in need*." Then he talked about how behavior so often responds to scarcity, or lack, or deficiency, how it must be "determined both in relation to the real and present factors which condition it and in relation to a present object, still to come, which it is trying to bring into being. This is what we call the project" (1963, p. 91).

When I first read Sartre and began noticing his stress on the connection between repairing deficiency, responding to need or to lack, and the securing of values, I thought I saw enormous relevance for a conception of educational philosophy as well as teaching. To "do philosophy" for me means responding to crucial questions having to do with social life, relationships, and the distribution of power. Without the consciousness of a gap between what is and what should be, problem-posing is likely to become purely analytical and abstract. Without an awareness of situatedness and lived experience, people are unlikely to ask the kinds of questions grounded in actuality, shaped by existential vantage points. Nor are they likely to concern themselves with the political sphere, with bringing into being a community that is rational, just, and humane.

Teaching, as I began to understand it, involves creating conditions in which teachers and learners both are provoked to construct, through shared inquiry and imaginative explorations, a range of meanings. Involved in such an effort are multiple processes of learning to learn; what follows ought to be a conception of what Dewey called "an articulate public" (1954, p. 184) and of a sustaining, multivocal community in which diverse persons are free to be. This means that they become increasingly conscious in the sense of reaching beyond where they are to different places, where they can renew, repair, and transform.

As I saw it, the barriers between private and public had to be overcome if this were to happen. Human beings had to be enabled, from their own locations and in the light of their own narratives, to bring into being what Hannah Arendt called an "in-between" (1958, p. 182). This meant that the pressures of old bureaucracies had to be resisted. It meant as well that those committed to the welfare and the journeys of young people had to gain the power to work *with* the young and on their behalf.

Because this led me to an interest in the way adults and the young carried the institutions within them and experienced them, I turned rather early to the work of Maurice Merleau-Ponty and, particularly, what he was writing about freedom. He said, for instance, that there is "free choice only if freedom comes into play in its decision, and posits the situation chosen as a situation of freedom. . . . The very notion of freedom demands that our decision should plunge into the future, that something should have been *done* by it" (1967, p. 437). Education, after all, has to do with time and futuring, and surely it has to do with something being done by and through acts of freedom. Viewed in that fashion, education can never be neutral. Positing certain kinds of obstacles blocking the realization of commitment, we need to realize that we—in the field of freedom we have projected—have constituted them as obstacles, and that we are free to make our way by climbing over them and (by doing so) transforming the world. We always, wrote Merleau-Ponty, have "the power to interrupt" what appears to be an inevitable movement; and this implies "a power to begin" (p. 438). Again, all this relates to the way we are in the world, the way we perceive the world in our intersubjectivity. A great deal depends on our awareness of being a worker or a bourgeois, a teacher-clerk or a professional. Our identifying of ourselves is done by means of an "implicit or existential project which merges into our way of patterning the world and co-existing with other people" (p. 447).

For me, and very possibly for Merleau-Ponty, that project is essentially a political one. We can pattern the world as technocratic, manipulative, and oppressive and see our students, in consequence, as mere functionaries-in-the-making, human resources to be molded in accord with the needs of the state. Or we can pattern the world as loosely knit with openings for interruptions and beginnings, for making a difference in what lies around.

When I was in graduate school and in the decade ending with the 1960s, numbers of teachers seemed to be choosing themselves as workers as they sought power through organizing trade unions, in the United States in both the American Federation of Teachers (AFT) and the National Education Association (NEA). Early on, it looked as if the turning to the unions was an aspect, for many, of the social activism of the period. Joining the AFT when I was at Brooklyn College, I was very aware of the hierarchical nature of the educational institution. Experiencing Brooklyn College that way and, somewhat indirectly, experiencing the New York schools that way when I worked with student teachers, I found it to be obvious that a life as a public employee was quite different from teaching lived as a "calling" by the largely female forces that came before. A clear need seemed to emerge for an identification *against* institutions that controlled and manipulated in the interests of forces outside.

Of course there were some who, in the 1960s, identified their commitment to social causes (the end of racism, the expansion of human rights, programs that might diminish terrible poverty) with the work of the trade unions; and teachers unions here and there did move beyond salary, hiring, and tenure issues. But then, of course, I remember the Ocean Hill-

Brownsville debacle in Brooklyn, New York, where the teachers' union came into conflict with the black community who were experimenting with decentralized, local community control of the schools their children attended (see Berube and Gittell 1969). The choices we made with respect to it were political; and, if you felt yourself to be allied to public education on any level, you found it impossible to be neutral. On the one hand, there were the old (and honored) traditions of civil service, of centralization, of professional policy-making. On the other, there was the voice of the local community and of the long-silenced minorities. It is hard to forget the upsurge of anti-Semitism (many of the teachers were Jewish) in the course of the struggle, even as it is difficult to forget the fearsome epithets, the humiliations still distorting much treatment of Blacks in the fourteen years following the 1954 *Brown v. Board of Education* decision by the U.S. Supreme Court and the associated struggles to desegregate racially Southern schools.

Of course, the climax of the fight about decentralization in New York came in the spring of 1968; and, like many of my colleagues, I held enduring memories from 1963 of going to Washington for the Civil Rights march, of hearing the "I have a dream" speech, of trying to do my political share of work for equal rights at home. Convinced as I was that a decent professor of any subject had to take sides, at least in the name of peace and civil rights, I remember being somewhat involved in establishing the so-called "Free Schools" in Harlem during the teachers' strike that year. I recall buttoning many children's sweaters during a brief, informal tenure as principal of one of those schools. All I know now is that, in the face of the stories and pictures coming out of the South, in the face of the new knowledge regarding inequities where schools and facilities were concerned, the pull of the Civil Rights movement and, yes, the student protest movements was irresistible.

I can, a quarter of a century later, list the deficiencies of the protest movements and even the peace movement that involved me so profoundly for so long: the lack of ideology, the influence of various anarchies, the spurts of unforgivable violence. I return now and then to Norman Mailer's (1968) *The Armies of the Night* to recapture the passion of the protests against the war in

Vietnam, the new questions being posed with respect to the country and its past and future, the metaphor of childbirth and the dreadful uncertainty about what finally would emerge.

There were the half desperate attempts to convince faculty members that the Vietnam War, like the uprisings in the slums, was indeed the business of the academic community. I remember the horrors and the high moments of the Columbia University "revolution" in 1968, speeches I made and friends made, the feeling we had that the old structures (like the statue of Alma Mater on the campus) would be put to new uses. Whatever "service" Teachers College offered to the military-industrial complex would be exposed. There would finally be the "Great Community" Dewey (1954) had described emergent from the endless conversations, the unending dialogues that marked the time. But there were the assassinations (e.g., Martin Luther King and Robert Kennedy). There were Kent State and Jackson State, where students were shot and killed by soldiers called upon to police campus protests. There were the troubling worries that our concerns and preoccupations were middle-class concerns and preoccupations, that we were not attending to the working class (to which some of us had yearned to belong when we were growing up) or to the disinherited, or even to the Blacks who had taught us so much.

When I look back now, I realize that we have, in our search for political actors, often overlooked the remarkable Afro-American women and the educational work they performed, the political work they did in schools and around the schools in the South and the North. I think now, with more than a little dismay at my own blindness, of my presidential address at the Philosophy of Education Society in the late 1960s. I called it "Morals, Ideology and the Schools: A Foray into the Politics of Education" (Greene 1967), and it involved a plea to educational philosophers to confront the effects of the war in Vietnam and racial discrimination on their own thinking as well as on the schools. It was a warranted enough charge to my fellow and sister philosophers; but it did not take into account the stubborn, often desperately courageous work already going on in schools and colleges by members of cultures long thought of as "cultures of silence" (as Paulo Freire [1970] would put it). It has taken the work of Michele Foster (1990), Gloria Ladson-Billings (1990), Joyce King (1990), and, lately, the summary work of Kathleen Casey (1993) to remind me of the diverse forms political action can take. Perhaps more importantly, these women and many others by now have made me wary of what Freire called "malefic generosity," or what he described as the belief that those converted from being among the oppressors believe "because of their background . . . that they must be the executors of the transformation. They talk about the people, but they do not trust them" (1970, p. 46).

Thinking back, particularly to the 1980s, I realize what a righteous pleasure so many of us took in taking a position antagonistic to the Reaganites, to the greed, to the mystifications in what Ira Shor, among others, termed "the restoration of the right" (1986). Most important for a reexamination of my own assumptions was the discovery of the texts associated with the Frankfurt School and what we learned to call "critical theory": the works of Adorno and Horkheimer (1972), of Marcuse (1966, 1968), of Walter Benjamin (1969), and—climactically, for many of us—of Jurgen Habermas (1970, 1971, 1973, 1987). It ought to be said that Henry Giroux (1988) and his associates (sometimes with the inspiration of Paulo Freire or the work of Antonio Gramsci) did a good deal to make the Frankfurt School writings accessible to educators and applicable to classrooms.

In my case, it was the original immersion in Marxist thought and the political action it entailed, along with the confrontation with the phenomena of consciousness, dread, and existential freedom that drew me towards critical theory. I was aware, however, that Adorno, Benjamin, Habermas, and the others were writing against very different lived biographies than ours. Not only had they been intimately affected by the Holocaust. They had lived through, with an immediacy unknown to us, the disillusionment and heartbreak due to the disclosures of what Soviet "communism" actually meant. Our history, though linked with theirs, was different. Our forefathers and foremothers were different. In the 1980s, I felt compelled to reenter Black history and Jewish history, along with the narratives of the many newcomers to this country. And, yes, perhaps belatedly, I abruptly became aware of feminist thought in what might be called its second or third phase. It had never been difficult to champion the cause of equal rights for women in this country. I must admit, however, that it was not near enough the surface of my consciousness to make me realize the ways in which my own rights had been ignored, my opportunities narrowed because of my gender. There were many years in which, for all my specialization in philosophy, I was thrust into departments of English or English Education because of my hostility to analytic philosophy, my interest in imagination, my ostensibly "private" focus on what was called "subjectivity." In a more or less typical female response, I thought I was not rigorous enough or systematic enough or bright enough to do what was expected of me; and, for many years, I complied (at least on the surface) with others' judgments. It was the second phase of feminism that awakened me, I believe. I mean the discovery of a "different voice" (Gilligan, 1981), the history of women's confinement to the "private" sphere, the internalization of men's infantilizing or object-making images of what we were.

I did not experience my election into the presidency of the American Educational Research Association (1981–82) as a political triumph, for all the fact that I was the first woman president in (I was told) thirty-one years. I did know enough to accept the nomination in the face of the nominating committee chair's reassurance that I would never be elected. It seems to me that I did find a voice through that experience and all the encounters it made possible (including those "on the Hill"). To be a political actor meant that I could integrate, at last, the subjective and objective, infuse the public space with what had so long been excluded as private (domestic, weak-minded, "soft"), open classrooms to passion and imagination as well as to open cognitive capacities, to reflection, to good habits of mind.

Today, confronting post-modernism and the problematic of the "subject," struggling like so many others to come to terms with "situatedness" (Benhabib, 1991) and the crying need for a democratic community, I find myself deeply uncertain about what can be done politically in schools. The "savage inequalities" (Kozol 1991) surrounding us require all kinds of public action if they are to be remedied. The racism and the new nativisms that underlie the talk of crime have to be dealt with in the streets as well as in the offices, agencies, and classrooms. "Race Matters," as Cornel West (1993) tells us, are for him (and should be for us) urgent questions "of power and morality." So are matters of multiplicity and multiculturalism; so are the AIDS epidemic, guns in the streets, the drug trade, homelessness, family break-ups, child molesting and wife-battering, the shortage of playgrounds and libraries. Promises of free market, cheese burgers, MTV, even of "authentic assessment" in the schools are not enough.

As I view it now, after all the years, we have to contextualize; we have to move back and forth between our families and our communities, our schools and other public institutions. We have to commit ourselves once more to incarnating our beliefs in freedom, equality, human rights, objectively grounded or no. We have to engage personally, authentically in the dialogues among concrete human beings that keep democracies alive. And, as I see it, we have to make the several arts more and more central in our lives. It is not that the arts hold solutions. It is that they open experience to new possibilities, to new perspectives on worlds-in-the-making. They may release all kinds of persons to shape richer and more complex narratives as they reach out to a public space and work to bring into being a common world.

This has come from the memory store of someone reaching back in time and at once reaching forward, trying to see, trying to transcend what is. The book to which this foreword is a small contribution is a significant act on the part of each one of the writers included. Yearning for the sense of commitment, yearning for a shared vision, I—like those around—can only continue developing my project, hoping to leave a footprint on the sand.

REFERENCES

Adorno, T. and Horkheimer, M. (1972) *Dialectic of Enlightenment*. New York: Seabury Press.

Arendt, H. (1958) *The Human Condition*. Chicago: University of Chicago Press.

Benhabib, S. (1992) *Situating the Self*. New York: Routledge.

Benjamin, W. (1969) *Illuminations*. New York: Schocken Books.

Berube, M. and Gittell, M. (1969) *Confrontation at Ocean Hill-Brownsville*. New York: Praeger.

Casey, K. (1993) *I Answer with My Life: Life Histories of Women Working for Social Change*. New York: Routledge.

Dewey, J. (1954) *The Public and Its Problems*. Athens, OH: Swallow Press.

Foster, M. (1990) "The Politics of Race Through the Eyes of Afro-American Teachers." *Journal of Education* 172 (3): 123–141.

Freire, P. (1970) *Pedagogy of the Oppressed*. New York: Herder and Herder.

Gilligan, C. (1981) *In a Different Voice*. Cambridge: Harvard University Press.

Giroux, H. (1988) *Schooling and the Struggle for Public Life*. Minneapolis: University of Minnesota Press.

Greene, M. (1965) "The Teacher and the Negro Child: 'Invisibility' in the School" *The Educational Forum*, March: 275–280.

———. (1967) "Morals, Ideology and the Schools: Foray into the Politics of Education." *Educational Theory* 17 (4): 271–288.

Habermas, J. (1970) *Towards a Rational Society*. Boston: Beacon Press.

———. (1971) *Knowledge and Human Interests*. Boston: Beacon Press.

———. (1973) *Theory and Practice*. Boston: Beacon Press.

———. (1987) *The Philosophic Discourse of Modernity*. Cambridge: MIT Press.

King, J.E. and Wilson, T.L. (1990) "Being a Soul-Freeing Substance: A Legacy of Hope in Afro-History." *Journal of Education*, 172 (2): 9–23.

Kinnell, G. (1985) *The Past*. Boston: Houghton-Mifflin.

Kozol, J. (1991) *Savage Inequalities: Children in America's Schools*. New York: Crown.

Kushner, T. (1994) *Perestroika*, Part II, *Angels in America*. New York: Theatre Communications Group.

Ladson-Billings, G. (1990) "Blurring the Borders: Voices of African Liberatory Pedagogy in the United States and Canada." *Journal of Education* 172 (2): 72–88.

Mailer, N. (1968) *Armies of the Night*. New York: New American Library.

Marcuse, H. (1966) *Eros and Civilization*. Boston: Beacon Press.

——. (1968) *Negations: Essays in Critical Theory*. Boston: Beacon Press.

Merleau-Ponty, M. (1967) *Phenomenology of Perception*. Evanston: Northwestern University Press.

Sartre, J.-P. (1956) *Being and Nothingness*. New York: Philosophical Library.

——. (1963) *Search for a Method*. New York: Alfred A. Knopf.

Shor, I. (1986) *Culture Wars: School and Society in the Conservative Restoration*. Boston: Routledge and Kegan Paul.

West, C. (1993) *Race Matters*. Boston: Beacon Press.

A Personal Introduction to *The Politics of Educators' Work and Lives*

Mark B. Ginsburg

This edited volume represents a collective effort to raise educators' consciousness and to encourage their active participation in the politics of everyday life in schools, educational systems, homes, and communities. *The Politics of Educators' Work and Lives* is the first book in Garland Publishing's Studies in Education/Politics series. Since educators—along with others, most notably students—are at the heart of the educational process, their work and lives should help us better understand the political dimension of education.

This volume—like other cultural productions—grows out of a struggle. In this case it is my (and my colleagues') struggle to understand and to participate in the transformation of the world in which we as educators work and live. Here I will first briefly sketch how I became involved in this project about the politics of educators' work and lives, and then I will provide an overview of the chapters of this book.

Personal/Political Journeys as a Scholar, Worker, Citizen, and Family Member

I would be engaging in "revisionist biography" if I claimed that my interest in the topic of this project evolved over a clear path during my academic career or my life. I find it easier to account for my interest in the politics of educators' work and lives in terms of an intersection of various paths. Some of these paths are etched in the sands of the academy, some in the gravel of community involvement, and some in the rocks of family life.

During my graduate studies at the University of California at Los Angeles (1972–76), I was involved in examining the political participation of parents and other community members in relation to controversies—still extant—concerning the equity and constitutionality of school funding programs (Ginsburg 1976). And as a co-president of the Graduate Students in Education Association, I had many opportunities to observe (and at times to intervene in) faculty members' political maneuvering over budgets, program content and requirements, positions, and promotion and tenure decisions. During the same period, our first child was born, and we entered another stage in our negotiation about the division of labor and power in our family—a division (and sharing) that seemed at this point to have been less gender "traditional" and more equal than is the case today.

After taking my first full-time appointment as a lecturer in the Educational Enquiry Department at the University of Aston in Birmingham, England (1976–78), I began to focus in my scholarly work on the work and lives of schoolteachers. Initially, I was more interested in what I would now term the micropolitical dynamics in classrooms and schools: teachers' socialization, evaluation and control of students and educators' socialization and control of their colleagues (see Ginsburg et al. 1977). However, because of the influence of colleagues, particularly Henry Miller and Bob Meyenn, but also as a result of developments in education and the state in Britain—a "Great Debate" on education, structural adjustments that led to massive cutbacks in social sectors' funding, and teachers' interpretations of and reactions to these—my gaze was widened to include collective action by teachers outside the school and even the school system (e.g., see Ginsburg, Meyenn and Miller 1979 and 1980). At this point, aside from becoming involved in some departmental level decision making and participating in a march and lobbying effort in London organized by the Association of University Teachers to force Parliament to give the pay raises previously negotiated, I was mostly a passive observer in teacher union politics. But I recall ruminating about how I would act (and how I would answer the interview questions I posed) if I were employed as a schoolteacher in the Midlands of England during that period. With greater demands from (or more attention to) my "public" sphere activities and especially after the birth of our second child the nature of my political role as a family member began to change. While I still was conscious of (and perhaps effective in) encouraging gender-neutral development with my children, the adult division of labor and power in the family moved toward a more gender traditional and less equal model—particularly with regard to relations with the extended family.

At the University of Houston (1979–87), I continued my scholarly focus on the political and ideological nature of professionalism and unionism among teachers (see Ginsburg 1987b; Ginsburg & Chaturvedi 1988; Ginsburg et al. 1988). Meanwhile, I expanded my concern about the classroom political activities of teachers to include the selection of curriculum knowledge and the construction of the hidden curriculum and to highlight the reproduction and transformation of gender as well as class and race relations (see Ginsburg 1987c; Ginsburg & Arias-Godinez 1984; Ginsburg & Clift 1990; Ginsburg & Giles 1984; Ginsburg & Newman 1985; Ginsburg & Sands 1985; Malmstad et al., 1983; Miller and Ginsburg 1989). These issues converged somewhat in my longitudinal ethnographic study of the socialization of preservice teachers (Ginsburg 1988a). While in Houston I devoted more time to reflecting/acting in relation to the political decisions other colleagues and I were making in terms of determining curriculum content, admitting and graduating students, and recruiting and promoting/tenuring colleagues. In a "right-to-work" state, my union/profession participation was focused primarily on academic freedom issues, and I eventually became president of the local chapter of the American Association of University Professors. I also became more active in progressive political movements, especially after the U.S. military invasion of Grenada in 1983. In part due to the stimulation from and solidarity with two visiting scholars, Ed Silva and Sheila Slaughter, I increasingly became engaged with student, faculty, and community activists on issues of peace, jobs, and justice—organizing a teach-in series on campus and a Peace and Justice Fair in the community as well as coordinating local, state, and national protest marches and rallies (see Ginsburg 1987a). I also continued to struggle with the growing responsibilities in the family (e.g., our third child was born) in the context of my spouse and myself pursuing an increasing range of activities outside the home. And the challenges negotiating the distribution of labor and of power within the family became more complex as our children became more visible and vocal members at the bargaining table. Included in the decisions were whether our children should attend public or private schools and how we should intervene in the structures, content, and processes of our children's schooling. These issues, for me, were always complicated by my wearing a variety of hats, including those of parent, professor, and union member.

In 1987 we moved from Texas to Pennsylvania, where I became director of the Institute for International Studies in Education at the University of Pittsburgh. Educators as workers and political actors (see Ginsburg 1988b; Ginsburg 1990; Ginsburg & Kamat 1994) and the political socialization of teachers have been the main themes that have guided my scholarship since coming to Pitt. The former theme also provided impetus for my involvement in examining educational reform (see Ginsburg 1991; Ginsburg et al. 1990)—an effort to combine national and world-system structural analyses with an action framework that calls attention to the agency of educators and other groups of political actors. The latter theme was explored primarily through a longitudinal ethnographic study in three institutions in Xalapa, Veracruz, Mexico (see Ginsburg 1994; Ginsburg 1995; Ginsburg and Tidwell 1990), and is currently expanding to consider policy formation and other aspects of the political dimension in teacher education (see Ginsburg and Lindsay 1995). As I engaged in this research, I continued to reflect on my own roles in developing the political ideas and actions of preservice and in-service educators. Such reflection and related action was complemented with my increasing role in campus politics, especially as I assumed leadership positions in the United Faculty, a local faculty union jointly affiliated with the American Association of University Professors and the American Federation of Teachers. The latter affiliation also offered opportunities to meet regularly with leaders of local, state, and national level schoolteacher unions. At the same time, through my active local involvement in the Alliance for Progressive Action, Faculty for Social Responsibility, Pittsburgh Cuba Coalition, and Pittsburgh Peace Institute, I joined with others in promoting peace and justice on a local, national, and global level. In this context the boundaries between being a professor and a community activist often blurred, in my judgment, to the benefit of both roles, with related lectures, discussions, meetings, and other activities occurring in and out of classroom settings and on and off campus. On the home front, thanks to the persistence of my spouse and children, I became more conscious of, if not always adept in, staying true to my progressive political commitments in my interaction (or lack thereof) with family members. This learning along with some readings encouraged me to take more seriously (at least in my thinking) "private sphere" politics. The family debates also continued regarding schooling. For example, having committed to enrolling our children in an urban public school district, we had to decide in what kinds of "special programs" (if any) they should be placed.

Crossing Paths and Seeking out Other Voices

This book project, however, is not a singular undertaking. Indeed, the collective nature of the project was signalled initially by my collaboration with colleagues (Sangeeta Kamat, Rajeshwari Raghu, and John Weaver), who at the time were graduate students with whom I was working, in preparing my presidential address to the Comparative and International Education Society (Ginsburg et al. 1992), which in revised form serves as the first chapter of this volume.

Drafts of this manuscript, moreover, were circulated to the authors of the other chapters of this book. This was done to obtain their input for revisions undertaken but also to encourage some coherence in this volume, to stimulate dialogue, but not to dictate (if this were even possible) how colleagues should frame their essays. I hope the subsequent chapters stretch the breadth and depth of the themes identified in the first chapter. At the same time colleagues, whose previous work considerably shaped my ideas sketched in the first chapter, have brought other themes and issues to the fore. Moreover, the poliphany of voices that came together to work on this book project is evidenced even in the style of their chapters—from personal accounts, to fictitious narratives, to more detached-appearing syntheses of literature.

Discussions and correspondence (via paper and electronic mail) have of course been extensive in carrying out this book project. In addition, many of the chapter authors have participated in formally organized panel sessions at one or both of the following conferences: Comparative and International Education Society (Annapolis, Maryland, March 12–15, 1992) and American Educational Research Association (Atlanta, Georgia, April 12–16, 1993). These conference sessions not only facilitated dialogue among chapter authors, but they also provided opportunities for other colleagues to raise questions, offer comments, or otherwise shape the thinking and writing of various members of the project group.

Overview of the Book

The nine chapters in this volume provide a range of analyses of the work and lives of educators. A variety of historical and national contexts are represented as the authors document and interpret the political action (and inaction) of educators in classrooms, schools, universities, households, and communities.

In the first chapter Sangeeta Kamat, Rajeshwari Raghu, John Weaver, and I analyze the concepts of politics and political status—stressing issues of power and the distribution of material and symbolic resources—in explaining why educators, in their work and lives, should be considered political. We then summarize a broad range of international literature, portraying the individual or collective, active or passive, and conservative or change-oriented nature of educators' political roles. These include curriculum decision making, pedagogy, student evaluation, research, employee/colleague and union/professional association participant, family member, and citizen. Madeleine Grumet uses her and her son's experience with a schoolteacher as an example of the problematics of exile and exclusion in which home-school relations are imbedded. She then examines issues of adults and children since they are differently dealt with by women and men in the separate, though interdependent and overlapping, public and private spheres of home, school, and workplace. She emphasizes that notions of the particular and the individual are sometimes drawn upon to "separate the family from politics." She then describes a model of teaching—an arrangement of duration, care, and instruction modeled directly on family relations— which she argues might overcome the problems that parents and teachers face, including the disregard of each others' practical knowledge and the artificial boundaries that limit their capacity to forge a community with and for children. Grumet also sketches how this model would provide opportunities for men and women teachers to construct more politically progressive roles in their interaction with children, parents, and colleagues.

Richard Altenbaugh uses the historical experience of rural and urban teachers in the United States to illustrate the "irony of gender"—that while women teachers have been treated like a minority, they comprise a numerical majority of educational workers. He describes the structural and ideological developments in education and society that facilitated the feminization of teaching, encouraging elites to promote the idea of women teachers at the same time women sought to expand the roles they played outside the home. Altenbaugh portrays the rich and contradictory texture of the personal lives of women teachers as they were engaged in political struggles against (and sometimes on behalf of) patriarchal relations in the home, school, and community. These struggles were not always individual or isolated; at times and with varying degrees of success, some female (and some male) teachers worked in and through their unions (and with other organizations and social movements) to confront gender inequities in power and material and symbolic resources in education and society.

Robert Connell proposes a theory of teachers' work as an approach to teachers' politics. He traces the place of teachers in social theories and analyses of education, noting that teachers have generally either not been taken into account or have been treated either (a) as pawns in dominant groups' efforts to reproduce their power, wealth, and status or (b) as society's specialized workforce who are more or less effective and efficient in preparing the larger workforce. He then uses examples from Australia, England, and the United States to illustrate another approach—one based on the notion of transformative labor. He examines the control of the labor process (particularly in relation to curriculum determination), the political order of the workplace and character of the workforce (especially in relation to gender), and the allocation of resources used in the work of teaching (in school programs with students of different racial/ethnic groups and social classes). In concluding on the relation between education and democracy, Connell emphasizes that the "main effect of educational labour is not the direct shaping of practice . . . [but] the formation and transformation of capacities for practice." Thus, the political impact of teachers' work, though salient, is neither direct nor predictable.

Martin Lawn, drawing in-depth on the case of Britain as well as on a range of other European societies, describes the development of schoolteachers' relations with the state, which depended in part on the ideological notion that teachers should be nonpolitical. State elites sought to enforce this model of the "good teacher" to prevent what they at times (mis)perceived as the "social danger of an organised teacher workforce." Many teachers joined state elites in promoting this model of the "good teacher," basing their view on one aspect of the "double-edged ideology of professionalism." Despite, or because of, such formal and informal, administrative and collegial enforcement of this model, Lawn reports, many teachers have been politically active—individually and collectively—in classrooms and schools, and through unions, political parties, and new social movements.

Carlos Torres draws on his extensive fieldwork observations of, as well as interviews and conversations with, educators in various settings in Latin America to create three dialogues with fictitious, but composite educators. He begins by sketching the context in which educators' work and lives are enacted: corporatist relations between the state and organized social groups (including educators) and uneven rates of economic growth and hyper-inflation, followed by "structural adjustment" policies—stipulated by the International Monetary Fund and the World Bank—which seek to stabilize economies by slashing spending in social sectors (including education). Torres then invites us to accompany him as he interacts with three colleagues and friends: Tomás Agustín, a professor of social science and political philosophy and the (elected) rector or president of the University of Buenos Aires (Argentina), who daily confronts declining material conditions and the "bastardization of university politics"; Luiza Amorosa, an elementary schoolteacher who turns down an offer to work in the São Paulo (Brazil) municipal education department, headed by Paulo Freire, in order to continue her involvement as a classroom teacher and an activist in community-based social movements; and Lupita, a vice-principal of a secondary school in Mexico City who affirms her support for the national teachers' union in the face of a movement for change initiated by "democratic" challengers to the long-time leadership of the union, in spite of recognizing how gender biases have affected her own and other women's careers in education. Through these fictitious dialogues we come to understand how and why educators in Latin America attempt to meet various challenges through various forms of political action.

Linda Dove, focusing on the context of developing countries, particularly in Africa and Asia, indicates how educators engage in political action through their curricular choices and screening of students for higher levels of education and work in higher status and financially rewarding jobs. She then delineates the political roles educators played during colonial and independence eras as community leaders, government officials, and participants in extraconstitutional radical move-ments. Dove analyzes the conditions underlying such active participation during these periods and discusses the structural and ideological changes (consolidation of state power, nationalization of educational systems, bureaucratization of schools, and teachers' status deflation) associated with the subsequent decline in educators' active political involvement outside of schools. She concludes with some predictions about the factors that may affect the future extent of classroom and community-based political activity among educators in developing countries.

Peter Darvas and Maria Nagy illuminate the political contexts and activities of teachers in Central and Eastern Europe (CEE)—a region that since World War II has witnessed the institution and dissolution of Stalinist, "Communist" regimes. While acknowledging the limits of existing research literature on teachers between 1945 and 1989, at least in part because "teachers were not typically placed on the central political agenda . . . in countries such as Bulgaria, East Germany, Hungary, and Poland," they sketch CEE teachers' contradictory experiences—for example, functioning in an elitist educational system in the context of a governing party's ideology of egalitarianism—during this era. Darvas and Nagy also examine some of the cross-national differences in how individual and organized teachers shaped and were affected by changes in education and society—for example, moves toward de-centralization and ideological changes in the curriculum—during the period immediately preceeding and following de-Stalinization. They end by suggesting alternative future scenarios for teachers' work and lives in these dynamic political and economic contexts.

Philip Altbach summarizes his encyclopedic knowledge of past and present political activity of university professors around the world. Although noting that the "vast majority of professors are not involved in public forms of activism," he draws attention to the political dimension of the "academic as expert" role that at least some "cosmopolitan" professors play through their writing activities in academic and popular media, their testimony to and consulting for government agencies, and their direct participation as elected or appointed government officials. He reminds us that such activities may be supportive of, or (less often) in opposition to dominant groups and existing authorities, as is the case with professors' participation in nongovernmental organizations and social movements. Altbach also examines the professoriate's involvement in local institutional or campus politics, including faculty governance bodies and unions, concerned with issues of curriculum, policy, salary, and working conditions.

Concluding Remarks

The contributors to this volume hope that these chapters will encourage educators to reflect on their own and colleagues' past, present, and future actions (and inactions). The authors would value receiving questions or comments about the ideas contained in this volume. We would also benefit by learning about other examples of educators' efforts to struggle for progressive social change—particularly efforts with which we can join to build a more peaceful, just, and environmentally sane tomorrow.

REFERENCES

Ginsburg, M. (1976). *An Investigation of Various Modes of Community Participation in School Affairs*. Unpublished doctoral dissertation, University of California, Los Angeles.

———. (1987a). "Contradictions in the Role of Professor as Activist." *Sociological Focus* 20:111–122.

———. (1987b). "Reproduction, Contradiction and Conceptions of Professionalism: The Case of Preservice Teachers." In *Critical Studies in Teacher Education*, edited by T. Popkewitz, pp. 86–129. New York: Falmer Press.

———. (1987c). "Teacher Education and Class and Gender Relations." *Educational Foundations* 1(2): 4–36.

———. (1988a). *Contradictions in Teacher Education and Society*. New York: Falmer Press.

————. (1988b). "Educators as Workers and Political Actors." *British Journal of Sociology of Education* 3:359–367.

————. (1990). "El Proceso de Trabajo y la Accion Politica de los Educadores: Un Analisis Comparado." *Revista de Educacion* (Extraordinario): 317–345.

————. (1994). "Aprendiendo a Ser Actores Politicos? La Educacion de Maestros en Mexico." *Punto y Seguido* 7: 17–20.

————. (1995). "Contradictions, Resistance and Incorporation in the Political Socialization of Educators in Mexico." In *The Political Dimension in Teacher Education*, edited by M. Ginsburg and B. Lindsay. London: Falmer Press.

Ginsburg, M. (Ed.). (1991). *Understanding Educational Reform in Global Context: Economy, Ideology and the State.* New York: Garland.

Ginsburg, M., and Arias-Godinez, B. (1984). "Nonformal Education and Social Reproduction/Transformation: Educational Radio in Mexico." *Comparative Education Review* 28(1): 116–127.

Ginsburg, M., and Chaturvedi, V. (1988). "Teachers and the Ideology of Professionalism in India and England: A Comparison of Case Studies in Colonial/Peripheral and Metropolitan/Central Societies." *Comparative Education Review* 32:465–477.

Ginsburg, M., and Clift, R. (1990). "The Hidden Curriculum in Teacher Education." In *Handbook of Research on Teacher Education* edited by W. R. Houston, pp. 450–464. New York: Macmillan.

Ginsburg, M., Cooper, S., Raghu, R., and Zegarra, H. (1990). "National and World-System Explanations of Educational Reform." *Comparative Education Review* 34(4): 474–499.

Ginsburg, M., and Giles, J. (1984). "Sponsored and Contest Modes of Social Reproduction in Selective Community College Programs." *Research in Higher Education* 21(3): 281–299.

Ginsburg, M., and Kamat, S. (1994). "Teachers' Work and Political Action." In *International Encyclopedia of Education: Research and Studies*, 2nd Ed., edited by T. Husen and T. Postlethwaite, pp. 4581–4587. New York: Macmillan.

Ginsburg, M., and Lindsay, B. (Eds.) (1995). *The Political Dimension in Teacher Education.* London: Falmer Press.

Ginsburg, M., and Newman, K. (1985). "Social Inequalities, Schooling, and Teacher Education." *Journal of Teacher Education* 36(2):49–54.

Ginsburg, M., and Sands, J. (1985). "Black and Brown Under the White Capitalist English Crown." In *Education and Intergroup Relations:*

An International Perspective, edited by J. Hawkins and T. La Belle, pp. 109–138. New York: Praeger.

Ginsburg M., and Tidwell, M. (1990). "Political Socialization of Prospective Educators in Mexico." *New Education* 12:70–82.

Ginsburg, M., Kamat, S., Raghu, R., and Weaver, J. (1992). "Educators/Politics." *Comparative Education Review* 36(4):417–445.

Ginsburg, M., Wallace, G., and Miller, H. (1988). "Teachers, Economy and the State." *Teaching and Teacher Education: An International Journal of Research and Studies* 4(4):1–21.

Ginsburg, M., Meyenn, R., and Miller, M. (1979). "Teachers and the Great Debate and Educational Cuts." *Westminister Studies in Education* 2:5–23.

————. (1980). "Teachers Conceptions of Professionalism and Trades Unionism: An Ideological Analysis." In *Teacher Strategies*, edited by P. Woods, pp. 178–212. London: Croom Helm.

Ginsburg, M., Meyenn, R., Miller, H., and Ranceford-Hadley, C. (1977). *The Role of the Middle School Teacher*. Birmingham, England: University of Aston Educational Enquiry Monograph.

Malmstad, B., Ginsburg, M., and Croft, J. (1983). "The Social Construction of Reading Lessons: Resistance and Social Reproduction." *Journal of Education* 165(4): 359–373.

Miller, D., and Ginsburg, M. (1989). "Social Reproduction and Resistance in Four Infant/Toddler Daycare Settings: An Ethnographic Study of Social Relations and Sociolinguistic Codes." *Journal of Education* 171(3): 31–50.

The Politics
of Educators'
Work and Lives

Educators and Politics: Interpretations, Involvement, and Implications[1]

Mark B. Ginsburg, Sangeeta Kamat,
Rajeshwari Raghu, and John Weaver

It is sometimes argued that educators can and should be apolitical. Some schoolteachers have claimed that "the realm of the 'political' [is or should be] removed from the educational sphere" (Lee 1987, p. 88). University educators, in lamenting and critiquing the "politicization" of education (Adler 1990; Sautman 1991), have asserted similarly that education is or should be "concerned with knowledge and understanding . . . which embod[y] criteria of truth and standards of excellence which . . . derive from the nature of the subject-matter and not from any political authority" (Dearden 1980, p. 151).[2]

Questioning the Assumptions That Educators Are Apolitical

Such arguments rest on three assumptions that need to be questioned as we examine the connection between politics and educators' work and lives. The first assumption is that *professional, intellectual,* and *technical* activity, on the one hand, and *political* activity, on the other, are mutually exclusive phenomena (Apple 1986; Dove 1986; Orlin 1981; Ziegler 1967). In contrast, we conceive of "technical" and "political" as referring

3

to different dimensions of phenomena rather than as constituting mutually exclusive phenomena. That is, we have a choice in how we focus our analysis of educators' work and lives. For example, we might consider the technical dimension, perhaps examining the effectiveness and efficiency of educators' paid work (as teachers, scholars, administrators, consultants, etc.) as well as unpaid work (e.g., as family members and citizens). Our concern here, however, is with the political dimension, which (as we will discuss further) focuses our attention on relations of power and the distribution of symbolic and material resources.

In emphasizing the political dimension of educators' activity, though, we do not consider ourselves "new politicized vulgarians who raucously disclaim everything is essentially a question of interest and power" (Adler 1990, p. 104). We posit that all actions (and inaction) by educators reflect and have implications for politics (viz., power, interests, and the distribution of resources), though the work of educators is not *only* a question of politics. The work and lives of educators also reflect and have implications for technical, professional, and intellectual as well as aesthetic issues (Hackett 1988).[3]

At the same time we need to understand that efforts to represent education and the work of educators as neutral (as only professional, intellectual, technical, etc.) can be interpreted as political acts, having consequences for the distribution of power and of material and symbolic resources both for educators and other groups. For instance, during the first decades of this century in the United States, the "cry 'Keep the schools out of politics' was used by professional administrators in their attempt to consolidate their power over the educational system" (Spring 1986, p. 256). The construction of an image of educators as "apolitical" and "classless" during the nineteenth century in England and the United States not only facilitated some improvement in educators' status, but also helped to preserve the wealth and power of the dominant class (Cook 1984; Mattingly 1975). University-based social scientists, at least in the United States, can also be seen to have acquired material and symbolic resources, while becoming "servants" of economic and state elites, through their disciplinary organization efforts to represent themselves as "neutral and objective" purveyors of profit-enhancing or policy-relevant expertise (Silva and Slaughter 1984). And we should note that state elites in a variety of historical and societal contexts tend to criticize schoolteachers for being political when they oppose (but not when they support) government policies (Duclau-Williams 1985; Fuhrig 1969).

A second questionable assumption buttressing the argument that educators are or should be apolitical is that *personal* and *political* matters or *private* and *public sphere* activity can be clearly separated. Educators are not (or should not be) considered to be political because many of them, especially women (Howe 1991; Ozga 1987; Strober and Tyack 1980), are not (or should not be) actively or visibly involved in public-sphere activity, such as participation in union/professional organizations, political parties, and other community-based citizen groups and movements. The implicit assumption here is that the personal-level interactions that educators have with students, colleagues, and educational authorities in the private sphere of classrooms and schools are excluded from the political realm (Corr and Jamieson 1990; Howe 1991; Turner 1990).[4]

We do not accept such a narrow definition of the concept of political. Our position is in line with feminist ideas: (1) the personal is political and the political is personal and (2) public and private are not separate spheres. What educators do in the private spheres of classrooms, laboratories, libraries, meeting rooms, and offices is a form of political action, as is public sphere participation or nonparticipation in picket lines, demonstrations, lobbying, voting, running for office, and (armed or unarmed) revolutionary or anticolonial struggle (Weiler 1989; Howe 1991).[5] For us, the terms *politics* and *political*, are not limited to considerations of the state, governments, parties, constitutions, and voting (see also Corr and Jamieson 1990; Dearden 1980). "Politics is how you live your life, not whom you vote for" (Nichols 1977, p. 183). All aspects of human experience have a political dimension.

The third questionable assumption supporting the argument that educators are or should be apolitical actors is that domination (dominating or being dominated) is the only type of relationship involved in politics. This assumption is evidenced, for instance, when prospective educators say that they want to avoid engaging in political activity because it would involve them with people whose primary concern is to control others or to accumulate material and symbolic resources at the expense of others (Ginsburg and Tidwell 1990). Educators and others may prefer to be engaged in activities that are mutually enhancing to participants, rather than those that necessarily produce winners and losers (Miller 1992).[6]

We agree that at its core politics is intimately linked to power (see Dallmayr 1984; Lasswell 1977; Mills 1956). As Foucault (1980, p. 189) observes, "the set of relations of [power] in a given society constitutes the domain of the political. . . . To say that 'everything is political' is to affirm this ubiquity of relations of [power] and their immanence in a political field."[7] Politics is concerned with the control of the means of producing, reproducing, consuming, and accumulating material and symbolic resources (Bacharach and Lawler 1980; Dearden 1980; Dove 1986). That is, politics "is about who gets what, when and how" (Osborne 1984, p. 17). To locate power relations at the heart of political activity, however, is not tantamount to equating politics with dominant–subordinate relations (Young 1992).[8] Hence, we do not agree with John Stuart Mill that there are *only* two "inclinations . . . one the desire to exercise power over others; the other . . . to [not] have power exercised over themselves" (Mill 1861; quoted in Arendt 1969, p. 39). We contend that *power over* is only one aspect of power, the other aspect of power being *power with*. Both aspects of power exist in dialectical relationship to each other at the core of politics, although one aspect may be more clearly evidenced in any given situation.

Power over is the aspect of power that has been emphasized more often by theorists and perhaps by political actors. It involves the capacity to get people to do something, to not do something, or to not even consider doing something such that their action or inaction is contrary to their interests (Lukes 1974).[9] In contrast, according to Kreisberg (1992, p. 85):

> Power with is manifest in relationships of co-agency. These relationships are characterized by people finding ways to satisfy their desires and to fulfill their interests without imposing on one another. The relationship of co-agency is one in which there is equality: situations in which individuals and groups fulfill their desire by acting together. It is jointly developing capacity. [10]

While the notion of *power over* implies that power "is a scarce resource to be coveted, hoarded, and used in one's own interest [so that] there are winners and losers," the idea of *power with* characterizes power as "an expanding renewable resource available through shared endeavors, dialogue, and cooperation" (Kreisberg 1992, pp. 32 and 63).

Conceptualizing Educators as Political Actors

Educators, like other people, work and live within power relations, including both the *power over* and the *power with* aspects. Whether characterized in terms of capitalism, patriarchy, racial or ethnic oppression, religious- or secular-state authoritarianism, or imperialism, the unequal, dominant-subordinate aspect of power relations is imbedded currently not only in local, national, and global communities. They also are extant in educators' immediate work sites (classrooms and campuses) as well as in educational systems more generally. At the same time, but not always as prominently, educators work and live in the context of interpersonal and broader *power with* relations, through which efforts to achieve mutual empowerment and mutual enhancement of symbolic and material resources are undertaken.

Once we discard the three questionable assumptions (distinguishing technical and political activity, separating public and private spheres, and associating power only with the *power over* aspect), it should be clear that educators can and should be considered as political actors. Educators do not operate in a political vacuum and educators are not neutral (Ota 1985; Freire 1970). What educators do occurs in a context of power relations and distributions of symbolic and material resources, and what

action (or inaction) educators engage in has political implications
for themselves and others. Everything that educators do in and
outside their workplaces is dialectically related (a) to the
distribution of structural and ideological power used to control
the means of producing, reproducing, consuming, and
accumulating material and symbolic resources and, thus, (b) to
the distribution of material and symbolic resources. Educators'
actions (and inaction) are constrained and enabled by such
relations of power and resource distributions, while at the same
time through their daily activity and historical struggles
educators are engaged in reproducing, resisting, and transforming existing power relations and resource distributions.
Casting the notion of educators and politics in this way means
that educators are political actors regardless of whether they are
active or passive; autonomous or heteronomous vis-à-vis other
groups; conservative or change-oriented; seeking individual,
occupational group, or larger collectivities' goals; and/or serving
dominant group, subordinate group, or human interests.

In the remainder of this chapter we provide illustrations
from different historical periods in various societies of the
political dimension of educators' work and lives. And like other
similar efforts, our "emphasis on political . . . practices is to
register a concern with that type of research that isolates the
world of the school (the teacher's domain) from the outside
world of political antagonisms" (Darmanin 1985, p. 183). We
organize our discussion around the following aspects of the
educators' role: curriculum decision making, pedagogy, student
evaluation, research, employee/colleague, union/professional
association participant, family member, and citizen.

Curriculum Decision Making as Political Work

Curriculum content represents a selection of topics and a
selection of ways of viewing these topics. Power relations are
imbedded in curriculum both in terms of who makes the
decisions and whose interests are served by the topics and
perspectives included or excluded (Giroux 1988). We emphasize
the content of the curriculum here, but it should be remembered
that the process of constructing the curriculum is a power

struggle in which teachers play a more or less active role. While teachers generally do not have full autonomy to determine officially the curriculum, they do, to varying extents, choose to accommodate, resist, or create alternatives to the curriculum determined by others.

Knowledge and power can be seen as inextricably linked (Foucault 1980). The content of curriculum knowledge may serve to legitimate or challenge existing relations of power. Similarly, existing relations of power constrain or enable the representation of particular kinds of curriculum knowledge (Apple 1982; Young 1971). A variety of studies have shown how capitalist relations are preserved by promoting its positive features, ignoring or rationalizing as individuals' failings its negative features, or limiting what is known about groups who have struggled to create a more just and humane economic arrangement (Anyon 1981; Apple 1979; Fisher 1983; Osborne 1984; Silva and Slaughter 1984). Class relations are also reproduced through the inclusion and greater valuing of the knowledge or cultural capital of dominant classes (Bourdieu and Passeron 1977). In contrast, a study in New Zealand documents how some teachers, who were active in social movements, developed their curriculum to analyze critically not only the exploitation of workers and indigenous groups under capitalism but also to draw attention to the role of union activity and class ethnic group struggle in seeking to change or transform the system (Sultana 1987).

Studies in a range of societies have documented how unequal gender relations have been legitimated through the knowledge that educators include in or exclude from the curriculum, portraying in an unproblematic manner males' paid labor and dominance in the economy and government and females' unpaid labor with respect to family care and house maintenance (Anyon 1983; Biraimah 1982; Dale et al. 1981; Kelly and Elliot 1982; Kelly and Nihlen 1982). Other educators have problematized gender relations, by developing or using antisexist curricular materials, by focusing attention on how patriarchal relations limit females' (and males') lives, and by encouraging students to consider alternatives to stereotyped gender roles in schools and society (Crumpacker and Haegen 1990; Joyce 1987; King 1987; Weiler 1988, 1990).

Educators have developed and/or transmitted curricular knowledge that has either supported or undermined unequal racial/ethnic group relations. For example, in South Africa some educators have promoted racist stereotypes and ideologies in their classrooms, while others have sought to "redefine curriculum content from its racist, sexist, and classist bias to the emancipatory goal of social relevance, political liberation, and social equality" (Jansen 1990, p. 67). Different groups of educators in Nazi Germany also worked either to legitimate or to critique racial stereotypes and ideologies (Jarausch 1990).

What knowledge and perspectives educators communicate to students may encourage supporting governing elites and their actions. Schoolteachers in the United States are seen more often as "promulgators of social myths than critical examiners of the political process," and thus "the classroom operates basically to reinforce a belief in the desirability of maintaining the status quo" (Ziegler 1967, pp. 96 and 119). The curricular work of educators in many developing countries is similarly described as "the promotion of values and deeds of the government of the day" (Dove 1986, p. 186). In the People's Republic of China many educators have promoted the ideas and values that during a particular period were in line with those prescribed by party and state officials (Sautman 1991; White 1981). There is evidence that during World War II academic secondary teachers joined higher education colleagues in "waging spiritual warfare for the fatherland" in Germany (Jarausch 1990, p. 29); educators "carried out ultranationalist indoctrination" for the military regime in Japan (Levine 1969, p. 148); and schoolteachers in England implemented curricular changes dictated by central government officials needed to support the war effort both materially and ideologically (Lawn 1987). After World War II those schoolteachers in Japan who retained their jobs served the allied occupation-controlled government by promoting views in the classroom, this time against nationalism and militarism (Levine 1969, p. 148).

The curriculum that teachers present to students sometimes challenges elites, their ideologies, and their actions. For example, during World War I primary schoolteachers affiliated with the revolutionary syndicalist movement in France challenged French authorities and sought to replace positive and romantic views of war with a view of it as barbaric, destructive, and not resolving anything; some of these educators were arrested for challenging the order that they read "anti-German propaganda" to students (Feeley 1989). In the People's Republic of China at various times since 1949, school government and party officials have criticized some teachers and teacher educators for subverting the revolution by promoting capitalist values, elitism, and bourgeois ideology through their teaching (Paine 1981; Tucker 1981; White 1981). And because they have been perceived to be critics of authoritarian regimes, university teachers have at various times been the target of restrictions on academic freedom and instructional activities, firings, institutional closures, jailings, and killings (Altbach 1990).

The concept of *cultural imperialism* (Carnoy 1974) seems apt for describing some educators' role in legitimating colonial and neocolonial rule through their curricular choices. Such classroom-based political activity occurred before as well as after "independence" in African societies (Bagunywa 1975). And in the Philippines, schoolteachers, who were tightly controlled through training, curriculum guides, and inspection, transmitted the technical and cultural knowledge and skills required by the United States' colonial rule there (Caniesco-Doronila 1987). Many university professors in former colonial societies have continued to deliver a "curriculum [which] was imposed from the outside" (Altbach 1990, p. 24). There is also contrasting evidence of educators' curricular work challenging imperialism. For example, rural teachers in Vietnam, in the face of efforts by French colonial authorities to impose a curriculum that denigrated Vietnamese culture and justified French rule, resisted and developed a curriculum that challenged French colonialism by celebrating Vietnamese culture and their capacity for self-rule (Kelly 1982).

The Politics of Pedagogy

How educators seek to organize their classrooms and how they relate to different groups of students also is a form of political activity. Research in Israel demonstrates that different forms of classroom social relations facilitate or impede the development of students' political efficacy and orientation to public forms of political involvement (supporting candidates and lobbying) (Ichilov 1991). Instituting authoritarian or democratic forms of classroom organization may either reinforce or contradict the political structures of the local, national, and global communities in which the educator works. This point can be clarified by examining the pedagogy of "People's Education" developed by the African National Congress in South Africa, which seeks "to restructure classroom relationships from the standard teacher-centered and authoritarian climate to a more student-centered, democratic form" (Jansen 1990, p. 67). And in Zimbabwe from independence until about 1980, teacher-student relations were "characterized by participation, productive work, and critical reflection," while after the onset of the military conflict a different pedagogy was put in place, one that "restores elitism, conforms to authority, and stifles critical thinking" (Jansen 1990, pp. 68–69).

Pedagogical relations have been found to vary by the social class of the secondary and preschool students in the United States (Bowles and Gintis 1976; Miller and Ginsburg 1989), as well as primary and preschool students in England (Bernstein 1977; Sharp and Green 1975), in ways that seem to reproduce the social relations of work experienced by members of working, professional/managerial, and capitalist classes. To illustrate, for working class students the dominant mode of social control employed by teachers was likely to be more formal and based on the authority of their position as an adult, while for the professional/managerial class, social control in the classroom tended to be more often organized on an interpersonal, negotiated basis.

When teachers use a particular language as the medium of instruction (Hawkins and La Belle 1985; Spolsky and Cooper 1978), when they engage in other styles of interaction that privilege the culture of one group of student over another (Giroux 1981), or when they devote more positive (or negative) attention to one type of student than another (Rist 1970), they are engaged in perpetuating or challenging existing power relations and the extant distribution of symbolic (and thus perhaps also material) resources. They help members of some groups more or less than others. Studies focusing on primary schools in England (Bernstein 1971; Lee 1984) and higher education institutions in France (Bourdieu and Passeron 1977) have identified how the dominant forms of pedagogy employed by teachers embody notions of individualism, linguistic codes, and forms of "cultural capital" that favor the involvement and achievement of middle- or upper-class versus working-class students.

The distribution of power and of symbolic and material resources among racial and ethnic groups is also shaped by pedagogical activity of educators (Ianni and Storey 1973; Ogbu 1978; Roberts and Akinsanya 1976; Spindler 1974). In the United States, for instance, it has been observed that the way teachers group students for instruction and the relationships they establish with different groups of students help subordinated racial/ethnic minority students to "achieve" school failure through a "rational adaptation" to their experience in schools controlled by dominant racial/ethnic groups (McDermott 1974, p. 87).

In terms of gender relations, studies focused on higher education in Canada and the United States show how pedagogical relations privilege male forms of discourse, such that women students may be either silenced or required to engage in the less personal and connected styles of talking and relating in order to participate in seminar discussions (Belensky et al. 1986; Lewis and Simon 1986). Research carried out in Australia suggests that teachers' efforts to manage or discipline students, which may require emotionally detached relations, and to motivate student learning, which may necessitate emotionally engaged relations, involve male and female teachers (and their students) in contradictory forms of social relations that have implications for maintaining or altering unequal gender relations (Connell 1985).

The Politics of Student Evaluation

There is little disagreement that schooling, in part through the work of educators, functions to sort and select students and to allocate symbolic resources (e.g., grades, credentials, status), which under certain conditions, at least, can be cashed in for or used to legitimate power and material resources (viz., income) (Bowles and Gintis 1976; Collins 1979; Cummings and Amano 1977; Halsey, Flood and Anderson 1961; Holmes 1985; Hopper 1981; Persell 1977). A debate centers around whether the sorting and allocation functions of schooling reflect a meritocratic system, where success or failure is based primarily on effort and ability, versus a reproductive system, where the individual's position within the social structure (i.e., class, gender, and race/ethnic, center/periphery relations) is the main determinant of who receives schools' symbolic resources. Regardless of which argument one adopts on the nature of education's allocation function, it should be clear that educators' role in student evaluation and credentialing has a political dimension.

The distribution of power and of symbolic and material resources are affected by those students whom educators deem worthy of admission into certain educational institutions (Dove 1986), whom they identify as having achieved more, and on whom they confer academic credentials (Altbach 1990). Analyses of the (former) Soviet Union and other countries lead to the conclusion that "Schooling is a social enterprise concerned with constructing and legitimating categories of competence in society, defining public classifications of people . . . , and providing differential access to valued positions in society through its credentialing authority" (Popkewitz 1982, p. 44). Australian researchers conclude similarly that the "competitive academic curriculum . . . helps to legitimate the idea of unequal ability and unequal reward" (Ashendon et al. 1987, pp. 257–258). In the South African context, although the dominant pedagogy has been one that demeaned and oppressed the majority of students who are black, some schoolteachers, representing different racial groups, labored to prepare black students to pass state exams, while also seeking to help them develop alternative ways of knowing and thinking about the world (Jansen 1990).

Research as Political Work

As noted in the discussion about curriculum decision-making, knowledge and power are closely linked. This bears on educators' work as researchers and scholars (producers or discoverers of knowledge), as it does on their activity as curriculum decision-makers (selectors and organizers of knowledge) (Orlin 1981). This is not always recognized, or acknowledged, however, because "the relations between power and knowledge were made invisible by distancing [scholarly] work from social interest through rhetoric about autonomy and responsibility" (Popkewitz 1991, p. 225). While not wanting to claim that research is *only* a political activity, we do want to examine the ways in which scholarly work reflects and has implications for the distribution of power and the distribution of material and symbolic resources. This occurs in part because of scholars' "need" for external support to undertake research. For example, social scientists in the United States have been "ardent in their search for material and symbolic resources" from corporations, foundations, and governments (Silva and Slaughter 1984, p. 75).

Research is political both through the "determination of the results of research" and by "determining the directions and topics of research" (Pan 1990, p. 12; see also Calhoun 1980; Elias 1982). The issues are often discussed in terms of infringements on academic freedom. For example, during the time of the Protestant Reformation in Europe, elite groups "pushed members of the university community to become propagandists in the religious and political debates and . . . reached out to punish academics who espoused views repellent to the civil or ecclesiastical authorities" (Altbach 1990, p. 25). During the twentieth century in Latin America, "[t]raditions of university autonomy and academic freedom have been repeatedly violated by hostile political regimes" (Pelczar 1977, p. 134). And in Canadian universities in the 1980s, the "professoriate [lost] . . . its academic freedom as academia [was] increasingly forced to pursue applied fields while more critical endeavors remain[ed] underfunded" (Filson 1988, p. 315).

We also need to examine how knowledge, particularly that which supports or critiques existing power relations and distributions of wealth and status, is or is not disseminated. For example, while university-based scholars may publish critical analyses of the status quo, many do so primarily in academic journals that have a limited circulation to a relatively small, privileged group rather than in mass circulation newspapers or magazines (Altbach 1990). More generally, publishers, editors and reviewers are in a position to determine whose work is (or is not) published. In the attendant "struggle in which [scholars] must engage in order to force recognition of [their] products and [their] own authority as a legitimate producer, what is at stake is in fact the power to impose the definition of science (i.e., the delimitation of the field of problems, methods and theories) that may be regarded as *scientific* (Bourdieu 1975, p. 19, italics added). An example of this is the domination of logical positivism in many intellectual fields throughout much of this century. Scholars who faithfully adhered to the canons of positivism have drawn conclusions from their "data" without having to articulate, let alone defend, the assumptions that underlined their method and, in many ways, determined their research results. Yet, scholars who based their work in other paradigms were labelled as reductionists or nonscholars, even as they have struggled to describe and justify the assumptions on which their work is based (Popkewitz 1984; Shank and Vampola 1992; Simons 1990). [11]

There is also a hierarchical structure internationally that shapes the circulation of knowledge, in which the high-prestige academic institutions, professional societies, and multinational corporations located in economically dominant nations publish most of the journals and books (Altbach 1980). The existence of center-periphery relations in the publishing field clearly has implications for which scholars in which countries exercise power in various disciplines and accumulate status and other rewards. The stratified world system of knowledge production and circulation also helps to determine which scholars promoting which ideas will likely be brought in as technical assistants or consultants to inform the development of cultural, educational, economic, educational, and political institutions in various nations. And while one may debate about who really benefits from such activity, it is clear that "development" work is (by our definition) political, having implications for the distribution of power, material resources, and symbolic resources (Berman 1983; Gonzales 1982). [12]

The Politics of Being an Employee/Colleague in the Workplace

That educators are workers and educational institutions are workplaces is generally agreed (Connell 1985; Dreeben 1988; Lawn and Ozga 1981; Tipton 1988). And like those employed in other organizations, teachers, administrators, and others who work in educational institutions are immeshed in interpersonal or micropolitics, involving the "tactical use of power to retain or obtain control of real or symbolic resources" (Blase 1987, p. 288). For instance, in England, different groups of schoolteachers, those whose careers are tied to academic subjects versus those identified with pastoral care or counseling responsibilities, have competed for material resources (salary levels and program funds), symbolic resources (status and recognition), and power to shape the direction of their schools (Redican 1988). Collegial relations among teachers in (at least) the United States have been found to involve strategies to acquire or protect symbolic resources, such as status and psychic rewards that come from feelings of success in working with students. Diplomatic friendliness, avoiding controversy and conflict, and mutually recognizing the sanctity of individual teachers' classrooms enable teachers to survive and obtain some level of satisfaction and control by retreating from the larger institutional setting that might otherwise be openly laden with struggles over material as well as symbolic resources (Blase 1991; Lortie 1975). And although teachers' retreat into the security of the classroom may be a creative strategy, it is one that likely allows miseducative and inequality-reinforcing aspects of the system to go unchallenged (Bullough 1987; Steedman 1987).

Research in schools around the world has illuminated how administrative power over teachers has been constructed, accommodated, and resisted (Filson 1988; Joyce 1987; Kale 1970; Kanpol 1988; Smyth 1987; St. Maurice 1987; White 1981). There is also evidence of how at different times the state or international organizations have intervened in these power relations on behalf of teachers or administrators (Archer 1979; Ginsburg 1991; Grace 1987; Lawn 1988). Studies in Latin America, for example, make clear that such power relations have implications for material resources, including employment, salary, and promotions, in that teachers "depend on the goodwill of their supervisors . . . to remain [and advance] in the profession [and] that goodwill in turn is paid for in loyalty and by 'not creating problems'" (Oliveros 1975, p. 231).

Despite or because of such a reality, at various times in some settings, schoolteachers and administrators have worked in alliance on projects inside and outside of schools. For example, until the 1960s both teachers and administrators were members of one of the major teacher organizations in the United States, the National Education Association (NEA) (Spring 1986). In contrast to the United States' case, where teachers forced the administrators out of the NEA, in Japan teachers and administrators jointly resisted efforts by the Ministry of Education and the International Labor Organization to end administrators' membership in Nikkyoso, the Japanese Teachers Union (Levine 1969; Ota 1985; Singleton 1976). The leadership of the Korean Federation of Teachers' Associations continues to celebrate the advantages of membership composed of both teachers and administrators (Korean Federation of Teachers' Associations 1991).[13]

In higher education institutions the relationships both among and between instructors and administrators also evidence a political dimension (Altbach 1991; Fuhrig 1969; Rabkin and Eisemon 1977). While some inter-educators' relations might be characterized as collegial or horizontal, others are vertical or hierarchical, both within and across institutions (Clark 1984; Perkin 1987). Policy setting, program and course approval, resource allocations, instructional and other load assignments, hiring and firing decisions, and promotion and tenure deliberations are clearly linked to the distribution of power and of symbolic and material resources within (and outside) universities and colleges (Altbach 1977, 1990; Filson 1988; Friedberg and Musselin 1987; Martinotti and Giasanti 1977; Scarfe and Sheffield 1977). Personnel decisions have resulted in a predominantly male professoriate, and there is evidence that "staff who have nonmainstream positions and who speak out may find it difficult to secure promotion . . . [and] may find their teaching loads increased or their salary raises blocked" (Altbach

1990, p. 35; see also Bourdieu 1988; Habermas 1987; Simpson 1991).

Power relations between teachers and administrators reflects in part the struggle over the educational labor process. Studies in various societal and historical contexts have focused on the sometimes contested processes through which many teachers have become "proletarianized" (their work has been deskilled and depowered) and how some teachers have become "professionalized" (their work has been reskilled and repowered) (Apple 1988; Busswell 1980; Carlson 1987; Danylewycz and Prentice 1988; Filson 1988; Ginsburg 1988, 1990). Through such a lens it becomes apparent that administrator-teacher relations reflect and have implications for class relations (Ginsburg 1988; Sarup 1984). For instance, through the process of proletarianization

> teachers are not merely made more like other workers in economic terms, i.e., less economically advantaged, more vulnerable to redundancy and pressure toward increased workload. [It] also involves a loss of control over the work process, a loss of definition by the worker of the essential elements of the task. (Ozga and Lawn 1981, p. 143)

And given the gender regime of schools and universities, where often men manage women, administrator-teacher relations constitute a terrain on which patriarchy is reproduced and struggled over (Acker 1983; Apple 1983; Connell 1985; Kelly and Nihlen 1982; Mattingly 1975; Schmuck 1987; Strober and Tyack 1980; Weiler 1988). In the United States at least "[s]cientific management institutionalized and provided justification for the traditional educational harem of female schoolteachers ruled by male administrators" (Spring 1986, p. 259). And there is evidence that female teachers, like their sisters in other jobs, are more likely than their male counterparts to experience proletarianization (Acker 1983; Apple 1984; Busswell 1980). Gender (as well as class and race) relations are also implicated in workplace interaction involving educators and noneducator employees. For example, issues of power and the distribution of material and symbolic resources can be seen as ingredients of school secretaries' daily experience in dealing with administrators and teachers (Casanova 1991).

Educators' Unions/Associations and Political Work

Educators all over the world have formed associations and unions, at least in part as a collective response to their shared experiences as employees involved in the politics of educational workplaces (Altbach 1991; Cooper 1992; Cummings and Amano 1977; Fraser 1989; Singleton 1976). In community colleges in Ontario, Canada, for instance, Filson (1988, p. 312) observed that:

> Senior administrators . . . accelerated technical pro-
> letarianization of faculty during the early 1980s by
> demanding fiscal restraint and increased efficiency,
> thereby provoking dissent, unionism and willingness on
> the part of faculty to resort to strike action to protect
> professionalism.

It is reported that in a variety of West European and North American societies, schoolteachers comprise the highest organized category of workers, although the percentage of teachers belonging to unions or associations varies intersocietally (Duclau-Williams 1985; Johnson, 1988; Leiulfsrud and Lindbad 1991). Schoolteachers in less economically privileged countries of the "Third World" are also likely to belong to occupational group organizations (Dove 1979; Hurst and Rust 1990). University- and college-level faculty have increased their organizational efforts in recent decades, although on average they do not conceive of themselves as militant and labor union oriented (Altbach 1990; Archer 1979; Filson 1988).

Educators' union and association activity "cannot be divorced from political considerations" (Darmanin 1985, p. 158). Such activity is political in the sense that it involves relations with national and local states to shape the distribution of material resources to educators (versus other groups). Educators have worked through their organizations to demand and/or obtain higher salaries, pensions, additional positions or other material benefits (Alba 1969; Altbach 1977; Altenbaugh 1987; Archer 1979; Bergen 1988; Darmanin 1985; Dove 1979; Feeley 1989; Fraser 1989; Friedberg and Musselin 1987; Ginsburg, Wallace, and Miller 1988; Henderson 1969; Laudner and Yee 1987; Lawn and Ozga 1981; Levine 1969; Natarajan 1969; Oliveros 1975; Ota 1985; Pietrasik 1987; Rosenthal 1969; Siefert

1987; Skopp 1982; Urban 1989; White 1981). Sometimes such organizational efforts have been focused more on improving the salaries and benefits of the more privileged organizational members, thus reinforcing hierarchical divisions within society (Fuhrig 1969; Henderson 1969).

Not all organizations of educators during all historical periods have focused on increased material rewards for their members (Annunziato 1990).[14] For example, prior to (but not after) the early 1960s, many teachers belonging to the National Education Association in the United States could be characterized as "docile handmaidens[15] of public education" (Rosenthal 1969, p. 1) and functioned as "agents for the preservation of the status quo" (Ziegler 1967, p. 90). And the national teachers' union in Korea (KFTA) (Shin, Kim, and Park 1991) and in Mexico (SNTE) (Arriaga 1981; Campos et al. 1990; Ginsburg and Tidwell 1990; Torres 1991) are viewed, at least to members of dissident teachers' movements, as serving more effectively to legitimate the decisions of state elites than to promote the interests of educators. The national teachers' union in Thailand, Khuru Sapha, has been similarly described as having "quasi-official standing with the ministry . . . [and] blending governmental paternalism, individual self-interest, and professional aspirations" (Heenan and Wronski 1969, pp. 279–280).

Part of the collective political activity of educators has been directed toward obtaining and retaining the right to organize and engage in negotiations, collective bargaining, strikes, and other forms of "militant" action (Archer 1979; Feeley 1989; Filson 1988; Kelly 1982, Seregny 1989; Skopp 1982; Spaull and Mann 1985; Stoer 1985). At various times in many societies it has been illegal for educators to withhold their labor (Assie-Lumumba and Lumumba-Kasongo 1991; Darvas 1991; Dembele 1991; Hurst and Rust 1990), and teacher strikes continue to be proscribed by law in some states in the United States (Johnson 1988; Spring 1986). Historically, teacher unionism in Japan was the target of government repression before World War II, given the blessings of the United States and allied occupying forces and the Japanese Socialist government from 1945–48, and then undermined when the Conservative Party assumed power in

1948 (Levine 1969; Ota 1985). Similarly, in the year following the consolidation of the 1917 Bolshevik Revolution, the Soviet state dissolved as "counterrevolutionary" the All Russian Federation of Teachers and created a state-sponsored union in response to a three-month strike called by the twelve-year old organization (Archer 1979, p. 285).

Educators' organizations have also struggled with local and national state elites, educational administrators, parents, other citizens, as well as other organizations, over issues of power, control, and autonomy (Archer 1979; Bergen 1988; Darmanin 1985; Ginsburg et al. 1988; Grace 1987; Lawn and Ozga 1981). "All teachers' organizations are political organizations in the sense that they are concerned with the exercise of power within countries" (Adams 1982, p. 198). Such struggles have focused on the capacity to determine working conditions; teachers' responsibilities and management practices; the supply and entry level qualifications of teachers; programs for preservice and inservice education; pedagogy and curriculum; examination systems; teacher-appraisal systems; educational policy; salary-determination mechanisms; and the level of funding for education in general (Adams 1982; Altenbaugh 1987; Archer 1979; Carlson 1987; Dembele 1991; Fraser 1989; Fuhrig 1969; Ginsburg 1988; Ginsburg, Meyenn and Miller 1979; Ginsburg et al. 1988; Laudner and Yee 1987; Lawn 1987; Manzer 1973; Natarajan 1969; Ozga and Lawn 1981; Oliveros 1975; Pietrasik 1987; Rosenthal 1969; Seregny 1989; Siefert 1987; Skopp 1982; So 1990; Spring 1986; Urban 1989; Walsh 1987; Williams 1977).

Organized educators have engaged in political action in relation to the state to obtain symbolic resources, such as "professional status" associated with university-based preparation (Ginsburg 1988, 1990; Jarausch 1990; Kale 1970; Mattingly 1975; Nwagwu 1977; Ozga and Lawn 1981; N. Parry and J. Parry 1974; Skopp 1982). Such status symbols have been seen to be valuable assets in educators' (and other educated workers') professionalization projects, in which increased power/autonomy and remuneration are also sought (Larson 1977). While national and local-state action has sometimes functioned as a catalyst for or reinforced teacher professionalization, educators have also been the targets of deprofessionalization or proletarianization efforts by the state (Barrington 1991; Dove 1979; Filson 1988; Ginsburg 1990; Ginsburg and Miller 1991; Imaz and Salinas 1984; Laudner and Yee 1987; Lawn and Ozga 1981; Robertson and Woock 1991). A major ideological weapon used, at least in Britain and former British colonies, by both educators and the state in such struggles is *professionalism* (Connell 1985; Filson 1988; Ginsburg and Chaturvedi 1988; Ginsburg et al. 1980; Ozga and Lawn 1981).[16] And while there are multiple and contradictory meanings of the term, *professionalism*, both in social-scientific literature and in everyday discourse, the notion of a hierarchical division of labor, legitimated by a meritocratic conception of educational attainment, is often a central element. In drawing on and reproducing this ideology, educators help to legitimate a division of labor needed by (at least) capitalist relations of production (Ginsburg 1987b).

This tendency is strengthened due to the fact that some conceptions of professionalism distinguish professionals' organizational efforts from the "unionism" and strike actions of members of the working class (Corr 1990; Filson 1988; Fuhrig 1969; Ginsburg and Chaturvedi 1988; Ginsburg et al. 1980; Heenan and Wronski 1969; Henderson 1969; Johnson 1988; Kale 1970; Lawn and Ozga 1981; Natarajan 1969).[17] This is part of the reason why in some societies the issue of educators being affiliated to the broader labor movement or to working-class-identified political parties is such a divisive issue (Adams 1982; Darmanin 1985; Duclaud-Williams 1985; Feeley 1989; Filson 1988; Fuhrig 1969; Ginsburg et al. 1988, Henderson 1969; Mattingly 1975; Natarajan 1969; Ozga and Lawn 1981; Spaull and Mann 1985; Urban 1989; White 1981) even though organized educators have played a major leadership role in labor movements in certain societies (Alba 1969; Assie-Lumumba and Lumumba-Kasongo 1991; Boucher 1985; Darvas 1991; Dembele 1991; Filson 1988; Levine 1969; Spring 1986; Stoer 1985).

Race relations have also affected and been shaped by the discourse and action of organized educators. For instance, the interests of black schoolteachers in England were less well served by the various teacher unions and associations during the

1970s and 1980s, although the National Union of Teachers has developed materials to be used by teachers in the classrooms to encourage multiculturalism and combat racism (Lyon and Migniuolo 1989). In the United States, teachers' organizations were racially segregated until the 1950s, and organized white teachers did not play a supportive role in the black teachers' organizational struggles for equal pay. Moreover, there are instances, such as the struggle by organized teachers in New York City in 1968 against black-community efforts to control their schools locally, which indicate that teachers' desire for professional autonomy has implications for the distribution of power among racial groups (Urban 1989).

Teachers' organizational activity is also political with respect to perpetuating and challenging gender relations. Historically, some predominantly male teacher organizations sought to achieve and maintain professional status for their members by excluding and distancing themselves from the corps of female teachers (Corr 1990; Darmanin 1985; Jarausch 1990; Witz 1990).[18] Some organizations have tended to reflect male approaches to dealing with issues accorded more importance by male than female teachers, while ignoring concerns, such as child care and domestic responsibilities, that, *within present practices*, affect women more than men (Corr 1990; Fuhrig 1969; Littlewood 1989). Some schoolteacher organizations struggled for, while others worked against, equal pay for female and male teachers (Boucher 1985; Corr 1990; Feeley 1989; Littlewood 1989; Scarfe and Sheffield 1977; Urban 1989). Gender-segregated teachers' unions were formed in Britain, with both men and women teachers setting up separate organizations. The former did so in order to deny women equal pay, and the latter sought to strengthen their struggle for equal pay. With the achievement of equal wages in the 1960s and 1970s, these unions were merged, although gender inequality still seems to operate in the organizations there as elsewhere (Littlewood 1989).

While women have served in leadership roles in teachers' organizations in some societies, females are underrepresented in high positions in such organizations even in the same countries (Campos et al. 1990; Corr 1990; Cortina 1989; Fraser 1989; Littlewood 1989; Urban 1989; Weiler 1989; Ziegler 1967). This point, however, must be qualified with reference to the different ways in which male and female educators may play an active and essential role in organizing collective action, such as strikes. For example, in England during the mid-1980s female school-level representatives of teachers' organizations were not as active or visible to the public as their male counterparts, but they played a politically crucial role of "keeping up morale among school level colleagues, dealing with problems of individual members, negotiating with their head teachers and representatives of other unions, and maintaining the flow of information" (Ozga 1987, p. 131). While this qualification renders problematic the issue of what constitutes political action, it also points up how a gendered division of labor is reflected in and perhaps reproduced by teachers' involvement in teachers' organizations.

Some organized educators have drawn on and reproduced a key element in the ideology that supports patriarchy. In the nineteenth century, leaders of schoolteacher organizations in the United States played a role both in promoting teaching as an extension of the private sphere and in claiming that teaching is a "natural" role for women because of their maternal instincts. In the early twentieth century they helped fan the concerns of the "women peril" in education—decrying the fact that teaching had become too feminized, and thereby posed a threat to male students' development. The latter occurred when some women teachers began to take seriously their involvement in the public sphere, especially feminist teachers' struggling for sexual equality in education and society, an indication that some organized teachers offered a challenge to the ideological notion of separate spheres (Weiler 1989).

Political Work as a Family Member

"We know that teaching has been (and can still be) liberating as well as inhibiting for women, men, and racial and ethnic minorities. . . . The teaching occupation encompassed more than just the classroom [or even educational system], affecting teachers' personal lives and, in many cases, their families" (Altenbaugh 1992, p. 194). Grumet's (1988) analysis of teachers' lives illustrates how their activity with their own children in home settings parallels and is interdependent with their work with other people's children in classrooms. Like classroom activity, however, the involvement of educators and others in homes and other family settings is inappropriately often not regarded as political, because it occurs in the "private sphere" (Corr and Jamieson 1990; Gamarnikow et al. 1986; Millet 1977).

Although there is not an extensive literature examining the family life of educators, it is apparent that what male and female educators do in their roles as spouses, parents, children, and so on, has a political dimension in that it is related to power relations and distributions of symbolic and material resources. Research focused on family life has illuminated how unequal gender relations, in particular, are constituted by and constitutive of the day-to-day interactions between spouses (Belenky et al. 1986; Tannen 1986). Male and female children are often socialized differently, which has implications not only for the symbolic and material resources they accumulate during their lives (Chafetz 1984; Chodorow 1978), but also for the aspects of power (*power over* versus *power with*) toward which they are oriented and skilled (Brock-Utne 1989). Moreover, the forms and consequences of such socialization vary by social class and race of families, as well as by the gender of the child and parent (Cohen 1976; Farran 1982; Luttrell 1992; Miller and Ginsburg 1989).

Political Work as Citizens in Communities

Individually and through their associations and unions, because of either the dictates of political and economic elites or their own values and convictions, educators have come to play political roles in local, national, and global communities. And while we will focus here on examples of activity, we should remember that nonparticipation is also a political act. Sometimes nonparticipation stems from a voluntary stance adopted by educators. For example in Nigeria, the professionalism that the leadership of the Teachers' Union sought "steered their followers away from the broader struggles and bellicose tactics of political unionism" (Henderson 1969, p. 252). Similarly, professors have not "been involved in direct political activism of an oppositional nature [because they] typically see themselves as part of an established intellectual and academic community [and] are not often willing to take the risk of direct political action" (Altbach 1991, p. 6; see also Grumet 1990; Mommsen 1987; Scarfe and Sheffield 1977; Wexler 1982).[19] Other times nonparticipation occurs because governments restrict certain types of educators' community-based political action (Altbach 1990; Assie-Lumumba and Lumumba-Kasongo 1991; Archer 1979, Darvas 1991; Dove 1979; Fuhrig 1969; Jarausch 1990; Kolmes 1981; Levine 1969; Otero 1981; Seregny 1989; Shils 1972; Stoer 1985; White 1981; Ziegler 1967). As Dove (1979, p. 4) comments with reference to developing countries, in some contexts educators "have to pass inspection by political screening of authorities before appointments are confirmed, . . . [and that] professional freedoms and personal liberties of teachers are circumscribed by restrictive rules concerning professional association, freedom of expression and political participation."

In contexts as diverse as Africa, Asia, Europe, and Latin America, educators have played leadership and other activist roles in nationalist, independence movements and anticolonial or anti-imperial struggles (Aguilar and Retamal 1982; Alba 1969; Altbach 1991; Dove 1979, 1986; Imaz and Salinas 1984; Kelly 1982; Lauglo 1982; Shils 1972). Historically and more recently, educators have also been prominent actors (militarily and otherwise) in revolutions in a variety of countries (Alba 1969; Altbach 1990, 1991; Assie-Lumumba and Lumumba-Kasongo 1991; Darvas 1991; Dembele 1991; Feeley 1989; Fuhrig 1969; Seregny 1989; Skopp 1982; Stoer 1985; White 1981). As Jansen (1990, p. 63) reports about his own and colleagues' recent experiences in the revolutionary context of South Africa, at "moments of student-teacher-police confrontation [we] made the transition from the technocratic teacher to political activist and, on occasion, to comrade in armed struggle."

Educators have served as community leaders, animateurs, and agents of social change and community and national development (Antler and Biklen 1990; Dove 1979, 1986; Hurst and Rust 1990; Kale 1970; Lauglo 1982; Seregny 1989; Stoer 1985; Watson 1983). Sometimes they have challenged "the political and cultural hegemony of the upper class" (Lauglo 1982, p. 235), assumed "leadership positions in the workers' struggle against a very procapitalist government" (Filson 1988, p. 307), or "associate[d] with organized labor . . . [in] a common struggle against corporate managers and control by the rich" (Spring 1986, p. 260; see also Ross 1991). Other times they have operated as agents of state and economic elites (Imaz and Salinas 1984; Lauglo 1982; Watson 1983). Similarly, educators have functioned as mediators between national state elites and the local citizenry, while trying to find space for autonomous action in the middle of a conflict between a secular state and the church (Alba 1969; Archer 1979; Fuhrig 1969; Meyers 1976; Seregny 1989; Skopp 1982; Stoer 1985). Dove (1986) concludes that schoolteachers more often served in community leadership roles during the pre- and immediate postindependence periods in developing countries than more recently, and Lauglo (1982) reports that historically European and North American rural schoolteachers have varied widely in the extent they performed such roles. In both cases the relative level of education of teachers compared to community members is seen as part of the explanation, with teachers being more active when they are more educated than community members.

In a variety of contexts, heads of state, legislators, and other government officials worked as schoolteachers or university professors at one point in their lives (Altbach 1990, 1991; Antler and Biklen 1990; Berube 1988; Clifford 1987; Dove 1979, 1986; Jarausch 1990; Nwagwu 1977; Shils 1972). Educators have also been leaders of political parties (Assie-Lumumba and Lumumba-Kasongo 1991; Darvas 1991) as well as over-represented (compared to other occupational groups) as active members in party organizations (Leiulfsrud and Linblad 1991; Urban 1989).[20] To varying degrees, individual and organized educators devote considerable time to lobbying and candidate electoral work (Adams 1982; Berube 1988; Levine 1969; Pietrasik 1987; Spaull and Mann 1985; Urban 1989; Ziegler 1967). This involvement varies internationally as well as historically. For instance, in the United States before the 1960s schoolteachers' involvement in unions and associations was for the most part not concerned with lobbying and electoral work (Ziegler 1967), but by the 1980s it could be reported that teachers "are a powerful force in American politics . . . powerful lobbying arms seeking favored legislation and political machines supporting local, state, and national candidates with [person] power and money" (Berube 1988, p. 1).

Educators, particularly those employed in higher education institutions, have played political roles as advisors to candidates, government officials, and corporate elites, or have through their writings and speeches shaped policy-relevant discourse (Altbach 1977, 1990, 1991; Mommsen 1987).[21] For instance, during and after the Second World War German academic exiles served as government advisors and other roles in shaping the United States' strategies for dealing with Germany (Sollner 1991). And social science "experts were able to counter their dependence on resource holders by constructing an ideology of expertise . . . [which] contributed to the technical rationalization of the economy and at the same time legitimated the existing order by demonstrating its capacity for limited reform" (Silva and Slaughter 1984, p. 159).

Educators' political work has focused on different sides of a variety of issues. Educators fit the portrait of intellectuals more generally, in that they have not all "been equally attracted by revolutionary politics. Moderates and partisans in civil politics, quiet apolitical concentration on their specialized intellectual preoccupation, cynical antipolitical passivity, and faithful acceptance and service of the existing order, are all to be found in substantial proportions among modern intellectuals" (Shils 1972, p. 9).[22] For instance, in Britain, South Africa, and the United States they have been active members in feminist and civil rights movements, fighting for universal suffrage, emancipation, racial desegregation, and tax reform (Altbach 1991; Antler and Biklen 1990; Clifford 1987; Fraser 1989; Jansen 1990; Joyce 1987; King 1987; Spring 1986; Urban 1989).

In Germany in the 1930s some secondary school and higher education teachers took a public stand against the Nazi's fascist and racist project, but others rationalized their duty to at least make minimal concessions to Hitler's demands, while still other educators publicly endorsed and supported the Nazi regime (Jarausch 1990; Mommsen 1987). Similarly, in the 1950s in the United States, some (but not all) university teachers actively or passively helped "to legitimize domestic repression before and during the McCarthy years" (Ross 1991, p. 114; see also Schecker, 1986). And during World War I and World War II educators in Germany, England, and the United States contributed time and energy to community-based work to support opposite sides in the war effort (Jarausch 1990; Lawn 1987; Ross 1991). Some educators have also become involved in antimilitarist peace movements, for example, in France during World War I, in England in the 1930s, in Japan before and after the Second World War, and in the United States in the 1960s and 1970s (Altbach 1991; Cummings and Amano 1977; Feeley 1989; Levine 1969; Ross 1991). Most recently, the 1990–91 war in the Persian Gulf attracted active and passive support or opposition from educators around the world (Epstein 1992).

Conclusion

In this chapter we have sought to clarify and to document the claim that the actions educators engage in, or refrain from engaging in, are political. This is not to say that such actions and inactions are *only* political, but that it is theoretically incorrect (and politically charged) to claim that educators' activities are apolitical. The issue to be addressed, therefore, is not whether educators are (or should be) political actors, but for what ends, by what means, and in whose interests should teachers engage in political work.

To develop our argument we have focused on different aspects of educators' role: curriculum decision making, pedagogy, student evaluation, research, employee/colleague, unions/association participant, family member, and citizen. And although we have discussed each aspect separately, these aspects of the educator's role should not be considered as separate or unrelated.

For example, educators' involvement in community-based social movements may be reinforced or contradicted by how they select and organize curriculum knowledge. Being active or inactive in the community may be related to focusing students' attention on or ignoring inequalities, exploitation, and oppression and the role subordinate groups play in challenging such relations of power (Alba 1969; Connell 1985; Grace 1979; Kelly 1982; Sultana 1987; Ziegler 1967). It has been noted as well that university-based scholars, who offer critiques of the inequalities of existing power relations and the extant distribution of material and symbolic resources, may not always play an active role in community-based progressive social movements and may at times act to reproduce inequalities through their decisions about curriculum and student evaluations (Ginsburg 1987a; Popkewitz 1984; Wexler 1982).

Additionally, in terms of the connections between educators' union/association activity and their involvement as citizens, we noted educators whose occupationally focused collective efforts served as a catalyst to mobilize them for active participation in broader based struggles in local, national, and global communities (Assie-Lumumba and Lumumba-Kasongo 1991; Berube 1988; Darvas 1991; Feeley 1989; Skopp 1982). We also presented evidence of schoolteacher organizations giving up (or having taken away) their rights to engage in independent electoral politics in order to secure some degree of attention from state and party elites to teachers' work-related demands (Jarausch 1990; Levine 1969; Rosenthal 1969; Torres 1991).

In discussing the political work of educators we have tried to keep in mind that educators are not a homogeneous group, and thus we have been careful to search for multiple means and ends of their political activity.[23] Although some patterns and similarities exist across a range of countries, over time, and among different groups of educators in the same location and time period, there are also important differences internationally, historically, and intra-occupationally. Here we have emphasized international comparisons, but historical comparisons are also instructive. For example, it has been noted that the relations between schoolteachers and the state have varied across different historical periods in countries such as Australia, Britain, Côte d'Ivoire, Germany, Hungary, Japan, Mexico, and the United States (Assie-Lumumba and Lumumba-Kasongo 1991; Berube 1988; Darvas 1991; Imaz and Salinas 1984; Grace 1987; Jarausch 1990; Levine 1969; Robertson and Woock 1991).

Divisions among educators and their organizations also make general statements about their political work problematic. In a range of societies there are examples of educators' unions and associations fractionated by gender, race/ethnicity, social class, sector of the education system, subject matter taught, regional location, religious identification, political ideology or party affiliation, militancy, and orientation to alliances with other groups of organized labor (Alba 1969; Altbach 1977; Archer 1979; Assie-Lumumba and Lumumba-Kasongo 1991; Bergen 1988; Darvas 1991; Duclau-Williams 1985; Feeley 1989; Ginsburg and Miller 1991; Grace 1987; Heenan and Wronski 1969; Jarausch 1990; Levine 1969; Littlewood 1989; Natarajan 1969; Nwagwu 1977; Stoer 1985; Urban 1989; White 1981; Ziegler 1967). Thus, different groups of educators at different times and places have engaged and continue to engage in a wide range of active and inactive forms of political work. Intragroup variation also means that the consequences of the political work by different groups of educators may sometimes reinforce and at other times challenge the existing distribution of material resources, symbolic resources, and power among various groups from local to global levels.[24]

And while recognizing such divisions among educators and the potentially countervailing tendencies in their political activity may lead some to believe that on average educators are a "neutral" political force (e.g., the conservatives balance out the progressives), two points must be kept in mind. First, concluding that some educators reinforce and others challenge the status quo is *not* tantamount to determining the proportion of educators reinforcing or challenging, nor the relative strength of the impact of their actions. Such mathematical assessments, if possible, would have to be conducted for each specific historical and societal context as well as for an overall conclusion about educators. Second, although there have been efforts by the state elites and some educators to form unitary national organizations (Alba 1969; Campos et al. 1990; Levine 1969; Natarajan 1969; Torres 1991),[25] the extant divisions and disunities among educators need to be understood as partly the result of state policy and practice (Lawn 1985).

Having reemphasized that educators, like other people, work and live within relations of power, we do not want to conclude with some image of educators as "objects rather than subjects [or as] . . . the unknowing tools of the social elite" (Quantz 1985, p. 439). Rather, we want to encourage a more dialectical perspective, one that focuses on both the "ways in which political authorities have sought to reshape . . . the social, political and cultural identity of teachers . . . [and] the methods by which teachers themselves have sought to ameliorate or defend their [and sometimes others'] access to scarce social goods and the nature of political resources they have mobilized" (White 1981, p. 3). Our point is not that, because everything is political, we are imprisoned within structures of power or are the pawns of dominant groups. Instead we seek to highlight the political nature and effects of activities that are routinely required of us as educators, and the ways in which their potential has been, and can be, seized at various points in time by different people to create the history we live. The many instances we have cited reflect the shifting ground of these power relationships and the ruptures and fissures these make possible.

The examples we have referenced also help clarify the choices we educators make. And while there are other dimensions to consider, we urge careful and continual reflection on the political dimension of our actions. We need to ask some general questions, such as: How do existing power relations shape what we do and how are they shaped by what we do? How are our actions constituted by and constitutive of the unequal distribution of material and symbolic resources? Under what conditions and through what strategies can we promote a *power with* rather than a *power over* orientation to politics?

We also need to identify the political implications of the following kinds of decisions that each of us makes on a daily basis: What ideas and perspectives should I include in school or university curriculum? What form of pedagogy and classroom social relations should I seek to institute in classrooms? What kind of system should I adopt or encourage for evaluating the performance of students? What topics should I research, from what perspective, gathering data from what sources, and to whom should I report the findings of my own and others' research? How should I operate in relation to colleagues and others in my workplace? Should I belong to and be active in unions and associations, and what goals and strategies should I encourage such groups to pursue? How should I behave in relation to spouse/companions, children, grandchildren, parents, grandparents, and so on? Should I be active or passive in my role as a citizen of local, national, and global communities; on what issues should I focus attention; with what other people should I ally; and what ends and means should I emphasize?

The use of the "I" in the above questions is to remind us that these political decisions are personal, although best made in dialogue with others. At the same time we want to reemphasize that personal decisions have a political dimension. We need to reflect on our own and others' activity, and we need to consider seriously the political implications of what we do or refrain from doing. We urge you to reject "the educational form of spectatorship . . . in favor of the reflexive, socially concrete individual struggling, always and inevitably in interaction, to understand and act upon her/his own social limitations and possibilities" (Wexler 1982, p. 65).[26] We agree with Shakespeare that to be or not to be *is* the question. But the choice is not about being political or apolitical, but about being relatively active or passive; autonomous or heteronomous vis-à-vis other groups; conservative or change-oriented; focused on individual, occupational group, or larger collectivities' goals; and allied to dominant group, subordinate group, or human interests.

NOTES

1. This is a revised version of Ginsburg et al. (1992). For an abridged version see Ginsburg and Kamat (1994). We want to thank Yvonne Jones for her assistance in word processing these manuscripts. Thomas Clayton also contributed to the editing of this chapter.

2. Note, however, that this argument, which Dearden (1980) counters, is based on a narrow conception of the political as only concerning state action.

3. Peter Hackett (1988) recommends that we attend to the aesthetic dimension, analyzing from multiple perspectives educators' past, present, and future lives, cultures, and institutions in terms of their beauty.

4. More generally, the distinction between public and private spheres must be problematized, in that the "categories of public and private spheres . . . were historically formulated in the nineteenth century" (Corr and Jamieson 1990, p. 2). The social construction of the private sphere (home, family life, devotional religious practice, etc.) as distinct from the public sphere (state, economic activity, etc.) has been linked both to the emergence of capitalist relations (Howe 1991) and to the rise of Protestantism (Turner 1990). It is interesting that at least in the United States during a period of capitalist industrialization, when many men were pulled into the public sphere of factory work and many women were pushed into the private sphere of the home, many women entered teaching and assumed roles in the private sphere of classrooms in "egg crate" schools, while in the more public sphere roles of administrators were dominated by males.

5. By considering both the public and private spheres as political realms, we can begin to challenge notions, such as "nineteenth century definitions [in at least the United States] of what constituted the political sphere, [which focused] exclusively on male activities in partisan electoral politics [and ignored] . . . the actions of women who organized and worked in many ways for social ideals" (Weiler, 1989, p. 14; see also Howe 1991).

6. Miller (1992, pp. 247–248), a major contributor to the concept of *power with* to be discussed, concludes that "there is enormous validity in women's [and we would add men's] not wanting to use power as it is presently conceived and used. Rather, women [and men] may want to be powerful in ways that simultaneously enhance, rather than diminish, the power of others."

7. In this quotation we substitute the term *power* for *force* because we believe it is the more central concept for Foucault.

8. Young (1992, p. 174) offers the useful reminder that "[p]olitics is partly a struggle over the language people use to describe social and political experience."

9. See Lukes (1974) on distinctions between *structural power*, exercised through overt behaviors to influence decision making or to

block decisions (i.e., nondecision making), and *ideological power*, exercised through the circulation of ideas that may create desires, goals, or orientations that are contradictory to an individual's or a group's interest.

10. Kreisberg (1992) effectively reviews a wide range of feminist and other theoretical analyses of power in clarifying the distinction between *power over* and *power with*, while arguing how the latter provides a more appropriate basis for empowerment efforts in education and other fields.

11. For an excellent discussion of the different assumptions of positivist, interpretive, and critical sciences in the context of the study of education, see Popkewitz (1984).

12. On the political dimension of university-based educators' involvement in *development* work, see Berman (1983) and Gonzales (1982).

13. Relevant information was also obtained during a personal meeting with the General Secretary and other officers of KFTA on January 17, 1992.

14. Even while seeking salary and benefits for teachers, unions may be seen to operate against the interests of their membership. For instance, generally in the United States unions have been characterized as engaged in *commodity unionism*, a practice that helps to reproduce capitalist relations which are argued to rest on the exploitation of workers. "Contemporary American unions . . . have evolved into producers and distributors of a peculiar commodity which is called "union representation." . . . Through the act of becoming union members, workers . . . continue their societal roles as consumers of commodities produced by others . . . under capitalist class conditions" (Annunziato 1990, p. 9).

15. Note the gendered terminology employed here. We will discuss later the role played by male and female teachers in organizational activity.

16. Ozga and Lawn (1981, p. vi) clarify that "professionalism could both operate as a strategy for control of teachers manipulated by the state, while also being used by teachers to protect themselves against dilution."

17. Kale (1970, p. 372) reports that the concept of *guru* functions similarly to produce "a sense of shame and guilt as [teachers] talked about teachers' militant attempts to demand higher pay."

18. These are examples of what Witz (1990, p. xx) terms a "gendered professional project of closure."

19. Grumet (1990, p. xii) reminds us that such claims that intellectuals are "retreating to their university offices, research grants and suburban homes" ignores the "two decades of vibrant, courageous and committed feminist scholarship . . . [and] recapitulates the sexism that has exacerbated the very division of public and private life that he laments."

20. Sometimes political parties create their own teachers' organizations (see Fuhrig 1969, p. 96).

21. This view of educators seems to characterize them as autonomous agents, independently framing political discourse. We also need to consider the possibility that certain intellectual ideas—those that serve to legitimate certain policies and institutional practices—are selected and widely distributed by those who own and control the means of mass communications (see Gramsci 1971).

22. Note, however, that we do not view "quiet . . . concentration on their specialized intellectual preoccupation" or "passivity" as apolitical or antipolitical.

23. In this and perhaps other senses our analysis is informed by postmodernist or poststructuralist approaches (see Cherryholmes 1988; Rust 1991).

24. Moreover, because of the contradictions in power relations that are constitutive of and constituted by educators' individual and collective action, it is often the case that a given educator in a given time and place operates in a manner that services partially the interests of both dominant and subordinate groups.

25. As noted above, however, these efforts to unify educators can also be seen as strategies for bringing the organizations under state control.

26. Moreover, we concur with Foucault and Popkewitz that our reflection and action must be creative and not just framed on current interpretations of existing possibilities. "If 'politicization' means falling back on ready-made choices and institutions, then the efforts of analysis involved in uncovering the relations of force and mechanisms of power are not worthwhile" (Foucault 1980, p. 190; discussed in Popkewitz 1991, p. 244).

REFERENCES

Acker, S. (1983). "Women and Teaching: A Semi-detached Sociology of a Semi-Profession." In *Gender, Class and Education,* edited by S. Walker and L. Barton, pp. 123–140. London: Falmer Press.

Adams, R. (1982). "The Future of Teachers' Unions." *Comparative Education* 18:197–204.

Adler, F. (1990). "Politics, Intellectuals and the University." *Telos* 82:103–109.

Aguilar, P., and Retamal, G. (1982). "Ideological Trends and the Education of Teachers in Latin America." In *Changing Priorities in Teacher Education,* edited by R. Goodings, M. Bryan, and M. Partland, pp. 140–159. London: Croom Helm.

Alba, V. (1969). "Mexico." In *Teacher Unions and Associations,* edited by A. Blum, pp. 200–232. Urbana: University of Illinois Press.

Altbach, P. (1977). "In Search of Saraswati: The Ambivalence of the Indian Academic." In *Comparative Perspectives on the Academic Profession,* edited by P. Altbach, pp. 146–165. New York: Praeger.

———. (1980). "The University as Center and Periphery." In *Universities and the International Distribution of Knowledge,* edited by I. Spitzberg, pp. 42–60. New York: Praeger.

———. (1991). "The Politics of Students and Faculty." Unpublished manuscript.

Altbach, P. (Ed.). (1990) "The Academic Profession." In *International Higher Education: An Encyclopedia,* pp. 23–46. New York: Garland.

Altenbaugh, R. (1987). "Teachers and the Workplace." *Urban Education* 21:365–389.

———. (1992). "The History of Teaching: A Social History of Schooling." In *The Teacher's Voice: A Social History of Teaching in Twentieth Century America,* edited by R. Altenbaugh, pp. 191–194. New York: Falmer Press.

Annunziato, F. (1990). "Commodity Unionism." *Rethinking Marxism* 3(2):8–33.

Antler, J., and Biklen, S. (1990). Foreword and Introduction. In *Changing Education: Women as Radicals and Conservators,* edited by J. Antler and S. Biklen, pp. ix–xxcii. Albany: State University of New York Press.

Anyon, J. (1981). "Social Class and School Knowledge." *Curriculum Inquiry* 11:2–42.

———. (1983). "Intersections of Gender and Class." In *Gender, Class and Education*, edited by S. Walker and L. Barton, pp. 19–38. London: Falmer Press.

Apple, M. (1979). *Ideology and the Curriculum*. Boston: Routledge and Kegan Paul.

———. (1982). *Education and Power*. Boston: Routledge and Kegan Paul.

———. (1983). "Work, Gender and Teaching." *Teachers College Record* 84:611–628.

———. (1984). "Teaching and Women's Work: A Comparative Historical and Ideological Analysis." In *Expressions of Power in Education*, edited by E. Gumbert, pp. 24–49. Atlanta: Center for Cross Cultural Education, Georgia State University.

———. (1986). *Teachers and Text*. Boston: Routledge and Kegan Paul.

———. (1988). "Work, Class and Teaching." In *Schoolwork*, edited by J. Ozga, pp. 101–151. Milton Keynes: Open University Press.

Archer, M. (1979). *The Social Origins of Educational Systems*. London: Sage.

Arendt, H. (1969). *On Violence*. New York: Harcourt, Brace and World.

Arriaga, M. (1981). "El Magisterio en Lucha." *Cuadernos Politicos* 27:79–101.

Ashendon, D., Connell, R., Dowsett, G., and Kessler, S. (1987). "Teachers and Working-Class Schooling." In *Critical Pedagogy and Cultural Power*, edited by D. Livingstone, pp. 245–268. South Hadley, MA: Bergin and Garvey.

Assie-Lumumba, N., and Lumumba-Kasongo, T. (1991). "The State, Economic Crisis and Educational Reform in Côte d'Ivoire." In *Understanding Educational Reform in Global Context*, edited by M. Ginsburg, pp. 257–284. New York: Garland.

Bacharach, S., and Lawler, E. (1980). *Power and Politics in Organizations*. San Francisco: Jossey-Bass.

Bagunywa, A. (1975). "The Changing Role of the Teacher in African Renewal." *Prospects* 5:220–226.

Barrington, J. (1991). "Educational Reform in New Zealand." In *Understanding Educational Reform in Global Context*, edited by M. Ginsburg, pp. 285–316. New York: Garland.

Belenky, M., Clinchy, B., Goldberger, N., and Tarule, J. (1986). *Women's Ways of Knowing*. New York: Basic Books.

Bergen, B. (1988). "Only a Schoolmaster: Gender, Class and the Effort to Professionalize Elementary Teaching in England, 1870–1910." In *Schoolwork*, edited by J. Ozga, pp. 48–68. Milton Keynes: Open University Press.

Berman, E. (1983). *The Influence of the Carnegie, Ford, and Rockefeller Foundations on American Foreign Policy.* Albany: State University of New York Press.

Bernstein, B. (1971). *Class, Codes and Control, Volume 1: Theoretical Studies Toward a Sociology of Language.* London: Routledge and Kegan Paul.

———. (1977). "Class and Pedagogies: Visible and Invisible." In *Class, Codes and Control, Volume 3: Toward a Theory of Educational Transmissions*, 2nd ed., pp. 116–150. London: Routledge and Kegan Paul.

Berube, M. (1988). *Teacher Politics: The Influence of Unions.* New York: Greenwood Press.

Biraimah, Karen. (1982). "Different Knowledge for Different Folks: Knowledge Distribution in a Togolese Secondary School." In *Comparative Education*, edited by P. Altbach, R. Arnove, and G. Kelly, pp. 161–175. New York: Macmillan.

Blase, J. (1987). "Political Interaction Among Teachers: Sociocultural Contexts in the Schools." *Urban Education* 2:286–309.

———. (Ed.). (1991). *The Politics of Life in Schools.* Newbury Park, CA: Sage.

Boucher, L. (1985). "Teacher Unions: Some Swedish Perspectives." In *The Politics of Teacher Unionism*, edited by M. Lawn, pp. 141–157. London: Croom Helm.

Bourdieu, P. (1975). "The Specificity of the Scientific Field and the Social Conditions of the Progress of Reason." *Social Science Information* 14(6):19–47.

———. (1988). *Homo Academicus.* Oxford: Polity Press.

Bourdieu, P., and Passeron, J.C. (1977). *Reproduction in Education, Society and Culture.* London: Sage.

Bowles, S., and Gintis, H. (1976). *Schooling in Capitalist America.* Boston: Routledge and Kegan Paul.

Brock-Utne, B. (1989). *Feminist Perspectives on Peace and Peace Education.* New York: Pergamon Press.

Bullough, R. (1987). "Accommodation and Tension: Teachers, Teacher Role, and the Culture of Teaching." In *Educating Teachers*, edited by John Smyth, pp. 83–94. London: Falmer Press.

Busswell, C. (1980). "Pedagogic Change and Social Change." *British Journal of Sociology of Education* 1(3):293–306.

Calhoun, M. (1980). "Struggles and Negotiating to Define What Is Problematic or What Is Not." In *The Social Process of Scientific Investigation*, edited by K. Knorr, R. Krohn, and R. Whitley, pp. 197–219. London: Reidel.

Campos, J., Cano, A., Hernandez, L., Perez Arce, F., Rojo, C., Salinas, G., Street, S., Ignacio Taibo II, T. P., Varga, R., and Vasquez, P. (Eds.). (1990). *De las Aules a las Calles*. Pueblo, Mexico: Informacion Obrera.

Caniesco-Doronila, M. L. (1987). "Teachers and National Identity Formation: A Case Study from the Philippines." *Journal of Educational Equity and Leadership* 7:278–300.

Carlson, D. (1987). "Teachers as Political Actors: From Reproductive Theory to the Crisis in Schooling." *Harvard Education Review* 57:283–307.

Carnoy, M. (1974). *Education as Cultural Imperialism*. New York: David McKay.

Casanova, U. (1991). *Elementary School Secretaries: The Women in the Principal's Office*. New York: Corwin.

Chafetz, J. (1984). *Sex and Advantage: A Comparative Macro-Structural Theory of Sex Stratification*. Totowa, NJ: Rowman and Allanheld.

Cherryholmes, C. (1988). *Power and Criticism: Poststructural Investigations in Education*. New York: Teachers College Press.

Chodorow, N. (1978). *The Reproduction of Mothering: Psychoanalysis and the Sociology of Gender*. Berkeley: University of California Press.

Clark, B. (1984). *The Higher Education System*. Berkeley: University of California Press.

Clifford, G. (1987). "'Lady Teachers and Politics in the United States, 1850–1930." In *Teachers: The Culture and Politics of Work*, edited by G. Grace, pp. 3–30. London: Falmer Press.

Cohen, R. (1976). "Conceptual Styles, Culture Conflict, and Nonverbal Tests of Intelligence." In *Schooling in the Cultural Context*, edited by J. Roberts and S. Akinsanya, pp. 290–322. New York: McKay.

Collins, R. (1979). *The Credential Society: A Historical Sociology of Education and Stratification*. New York: Academic Press.

Connell, R. (1985). *Teachers' Work.* Sydney: George Allen and Unwin.

Cook, C. (1984). "Teachers for the Inner City." In *Education and the City,* edited by G. Grace, pp. 269–291. London: Routledge and Kegan Paul.

Cooper, B. (Ed.). (1992). *Labor Relations in Education: An International Perspective.* New York: Greenwood.

Corr, H., (1990). "Politics of the Sexes In English and Scottish Teachers' Unions, 1970–1914." In *The Politics of Everyday Life: Continuity and Change in Work and the Family,* edited by H. Corr and L. Jamieson, pp. 186–205. London: Macmillan.

Corr, H. and Jamieson, L. (1990). *Politics of Everyday Life: Continuity and Change in Work and the Family.* London: Macmillan.

Cortina, R. (1989). "Women As Leaders In Mexican Education." *Comparative Education Review* 33(3):357–376.

Crumpacker, L., and Haegen, E. V. (1990). "Valuing Diversity: Teaching About Sexual Preference in a Radical/Conserving Curriculum." In *Changing Education: Women as Radicals and Conservators,* edited by J. Antler and S. Biklen, pp. 201–215. Albany: State University of New York Press.

Cummings, W., and Amano, I. (1977). "The Changing Role of the Japanese Professor." In *Comparative Perspectives on the Academic Profession,* edited by P. Altbach, pp. 43–64. New York: Praeger.

Dale, R., Esland, G., Fergusson, R., and MacDonald, M. (Eds.). (1981). *Education and the State, Volume 2: Politics, Patriarchy and Practice.* London: Falmer Press.

Dallmayr, F. (1984). *Polis and Praxis.* Cambridge, MA: MIT Press.

Danylewycz, M., and Prentice, A. (1988). "Teachers Work: Changing Patterns and Perceptions In the Emerging Systems of Nineteenth and Early Twentieth Century Central Canada." In *Schoolwork,* edited by J. Ozga, pp. 69–85. Milton Keynes: Open University Press.

Darmanin, M. (1985). "Malta's Teachers and Social Change." In *The Politics of Teacher Unionism: International Perspectives,* edited by Martin Lawn, pp. 158–190. London: Croom Helm.

Darvas, P. (1991). Perspectives of Educational Reform in Hungary. In *Understanding Educational Reform in Global Context,* edited by M. Ginsburg, pp. 229–246. New York: Garland.

Dearden, R. (1980). "Education and Politics." *Journal of Philosophy of Education* 14:149–156.

Dembele, M. (1991). "Political Instability, Economic Hardships, and the Preservice Education of Secondary Teachers in Burkina Faso, 1960–91." Unpublished Master's thesis, University of Pittsburgh.

Dove, L. (1979). "Teachers In Politics in Ex-Colonial Countries." *Journal of Commonwealth and Comparative Politics* 17:176–191.

————. (1986). *Teachers in Politics in Developing Countries.* London: Croom Helm.

Dreeben, R. (1988). "The School as a Workplace." In *Schoolwork*, edited by J. Ozga, pp. 27–47. Milton Keynes: Open University Press.

Duclau-Williams, R. (1985). "Teacher Unions and Educational Policy in France." In *The Politics of Teacher Unionism*, edited by M. Lawn, pp. 73–102. London: Croom Helm.

Elias, N. (1982). "Scientific Establishments." In *Scientific Establishments and Hierarchies*, edited by N. Elias, H. Martins, and R. Whitley, pp. 3–69. London: Reidel.

Epstein, B. (1992). "The Anit-War Movement During the Gulf War." *Social Justice* 19(1):115–131.

Farran, D. (1982). "Mother-Child Interaction, Language Development and the School Performance of Poverty Children." In *The Language of Children Reared in Poverty*, edited by L. Feagans and D. Farran., pp. 19–52. New York: Academic Press.

Feeley, F. (1989). *Rebels With Causes: A Study of Revolutionary Syndicalist Culture Among French Primary School Teachers Between 1880 and 1919.* New York: Peter Lang.

Filson, G. (1988). "Ontario Teachers' Deprofessionalization and Proletarianization." *Comparative Education Review* 32:298–317.

Fisher, D. (1983). "The Political Nature of Social Studies Knowledge." *History and Social Science Teacher* 18:219–225.

Foucault, M. (1980). *Power/Knowledge.* New York: Pantheon.

Fraser, D. (1989). "Agents of Democracy: Urban Elementary-School Teachers and the Conditions of Teaching." In *American Teachers*, edited by D. Warren, pp. 118–156. New York: Macmillan.

Freire, P. (1970). *Pedagogy of the Oppressed.* New York: Seabury Press.

Friedberg, E., and Musselin, C. (1987). "The Academic Profession in France." In *The Academic Profession: National Disciplinary, and Institutional Settings*, edited by B. Clark, pp. 93–117. Los Angeles: University of California Press.

Fuhrig, W. (1969). "West Germany." In *Teacher Unions and Associations,* edited by A. Blum, pp. 83–118. Chicago: University of Illinois Press.

Gamarnikow, E., Morgan, D., Purvis, J., and Taylorson, D. (Eds). (1986). *The Public and the Private.* Aldershot, Hampshire: Gower.

Ginsburg, M. (1987a). "Contradictions in the Role of Professor as Activist." *Sociological Focus* 20:111–122.

———. (1987b). "Reproduction, Contradiction and Conceptions of Professionalism: The Case of Preservice Teachers." In *Critical Studies in Teacher Education,* edited by T. Popkewitz, pp. 86–129. New York: Falmer Press.

———. (1988). "Educators as Workers and Political Actors." *British Journal of Sociology of Education* 3:359–367.

———. (1990). "El Proceso de Trabajo y la Accion Politica de los Educadores: Un Analisis Comparado." *Revista de Educacion* (Extraordinario): 317–345.

Ginsburg, M. (Ed.). (1991). *Understanding Educational Reform in Global Context.* New York: Garland.

Ginsburg, M., and Chaturvedi, V. (1988). "Teachers and the Ideology of Professionalism in India and England: A Comparison of Case Studies in Colonial/Peripheral and Metropolitan/Central Societies." *Comparative Education Review* 32:465–477.

Ginsburg, M., and Kamat, S. "Teachers' Work and Political Action." Forthcoming In *International Encyclopedia of Education: Research and Studies,* 2nd ed., edited by T. Husen and T. Postlethwaite, Vol. 8, pp. 4581–4587. New York: Macmillan.

Ginsburg, M., Kamat, S., Raghu, R., and Weaver, J. (1992). "Educators/ Politics." *Comparative Education Review,* 36(4):417–445.

Ginsburg, M., Meyenn, R., and Miller, M. (1979). "Teachers and the Great Debate and Educational Cuts." *Westminister Studies in Education* 2:5–23.

Ginsburg, M., Meyenn, R., and Miller, M. (1980). "Teachers Conceptions of Professionalism and Trades Unionism: An Ideological Analysis." In *Teacher Strategies,* edited by P. Woods, pp. 178–212. London: Croom Helm.

Ginsburg, M., and Miller, H. (1991). "Restructuring Education and the State in England." In *Understanding Educational Reform in Global Context,* edited by M. Ginsburg, pp. 49–84. New York: Garland.

Ginsburg M., and Tidwell, M. (1990). "Political Socialization of Prospective Educators In Mexico." *New Education* 12:70–82.

Ginsburg, M., Wallace, G., and Miller, H. (1988). "Teachers, Economy and the State." *Teaching and Teacher Education: An International Journal of Research and Studies* 4(4):1–21.

Giroux, H. (1981). "Teacher Education and the Ideology of Social Control." In *Ideology, Culture and the Process of Schooling*, edited by H. Giroux, pp. 143–162. Philadelphia: Temple University Press.

———. (1988). *Teachers as Intellectuals*. Branby, MA: Bergin and Garvey.

Gonzales, G. (1982). "Imperial Reform in the Neo-Colonies: The University of California's Basic Plan for Higher Education in Columbia." *Journal of Education* 164:330–350.

Grace, G. (1979). *Teachers, Ideology and Control*. London: Routledge and Kegan Paul.

———. (1987). "Teachers and the State in Britain." In *Teachers: The Culture and Politics of Work*, edited by M. Lawn and G. Grace, pp. 193–228. London: Falmer Press.

Gramsci, A. (1971). "The Intellectuals." In *Selections from Prison Notebooks*, pp. 5–23. New York: International Publishers.

Grumet, M. (1988). *Bitter Milk: Women and Teaching*. Amherst, MA: University of Massachusetts.

———. (1990). "Foward." In *Changing Education: Women as Radicals and Conservators*, edited by J. Antler and S. Biklen, pp. ix–xiii. Albany, NY: State University of New York Press.

Habermas, J. (Ed.). (1987). *Observations on the "Spiritual Situation of the Age."* Cambridge, MA: MIT Press.

Hackett, P. (1988). "Aesthetics as a Dimension for Comparative Study." *Comparative Education Review* 32:389–399.

Halsey, A., Flood, J., and Anderson, C. (Eds.). (1961). *Education, Economy and Society*. New York: Free Press.

Hawkins, J., and La Belle, T. (Eds.). (1985). *Education and Intergroup Relations*. New York: Praeger.

Heenan, D., and Wronski, S. (1969). "Thailand." In *Teachers Unions and Associations*, edited by Albert Blum, pp. 279–280. Chicago: University of Chicago Press.

Henderson, J. (1969). "Nigeria." In *Teacher Unions and Associations*, edited by A. Blum, pp. 233–270. Chicago: University of Chicago Press.

Holmes, B. (Ed.). (1985). *Equality and Freedom in Education: A Comparative Study*. London: Allen and Unwin.

Hopper, E. (1981). *Social Mobility.* Oxford: Basil Blackwell.

Howe, C. (1991). "Women and Collective Action." Paper presented at the annual meeting of the American Sociological Association, Cincinnati, August 23–27.

Hurst, P., and Rust, V. (1990). "Working Conditions of Teachers." In *Teachers and Teaching in the Developing World,* edited by V. Rust and P. Hurst, pp. 151–170. New York: Garland.

Ianni, F., and Storey, E. (Eds.). (1973). *Cultural Relevance and Educational Issues.* Boston: Little, Brown and Company.

Ichilov, O. (1991). "Political Socialization and Schooling Effects Among Israeli Adolescents." *Comparative Education Review* 35:430–446.

Imaz Gispert, C., and Salinas Alvarez, S. (1984). *Maestros y Estado, Volumes I and II.* Mexico City: Editorial Linea.

Jansen, J. (1990). "In Search of Liberation Pedagogy in South Africa." *Journal of Education* 172:62–71.

Jarausch, K. (1990). *The Unfree Professions: German Lawyers, Teachers, and Engineers, 1900–1950.* New York: Oxford University Press.

Johnson, S. (1988). "Unionism and Collective Bargaining in the Public Schools. In *Handbook of Research an Educational Administration,* edited by N. Boyan, pp. 603–622. New York: Longman.

Joyce, M. (1987). "Being a Feminist Teacher." In *Teachers: The Culture and Politics of Work,* edited by M. Lawn and G. Grace, pp. 67–89. London: Falmer Press.

Kale, P. (1970). "The Guru and the Professional: The Dilemma of the Secondary School Teacher in Poona, India." *Comparative Education Review* 14:371–376.

Kanpol, B. (1988). "The Concept of Resistance." *Critical Pedagogy Newsletter* 2:1–4.

Kelly, G. (1982). "Teachers and the Transmission of State Knowledge: A Case Study of Colonial Vietnam." In *Comparative Education,* edited by P. Altbach, R. Arnove, and G. Kelly, pp. 176–194. New York: Macmillan.

Kelly G., and Elliot, C. (Eds.). (1982). *Women's Education in the Third World.* Albany: State University of New York Press.

Kelly, G., and Nihlen, A. (1982). "Schooling and the Reproduction of Patriarchy: Unequal Workloads, Unequal Rewards." In *Cultural and Economic Reproduction in Education,* edited by M. Apple, pp. 162–180. Boston: Routledge and Kegan Paul.

King, S. (1987). "Feminists in Teaching." In *Teachers: The Culture and Politics of Work*, edited by M. Lawn and G. Grace, pp. 31–49. London: Falmer Press.

Kolmes, J. (1981). "Teachers and Human Rights in Latin America." *Education Digest* 66(9):19–22.

Korean Federation of Teachers' Associations. (1991). *What Is the KFTA?* Seoul: KFTA.

Kreisberg, S. (1992). *Transforming Power: Domination, Empowerment, and Education.* Albany: State University of New York Press.

Larson, M. (1977). *The Rise of Professionalism.* Berkeley: University of California Press.

Lasswell, H. (1977). *Harold D. Lasswell on Political Sociology.* Chicago: University of Chicago Press.

Laudner, H., and Yee, B. (1987). "Are Teachers Being Proletarianized?" In *Gender, Class and Education*, edited by S. Walker and L. Barton, pp. 58–71. London: Falmer Press.

Lauglo, J. (1982). "Rural Primary Teachers as Potential Community Leaders? Contrasting Historical Cases in Western Countries." *Comparative Education* 18:233–255.

Lawn, M. (1985). Introduction. In *The Politics of Teacher Unionism: International Perspectives*, edited by M. Lawn, pp. 1–9. London: Croom Helm.

———. (1987). "What Is the Teacher's Job? Work and Welfare in Elementary Teaching, 1940–45." In *Teachers: The Culture and Politics of Work*, edited by M. Lawn and G. Grace, pp. 50–64. Sussex: Falmer Press.

———. (1988). "Skill in Schoolwork." In *Schoolwork*, edited by Jenny Ozga, pp. 152–182. Milton Keynes: Open University Press.

Lawn, M., and Ozga, J. (1981). "The Educational Worker." In *Schools, Teachers and Teaching*, edited by L. Barton and S. Walker, pp. 45–64. Lewes: Falmer Press.

Lee, J. (1984). "Contradictions and Constraints in an Inner-City Infants School." In *Education and the City*, edited by G. Grace, pp. 243–268. London: Routledge and Kegan Paul.

———. (1987). "Pride and Prejudice: Teachers, Class and an Inner-City Infants School." In *Teachers: The Culture and Politics of Work*, edited by M. Lawn and G. Grace, pp. 90–116. London: Falmer Press.

Leiulfsrud, H., and Lindbad, S. (1991). "Teachers and Societies: A
    Comparative Study of Teachers' Positions and Orientations in the
    Social Structure. The Cases of Canada, Norway, Sweden, the U.S.,
    and West Germany." Paper presented at the 1991 annual meeting
    of the Comparative and International Education Society,
    Pittsburgh, PA.

Levine, S. (1969). "Japan." In *Teacher Unions and Associations: A
    Comparative Study*, edited by A. Blum, pp. 141–199. Urbana:
    University of Illinois Press.

Lewis, M., and Simon, R. (1986). "A Discourse Not Intended for Her:
    Learning and Teaching Within Patriarchy." *Harvard Educational
    Review* 56:457–472.

Littlewood, M. (1989). "The 'Wise Married Woman' and the Teachers
    Union." In *Women Teachers*, edited by H. de Lyon and F.
    Migniuolo, pp. 180–190. Milton Keynes: Open University Press.

Lortie, D. (1975). *School Teacher: A Sociological Analysis*. Chicago:
    University of Chicago Press.

Lukes, S. (1974). *Power: A Radical View*. London: British Sociological
    Association.

Luttrell, W. (1992). "Working-Class Women's Ways of Knowing: Effects
    of Gender, Race and Class." In *Education and Gender Inequality*,
    edited by J. Wrigley, pp. 173–191. Washington, DC: Falmer Press.

Lyon, H., and Migniuolo, F. (1989). "Introduction to Section IV:
    Teachers Unions." In *Women Teachers*, edited by H. Lyon and F.
    Migniuolo, pp. 169–179. Milton Keynes: Open University Press.

Manzer, R. (1973). "The Technical Power of Organized Teachers." In
    Education in Great Britain and Ireland, edited by G. Bell, G. Fowler,
    and G. Little, pp. 59–70. London: Routledge and Kegan Paul.

Martinotti, G., and Giasanti, A. (1977). "The Robed Baron: The
    Academic Profession in the Italian University." In *Comparative
    Perspectives on the Academic Profession*, edited by P. Altbach, pp.
    23–42. New York: Praeger.

Mattingly, Paul. (1975). *The Classless Profession*. New York: New York
    University Press.

McDermott, R. (1974). "Achieving School Failure." In *Education and
    Cultural Process*, edited by G. Spindler, pp. 82–118. New York:
    Holt, Rinehart and Winston.

Meyers, P. (1976). "Professionalization and Social Change: Rural
    Teachers in Nineteenth Century France." *Journal of Social History*
    9:524–558.

Mill, J. S. (1861). *Considerations on Representative Government*. London: Liberal Arts Library.

Miller, D., and Ginsburg, M. (1989). "Social Reproduction and Resistance in Four Infant/Toddler Daycare Settings." *Journal of Education* 171:31–50.

Miller, J. B. (1992). "Women and Power." In *Rethinking Power*, edited by T. Wartenberg, pp. 240–248. Albany: State University of New York Press.

Millet, K. (1977). *Sexual Politics*. New York: Virago.

Mills, C. W. (1956). *The Power Elite*. New York: Oxford University Press.

Mommsen, M. (1987). "The Academic Profession in the Federal Republic of Germany." In *The Academic Profession*, edited by B. Clark, pp. 60–92. Los Angeles: University of California Press.

Natarajan, S. (1969). "India." In *Teachers Unions and Associations*, edited by A. Blum, pp. 119–140. Chicago: University of Chicago Press.

Nichols, R. L. (1977). "Rebels, Beginners, and Buffoons: Politics as Action." In *Political Theory and Praxis*, edited by T. Ball, pp. 159–199. Minneapolis: University of Minnesota Press.

Nwagwu, N. (1977). "Problems of Professional Identity Among African School Teachers." *Journal of Educational Administration and History* 9:49–54.

Ogbu, J. (1978). *Minority Education and Caste*. New York: Academic Press.

Oliveros, A. (1975). "Change and the Latin American Teacher." *Prospects* 5:230–238.

Orlin, L. (1981). "The Concept of the Apolitical University." *The Journal of General Education* 33:93–101.

Osborne, K. (1984). *Working Papers in Political Education*. Winnipeg: University of Manitoba Press.

Ota, H. (1985). "Political Teacher Unionism in Japan." In *The Politics of Teacher Unionism*, edited by M. Lawn, pp. 103–140. London: Croom Helm.

Otero, M. (1981). "Oppression in Uruguay." *Bulletin of Atomic Scientists* 37(2):29–31.

Ozga, J. (1987). "Part of the Union: School Representatives and Their Work." In *The Culture and Politics of Work*, edited by M. Lawn and G. Grace, pp. 113–144. London: Falmer Press.

Ozga, J., and Lawn, M. (1981). *Teachers, Professionalism and Class*. London: Falmer Press.

Paine, L. (1981). "The Teaching of Teachers: Technocracy and Politics in China." Paper presented at the Comparative and International Education Society annual meeting, Stanford, California.

Pan, D. (1990). "Ivory Tower and Red Tape: Reply to Adler." *Telos* 86:109–117.

Parry, N., and Parry, J. (1974). "Teachers and Professionalism: The Failure of an Occupational Strategy." In *Education, Schools and Ideology*, edited by N. Flude and M. Ahier, pp. 160–185. London: Wiley.

Pelczar, R. (1977). "The Latin American Professoriate: Progress and Prospects." In *Comparative Perspectives on the Academic Profession*, edited by P. Altbach, pp. 125–144. New York: Praeger.

Perkin, H. (1987). "The Academic Profession in the United Kingdom." In *The Academic Profession*, edited by B. Clark, pp. 13–59. Los Angeles: University of California Press.

Persell, C. (1977). *Education and Inequality.* New York: Free Press.

Pietrasik, R. (1987). "Teachers' Action: 1984–86." In *Teachers: The Culture and Politics of Work*, edited by M. Lawn and G. Grace. London: Falmer Press.

Popkewitz, T. (1982). "The Social/Moral Basis of Occupational Life: Teacher Education in the Soviet Union." *Journal of Teacher Education* 33:38–44.

———. (1984). "Paradigms in Educational Science: Different Meanings and Purpose to Theory." In *Paradigm and Ideology in Educational Research: The Social Functions of the Intellectual*, pp. 31–58. New York: Falmer Press.

———. (1991). *A Political Sociology of Educational Reform: Power/Knowledge in Teaching, Teacher Education and Research.* New York: Teachers College Press.

Quantz, R. (1985). "The Complex Visions of Female Teachers and the Failure of Unionization in the 1930s: An Oral History." *History of Education Quarterly* 25:439–458.

Rabkin, J., and Eisemon, T. (1977). "Multiple Professional Roles of the Academic: A Canadian Case Study." In *Comparative Perspectives on the Academic Profession*, edited by P. Altbach, pp. 114–122. New York: Praeger.

Redican, B. (1988). "The Subject Teachers Under Stress." In *Schoolwork*, edited by J. Ozga, pp. 138–152. Milton Keynes: Open University Press.

Rist, R. (1970). "Student Social Class and Teacher Expectations: The Self-Fulfilling Prophecy in Ghetto Education." *Harvard Education Review* 40:411–451.

Roberts, J., and Akinsanya S. (Eds.). (1976). *Schooling in Cultural Context.* New York: McKay.

Robertson, S., and Woock, R. (1991). "The Political Economy of Educational 'Reform' in Australia." In *Understanding Educational Reform in Global Context*, edited by M. Ginsburg, pp. 85–114. New York: Garland.

Rosenthal, A. (1969). *Pedagogues and Power: Teacher Groups in School Politics.* Syracuse, NY: Syracuse University Press.

Ross, A. (1991). "Defenders of the Faith and the New Class." In *Intellectuals: Aesthetics, Politics and Academics*, edited by B. Robbins, pp. 102–132. Minneapolis: University of Minnesota Press.

Rust, V. (1991). "Postmodernism and Its Comparative Education Implications." *Comparative Education Review* 35:610–626.

Sarup, M. (1984). "Teachers: Class Position and Socialist Pedagogy." In *Marxism/Structuralism/ Education*, edited by M. Sarup, pp. 113–127. New York: Falmer Press.

Sautman, B. (1991). "Politicization, Hyperpoliticization, and Depoliticization of Chinese Education." *Comparative Education Review* 35:669–689.

Scarfe, J., and Sheffield, E. (1977). "Notes on the Canadian Professoriate." In *Comparative Perspectives on the Academic Profession*, edited by P. Altbach, pp. 92–113. New York: Praeger.

Schecker, E. (1986). *No Ivory Tower: McCarthyism and the Universities.* New York: Oxford University Press.

Schmuck, P. (1987). *Women Educators: Employees in Western Countries.* Albany, NY: State University of New York Press.

Seregny, S. (1989). *Russian Teachers and the Peasant Revolution: The Politics of Education in 1905.* Bloomington: University of Indiana Press.

Shank, M., and Vampola, D. (1992). "Negating Positivism: Language and the Practice of Science." In *The Philosophy of Discourse*, edited by C. Sills and G. Jensen, pp. 22–52. Portsmouth, NH: Heinemann.

Sharp, R., and Green, A. (1975). *Education and Social Control.* London: Routledge and Kegan Paul.

Shils, E. (1972). *The Intellectuals and the Other Powers and Other Essays.* Chicago: University of Chicago Press.

Shin, Yong-Kuk, Kim, K.-M., and Park, J.-H. (1991). *An Analytical Study of Teacher Trade-Union Movement: Focused on Political Involvement.* Changwon, Korea: Changwon University Press.

Siefert, R. (1987). *Teacher Militancy: The History of Teacher Strikes, 1896– 1987.* London: Falmer Press.

Silva, E., and Slaughter, S. (1984). *Serving Power: The Making of the Academic Expert.* London: Greenwood.

Simons, H. (1990). Introduction. In *The Rhetorical Turn*, edited by H. Simons, pp. 1–31. Chicago: University of Chicago Press.

Simpson, D. (1991). "New Brooms at Fawlty Towers: Colin MacCabe and Cambridge English." In *Intellectuals: Aesthetics, Politics and Academics*, edited by B. Robbins, pp. 245–271. Minneapolis: University of Minnesota Press.

Singleton, J. (1976). "Schools and Teacher Union Interaction." In *Schooling in Cultural Context*, edited by J. Roberts and S. Akinsarya, pp. 437–447. New York: McKay.

Skopp, D. (1982). "The Elementary School Teachers in 'Revolt': Reform Proposals for Germany's *Volksschulen* In 1848 and 1849." *History of Education Quarterly* 17(3):341–361.

Smyth, J. (1987). "Transforming Teachers Through Intellectualizing the Work of Teachers." In *Educating Teachers*, edited by J. Smyth, pp. 155–168. London: Falmer Press.

So, H. (1990). "Factors Affecting the Implementation of Teacher Union Policy in the Republic of Korea." Unpublished manuscript, University of Pittsburgh, April.

Sollner, A. (1991). "From Political Dissent to Intellectual Integration: The Frankfurt School in American Government." In *Intellectuals: Aesthetics, Politics and Academics*, edited by B. Robbins, pp. 225– 241. Minneapolis: University of Minnesota Press.

Spaull, A., and Mann, S. (1985). "Teacher Unionism in Australia: The Case of Victoria." In *The Politics of Teacher Unionism*, edited by M. Lawn, pp. 13–39. London: Croom Helm.

Spindler, G. (Ed.). (1974). *Education and Cultural Process.* New York: Holt, Rinehart and Winston.

Spolsky, B., and Cooper, R. (Eds.). (1978). *Case Studies in Bilingual Education.* Rowley, MA: Newbury House.

Spring, J. (1986). *The American School, 1642–1985.* New York: Longman.

St. Maurice, H. (1987). "Clinical Supervision and Power: Regimes of Instructional Management." In *Critical Studies in Teacher Education*, edited by T. Popkewitz, pp. 242–265. New York: Falmer Press.

Steedman, C. (1987). "Prisonhouses." In *Teachers: The Culture and Politics of Work*, edited by M. Lawn and G. Grace, pp. 117–130. London: Falmer Press.

Stoer, S. (1985). "The April Revolution and Teacher Trade Unionism in Portugal." In *The Politics of Teacher Unionism*, edited by M. Lawn, pp. 40–72. London: Croom Helm.

Strober, M., and Tyack, D. (1980). "Why Do Women Teach and Men Manage?" *Signs* 3:494–503.

Sultana, R. (1987). "Social Movements and the Transformation of Teachers Work: Case Studies from New Zealand." *Research Papers in Education* 6:133–152.

Tannen, D. (1986). "Talk in the Intimate Relationship." In *That's Not What I Meant! How Conversation Style Makes or Breaks Your Relations With Others*, edited by D. Tannen, pp. 133–151. New York: Morrow.

Tipton, J. (1988). "Education Organizations as Workplaces." In *Schoolwork*, edited by J. Ozga, pp. 3–20. Milton Keynes: Open University Press.

Torres, C. A. (1991). "State Corporatism, Educational Policies and Students' and Teachers Movements in Mexico." In *Understanding Educational Reform in Global Context*, edited by M. Ginsburg, pp. 115–150. New York: Garland.

Tucker, J. (1981). "Teacher Education Policy in Contemporary China." *Theory and Research in Social Education* 8:1–13.

Turner, B. (1990). "Outline of a Theory of Citizenship." *Sociology* 24:189–217.

Urban, W. (1989). "Teacher Activism." In *American Teachers*, edited by D. Warren, pp. 190–219. New York: Macmillan.

Walsh, K. (1987). "The Politics of Teacher Appraisal." In *Teachers: The Culture and Politics of Work*, edited by G. Grace, pp. 147–168. London: Falmer Press.

Watson, K. (1983). "Rural Primary Teachers as Change Agents in the Third World: Three Case Studies." *International Journal of Educational Development* 3:47–89.

Weiler, K. (1988). *Women Teaching for Change: Gender, Class and Power*. South Hadley, MA: Bergin and Garvey.

————. (1989). "Women's History and the History of Women Teachers." *Journal of Education* 171:9–30.

————. (1990). "You've Got to Stay There and Fight." In *Changing Education: Women as Radicals and Conservators*, edited by J. Antler and S. Biklen, pp. 217–236. Albany: State University of New York Press.

Wexler, P. (1982). "Ideology and Education: From Critique to Class Action." *Interchange* 13:53–68.

White, G. (1981). *Party and Professionals: The Political Role of Teachers in Contemporary China*. New York: M. E. Sharpe.

Williams, P. (1977). "Too Many Teachers? A Comparative Study of the Planning of Teacher Supply in Britain and Ghana." *Comparative Education* 13:169–179.

Witz, A. (1990). "Patriarchy and Professions: The Gendered Politics of Occupational Closure." *Sociology* 24:675–690.

Young, I. (1992). "Five Faces of Oppression." In *Rethinking Power*, edited by Thomas Wartenberg, pp. 174–195. Albany, State University of New York Press.

Young, M. F. D. (1971). *Knowledge and Control*. London: Macmillan.

Ziegler, H. (1967). *The Political Life of American Teachers*. Englewood Cliffs, NJ: Prentice-Hall.

At Home and in the Classroom: The False Comfort of False Distinctions

Madeleine R. Grumet

Exile and Intrusion

When our son was in school, maybe the fourth or fifth grade, he was asked to write an essay about what happened in our family when our rules were broken. He was indignant. Rather than answering the question as stated, he took exception to it, claiming that indeed we had no rules, and that in our home issues concerning behavior, property, and violence were negotiated.

I know that at the time I was flattered. Here he was, distinguishing our loving and rational home from an institution where rules and punishments are rehearsed in an inexorable algorithm of fear. I purred with pleasure to think that he celebrated our enlightened and open communication.

Now as I think about it again, our collusion seems obvious and outrageous. Of course we had rules.

Our kids knew they had to stay away from chemicals before they could talk. "Cacaca," one of my babes had called them. The back of the station wagon was dubbed "The Dangerous Back," and to this day I think they are nervous if they have to sit in it. They carry those cautions around with them in their adult hesitance to get on a motorcycle or to fly in small planes. I have noticed that my eldest daughter, victim of my first anxious motherhood, is still a little nervous when she lights a match. My kids are not bungee jumpers.

We had all sorts of rules, a kaleidoscope of typical and idiosyncratic cautions and commandments.

What Jason was repudiating was this teacher's attempt to translate family history into the code of institutional control. He was very proud of himself. He had detected a set of assumptions that framed the question, and recognized that those assumptions arrogated the culture of the family to the description and analysis of the classroom. He had stood his family ground and claimed authority to describe the one social structure about which he could claim superior knowledge, his own family—in his, or our, own terms. And challenged by the pedagogical intrusion, he defended the family code; he disclaimed his experience, and with our blessing, redescribed it out of the conversation.

We colluded in constructing what Halliday (1978) calls an antilanguage, claiming a privacy and ultimately an un-intelligibility to our own power relations so that they could escape the scrutiny of the school.

Now there is much to celebrate in this escape from public view. The control and manipulation and overgeneralizations of public power are present in school politics, in corporations and, as Foucault (1979) has argued, in military and police, mental health, and justice systems. Aries (1965) links these institutions to the development of large urban centers and argues that the family-as-refuge is a compensatory, though sentimental, response to the loss of small agrarian communities and the social relations they sustained.

As Jason and I participated in the mystification of our family's precepts, we also reinforced the popular, and ancient order that defines intimate, familial, and personal relations as apolitical. Proscribed as such, familial relations and signs escape intrusive readings, but then are also excluded from society's definitions of power.

The junction of family and polity is monitored by conflicting and contradictory signals as revealed in responses to issues dealing with family violence and reproductive rights. Exclusion from social scrutiny has made domestic battering and sexual abuse invisible, and it is only recently that we have begun to articulate the coordination of ethical and legal discourses and police intervention with the domestic relations within which abuse occurs. Many who support society's interventions to prevent domestic violence are nevertheless distressed when the state removes children from families, and the line between assistance, protection, and abduction is a wavy one.

The ancient separation of the *oikos* from the *polis* persists in these ethical struggles. In *Public Man, Private Woman* Jean Elshtain (1981) has argued that the very meaning of the term *politics* rests on the exclusion of women and children. In Greco-Roman culture *public* designated the interactions of men in the marketplace and in the forum. It excluded relations of reproduction. A strikingly similarly phallocentric definition of politics can be found in Agnes Heller's (1984) study, *Everyday Life*: "political activity is any activity which is performed directly with 'we-consciousness'." Ah, an inclusive definition, but the exclusion follows rapidly in the companion clause: "and is directed towards defending or attacking any social integration wider than the family" (p. 97). A Marxist Hungarian intellectual, Heller maintains the Marxian distinction between the social and the private division of labor throughout her text, a distinction that I will argue is specious and contradicts her project of elucidating the categories of everyday life, where, I will argue, the distinctions disappear. Heller's work, nevertheless, endows everyday life with the dignity of representation that facilitates my efforts to talk about the places where we work, as educators, with our own and other people's children.

From the Particular to the Individual

I want to explore two categories that Heller establishes, the category of the *particular* and the category of the *individual*. Both terms denote human conditions achieved through ministrations of care, but I will not keep them tethered to their places on either side of the wall that Heller has maintained to separate the family from politics. Heller uses particularity to designate interests and concerns that are tethered to each person's unique and specific existence. We are all particularistic as we go about the business of our lives, taken up with our own needs and interests. Maternal care sustains our particularity when sustenance answers a puny cry or a call in the night. Intentionality must be the necessary mode of consciousness of the particular, as we are swallowed into the object of our need or interest. Nevertheless, there are those, Heller (1984, p. 17) tells us, with a broader vision:

> who see themselves—from the point of view of species-being, from the point of the actual stage reached in the development of the species at a given time—as objects, who see that they should not be identified with the needs of their own existence, and that they should not make their being, the forces of their being, nothing more than a means of satisfying the needs of their existence. So, we give the name of "individual" to the person for whom his own life is consciously an object, since he is a conscious
> · species-being.

The sense of species-being that is interposed between the particular and the individual is constructed by history, as well as poetry. Species-being is the sense of what is possible for humanity, providing a general sense of humanity's possibilities that sets off one's own existence, action, and commitments as objects for reflection. Individuality is produced, then, through reflection, and, contrary to our current sense of individualism as a degenerate expression of competition, self-interest and isolation, individuality as Heller interprets the Marxian concept, rests on a vivid sense of the relation of oneself to the well-being and future of the species.[1] The teacher, presenting the accumulated wisdom of the culture, may provide the material through which individuality emerges, but I will argue that, contrary to Heller's assumptions, the shift from particularism to a species-being focus is also possible in families and often absent in classrooms.

Relations within the family are usually contained within particularism in psychological and social theory. Simultaneously romanticized and trivialized, family relations in classical psychoanalytic theory are collapsed into mother-child symbioses that admit little knowledge and less theory. Following the mind-body split in psychosocial theory, mothers get body, fathers get mind, and the development of children moves from body to mind, from mother to father, from particular to general, eliding individuality in the process of socialization.

These dichotomies rest on the illusion of the family's stasis. Hodge and Kress (1988) point out that family is often portrayed as an "eternal verity," a set of rules and roles located outside time and process. Like a Houdini box, it appears solid and impenetrable, even though it is rigged for escape.

There is an overall impression of the family as an immensely stable and stabilizing force, changing only slowly, if at all, resisting pressures for change outside itself. This impression of stability, however, needs to be put against a recognition of the intrinsically transformational

> processes which underlie it. . . . The eternal verity of the family has to cope with the ubiquitous presence of change, as new individuals are born and incorporated into specific places, and then redistributed into different places as they or others grow weaker or stronger, sexually active or quiescent, or dead. Given this endless change, the illusion of absence of change can only be achieved by homeostatic transformations. . . . The apparent absence of change, far from being a given, is itself one of the products of transformational processes, which must be precisely regulated and controlled if the trick is to be pulled off yet again. (Hodge and Kress 1988, p. 205)

Exiled from political space and political time, real families languish in the conservative fantasy of their natural and necessary arrangements, as the myth of family thrives. Held apart, sacrosanct, confined within the mythology of its privacy, contentment, and containment, the family is simultaneously isolated and mystified. Accordingly, public institutions are constrained from acknowledging and responding to the energy and change that moves in families and moves out from families to the other social institutions that engage their members.

In *Bitter Milk: Women and Teaching* I have argued that the very standard of success in the public world that schooling promises is funded by the politics and attachments that take place in the time and space that we have termed *private*. Whereas studies of schooling often designate it as the place and process that accommodates children to the codes and conventions that dominate the arena of production, that very process, I argue, is rooted in our responses to our own reproductive experience. There must have been moments in the history of culture, just as there have been moments in all of our lives, when caring for children and feeding them and providing shelter were intertwined in daily life, so that it would have been impossible to distinguish the hours filled with love from the hours filled with work.

Nevertheless, current conceptualizations of love and work depend on their mutual antagonism. They are presented to us as refuges from each other. In education the split is replicated in that teaching is understood as separate from the disciplines of knowledge. *Knowing* is seen as the ascetic ritual process that credentials the child as an adult, as a worker, as a citizen, and *teaching* is seen as a comfort designed to make this process tolerable.

Repudiating these divisions between reproduction and production, I suggest that curriculum is the deliberate attempt to transcend the limitations of our original relations to our own progeny. That relation differs for men and for women.

Gender distinctions may be traced to the biological constraints on the initial relations of men and women to their progeny. Prior to reproductive technologies, women, consigned to multiple pregnancies and nursing of the young, were engaged in a physical symbiosis with their children throughout their childbearing years. For men, on the other hand, paternity was merely inferential. Feminist theorists have suggested that rather than understanding so-called private relations as epiphenomena of political or productive systems, we should see those public systems as responses to the primordial production of our progeny.

In the feminist construction, the public domain evolves to compensate men and women for biology's constraints on their relations to their children. Women, seeking independence from the responsibilities of child care, turn to the public sphere for independence and differentiation. Men turn to the public sphere to find the absolute connection and control obscured in biological paternity—enter the model of industrial capital.

Education is drawn into the father's project to claim the child and into the mother's project to differentiate from the child. This schema, tethered to biology and early object relations, cannot encompass the reproductive relations of any one of us, for our own histories provide countless exceptions, variations, and interpretations of this structure. Furthermore, this dualistic narrative no longer fits the reproductive relations that technology has spawned. Reproductive technologies of birth control, surrogacy, *in vitro* fertilization, genetic tracing, and cloning have loosened the constraints on the relations of men and women to their progeny, allowing each sex to assume relations to their children that had hitherto been the exclusive entitlement of the other.

These technologies have made it possible to renegotiate absolute claims of reproductive powers and rights so that what were once discrete prerogatives of men and women are shared by both. Men and women who come together to form families are now challenged to form corporate units where each no longer is defined by a single relation of symbiosis or inferential paternity, by private nurture or public labor, but instead form a unit where each is able to identify with both terms rather than one or the other.

Despite these technological transformations of re-productive possibility and responsibility, we must not confuse the existence of technology with its accessibility or its impact on patterns of consciousness and gender that have persisted for centuries. The patterns persist, modified here, challenged there; they, like the conservative myth of the family, provide a scenario of gender roles against which we measure, justify, and imagine our own experience. This dialectic of the parental project intersects with yet another, as the relation of the subject to the objects of consciousness is also delineated along gender lines.

Freud (1966) and later Lacan (1968) have both argued that to be gendered is to subordinate one's consciousness to a system of oppositions encoded in culture, in perception, and in language.

Object relations theorists such as Nancy Chodorow (1978) maintain that when the mother is the primary parent for infants of both sexes, the development of gender is a process that is different for males and females. Males, the theory goes, must learn to differentiate from the one who has cared for them, who has been the world for them, the one with whom they have immediately identified. That one is mother and so male gender is the repudiation of that identification. What is male is what is not female. Disconnection becomes the theme of male gender identity and of male epistemology as subject and object are no longer seen as continuous, but as separate. Connection is the relation that remains to be proven, rather than taken for granted. Overgeneralization is the perspective of this project as know-ledge is split off from daily experience and the tension of the particular is relinquished to the rush to the abstract.

Women, on the other hand, need not repress their earliest connections. Although heterosexual women shift their erotic cathexis from mother to father, their gender identity permits them to maintain continuity with their earliest senses of connection to their mothers, and to the world. Particularity is the focus of this feminine perspective, if the world that is shared is taken up with the local and immediate world and the larger world is kept too distant for relation.

These contradictions between the projects of reproduction and the patterns of gender identity provide a space that invites our exploration and transformation. For if the father's project is to claim connection against an epistemological presupposition that assumes separation, and if the mother's project is to foster separation against an epistemological presupposition of attachment, then we no longer have a smooth transition between childhood and adulthood. Contemporary developmental theory assumes just the opposite, attributing dependent relations to mothers and children and independence to the adult domain of public, male-dominated culture.

It is reflection that mediates the particularistic motives of both mothers and fathers. It is reflection upon species-being that helps us to realize our own possibilities and prompts us to take up education as students or teachers to rectify, or enlarge, the relations that gender identifications have provided.

The "we-consciousness" that Heller (1984) designates as political is an unbroken continuum, stretching from the family to the school and the workplace. These domains must be understood as related in one system rather than as separate and opposed.

The Home/School Continuum

Furthermore, it is important to note that the relations and meanings that fill the rooms of home are hardly separate from the public culture that surrounds domesticity. Shared parenting requires negotiation. Whatever the gender, age, or generation of the parenting partners, when two or more people come together to raise children, there is a strong possibility that there will be differences of opinion and conversation framing the daily decisions of everyday life: Should we let him cry himself to sleep? Should she be out after dark? Must they do chores before watching TV? And in the spaces between genders, histories, and generations hover the possibilities of species-being. When conversation and experience move everyday knowledge out from the confines of the particularistic, we call it practical knowledge.

The problem with practical knowledge is that we do not know we have it until the context where we developed it is shifted and we find it somewhere else. Then, in the new place, seeing again the events, relationships, and configurations of the old, we experience recognition, re-cognizing the world we know and realizing that we know it well.

Too often, the practical knowledge that we bring with us from home remains lodged in intuition but is rarely articulated because it has not been resymbolized through processes that encode it for reflection. When home and school are dichotomized into the private and the public, the female and the male, the infantile and the adult, the familiar and the strange, both students and teachers are cut off from their experience and denied practical knowledge and a usable past.

Exiled from politics, the family and often the school, lacks conventions of discourse that can sustain conversation about the child. Teachers and parents do not know and do not trust each other. Parents are perceived and portrayed as merely particularistic, interested only in their own children. The history of schooling in the United States confirms this portrayal, peppered with policy documents that decry the limitations of the family and summon the state to compensate for its deficiencies, immorality, and language deficits. Familial particularism has been the dominant rationale for building a system of compulsory schooling that will bring children from diverse ethnicities, races, religions, and classes into a heterogenous and hegemonic "American" culture.

Despite the widespread perception of the family's particularism, often it is difficult to find the particular, even at home. In *The Children in Our Lives: Knowing and Teaching,* Jane Adan (1991) provides glimpses of how quickly the particularistic gives way to the general, even within and among families.

In one chapter, "Mark at Preschool," Adan (1991) describes the dread experienced by a neighbor's three-and-a-half-year-old son as he approached preschool. His reluctance was consistent, his wariness and ultimate terror unabated, despite efforts to make him comfortable. The author confesses to participating in an interpretation of Mark's resistance that depicted his mother as "overprotective," attributing his undaunted refusal, "I don't like that place," to her anxiety. Adan even took him to the school herself for his first orientation visit in order to diminish the separation trauma that his own mother's presence might have occasioned. His mother's overprotectiveness, she tells us, became a handy explanation for behavior that otherwise could not be explained, a stereotype of the clinging mother that even the bewildered maternal culprit entertained.

Adan's (1991) point is that this handy piece of everyday knowledge is itself a refugee from misogynist psychoanalytic theory that has seeped into everyday discourse. Mark's mother accompanied him to the second orientation visit, and it was only she, with intimate knowledge of his home world and his school world, who was able to pull her attention away from the overgeneralized interpretation to see the particularity that formed this child's response. It was Mark's mother who finally made the connection between the Walt Disney version of the "Three Little Pigs," a record that Mark played constantly, and her son's aversion to preschool. In that recording the big bad wolf blows in the house of sticks—the preschool was constructed of unfinished redwood—and only the house of bricks survives. Mark's own home was cement block.

Adan (1991) points out another feature of the Disney rendition that may have fueled Mark's fear. The pig's mother is present in the Volland text version of the tale, but absent in the Disney version. The Volland text ends decisively, "So he [the big, bad wolf] went away, and that was the end of him," but the Disney record ends with the wolf still alive and continuing to plot against the pigs.

I wish there were space here and time to provide the other details that Adan (1991) notes as she reports the unravelling of the mystery, for the details matter. They are the antidote to the facile and reductive generalizations that spring up to explain Mark and blame his mother. Furthermore, the culprit is hardly domesticity, but commercialized versions of folk culture. Adan is not a prig or a purist. Her point is not to remove Disney from the library shelves or record players, although Mark did make it to school once the record was stashed on a high shelf in the closet. Her point is that as a child moves from the door of his home, onto the bus, and into the classroom, he is continuous and integrated; it all goes along with him, and it all comes home again. If we are to understand the sense he makes of either world, we must accompany him on the journey. And her point resides as well in the exquisite detail of her text. It is the detail of this child's utter particularity that reveals how he may become a participant in the community of the school, and it is this detail that parents and teachers ignore or denigrate because it comes from home.

Because the particularistic always rests in the field of the subject's immediate needs and interests, both teacher and parent need to assume a phenomenological imagination that will permit them to inhabit the child's perspective for a while. There is nothing to be gained in ignoring the particularity of the child.

For should he accede, and stop kicking and screaming, and go to preschool and stay, we extract his compliance from what Winnicott (1971) has called a *false self*. The terrified Mark goes underground, ever vigilant, expecting the wolf, expecting the worst, always on the look-out.

So not only is the family not contained within the immediacy of its intimate relations, it too must seek out the particularity of its members, so invaded are we by overgeneralized media. Clearly, the system of meaning and signs that the family employs to symbolize and communicate its experience is continuous with culture that is external to it.

Furthermore, we need to take note of interventions, conversations, and politics that take place between Mark's mother and her friends. There is an informal collaboration at work among families who raise children of similar ages. Kids are swapped, carpooled, tutored, baby-sat. Over coffee, on the phone, leaning against the doorframe, the talk about them continues. Remedies are exchanged, exasperations confided, suggestions offered. All children are not loved, or even admired. But there is a tolerance that comes from knowing Mark's mother or father, glimpsing the system that enmeshes this child and sensing its effort, however great its failure, to love him.

If families have been portrayed as essentially apolitical, schools, clearly part of the socialization processes in capitalist societies, are understood as profoundly political, although there is an enduring presumption that the school and the teacher should be above politics. Self-abnegation has been the cultural standard for teachers, a tradition that has roots in the religious and church responsibilities associated with teaching as well as the accommodations to industrialization that required the cult of motherhood to rationalize bringing women out of their kitchens and into the classrooms of the common schools.[2] Always underpaid, teachers are expected to relinquish their own particularity, endlessly deferring their own individual needs to meet the needs of their students.

The politics of contemporary teaching continue the repudiation of the particularity of teachers and students alike. The ethos of self-abnegation fails to understand that we could not retrain teachers to deny their own particularity in the workplace and expect them to notice and support the particularity of the children they taught.

And if something larger than particularism is desired, the individuality that Heller (1984) sketches for us, where is the companionship that can provide teachers with the occasions for reflection that will generate their sense of their own individuality, each other's, and that of the children they teach?

Teachers have been isolated from their own interests, their own needs, from their histories, from the outside world and from each other. The relentless and redundant isolations that confine teaching cannot be the products of coincidence. They repeat the deliberate isolation of the family and denial of its power. The mediation that we require if particularity is to be transformed into individuality, requires rich and ongoing relations of parents and teachers as well as the pedagogical equivalent of shared parenting that is team teaching.

Duration and Community

I am calling for a model of teaching that sustains a community of sixty children, with at least three teachers, who stay together for three years. This is an arrangement of care and instruction modelled directly on family relations. This model of duration is not extended merely to the early grades where it has flourished now and then. It is alive and well in graduate school, you may remember, where our survival of grades K–16 testified to our adequate socialization and allowed relations that honored intimacy, development, and expression—within limits.

Frenetic mobility militates against politics. Every hour another subject, every year another teacher, another guidance counselor. The model proposed here is overtly political because within its relations of duration, parents, students, and teachers may assume the familiarity and security needed to express their needs and interests.

The model of duration that I propose allows time for door-to-door introductions. It creates a community in the classroom that parents can come to know over time as they can come to know each other and each other's child. The model for parents' interactions with each other must be established by the teachers themselves, for if the classroom is autocratic or hierarchical, it cannot provide the ground for a democratic community.

The triad of teachers promises multiplicity of opinion, response, and perspective, a condition that fosters the larger vision of species-being. Being seen by other teachers in the act of teaching invites self-consciousness that takes the act of teaching out of the grip of intentional consciousness and makes it an object of reflection. Teachers must have time to talk to each other, not only about the children, but about their responses to the children. Deprived of adult companionship, teachers are isolated from the conversation that can turn their experience into knowledge.

The fantasy of mother-child symbiosis that suggests a romantic dyad, cut off from the world and other relationships, has trapped the teacher-student relationship in a cocoon of sentimentality. Even children who are raised by single parents are raised amidst a complex set of adult relationships.

The teacher who works alone with a group of children is burdened with awesome power, for there is no other adult present to respond to endless demands for emotional support and engagement, for intellectual breadth and flexibility, and for instantaneous ethical judgment. We attempt to check the teacher's power through mechanisms that blunt its effects: standardized tests, individualized educational plans, vague and generalized home reports—and by the general denigration and undervaluing of the profession of teaching. Nevertheless, suppressed and disguised, the dilemmas and powers of teaching do not disappear, they just go on, unobserved, unacknowledged, and uncompensated.

Shared teaching invites its participants to acknowledge and to share their power. More openly and directly observed and contested, the power of pedagogy may become less threatening and the capacity of children, parents, and teachers to negotiate it may be encouraged. Whereas the isolated teacher cannot afford to appear weak, the team of teachers, finding comfort and support from each other, may be more open to both children and their parents. The team of teachers may also find the collective voice to address issues of school structure and policy that reach beyond their classrooms.

The dilemma of the isolated teacher is exacerbated when that teacher is working in a community that is not her own. Creating relationships with extended family, with religious communities, with community-based organizations, and with ethnic organizations may be daunting for the isolated teacher but challenging and productive for a team that is working itself within a model of pluralism and collaboration.

And duration is essential for parents to come to know and trust the teachers of their children, especially when there are class, ethnic and racial, and religious differences between parents and teachers. There, using Heller's (1984) language, a sense of each other's particularity will be the necessary ground for the collaboration needed to thread the child's specificity through the codes and conventions of school politics.

Finally, shared teaching promises to interrupt the motives that move us from our gendered experiences of reproduction to our work with other people's children. Male teachers, confronted with other interpretations of knowledge, may reflect on the path of their own opinions, recovering their own motives. Offered parity with other teachers, male teachers may relax the defensive project to wrest the child from its primary identification with mother, extending a friendlier knowledge to students.

Shared teaching may offer female teachers the companionship that will protect them from the inexorable and lonely work of care, giving them more energy and enthusiasm for the political work of school reform. In the company of peers, the particularity that flourishes behind the classroom door may give way to a collective vision of a school community and to a curriculum that expresses its possibilities.

Duration invites intimacy between teachers and parents and parents and each other. Maybe Jason's teacher would not have assigned that intrusive essay if we had known each other. If we had known each other, maybe it would not have seemed intrusive.

NOTES

1. This approach to individuality may be found as well in Richard Rodriguez's (1983) autobiography, *Hunger of Memory*. He criticizes bilingual education as confining foreign speakers to very narrow particularistic communities and claims that he found his individuality once he could express his world in written, literate English, defining and articulating his experience against a wider range of possibilities.

2. This argument is more fully developed in "Pedagogy for Patriarchy" in *Bitter Milk: Women and Teaching* (Grumet 1988, pp. 31–58).

REFERENCES

Adan, J. (1991). *The Children in Our Lives*. Albany: State University of New York Press.

Aries, P. (1965). *Centuries of Childhood*. R. Baldick, trans. New York: Random House.

Chodorow, N. (1978). *The Reproduction of Mothering*. Berkeley: University of California Press.

Elshtain, J. B. (1981). *Public Man, Private Woman*. Princeton, N.J.: Princeton University Press.

Fernandez, J., and Underwood, J. (1993). *Tales Out of School*. Boston: Little, Brown and Company.

Freud, S. (1966). *The Complete Introductory Lectures on Psychoanalysis*. James Strachey, trans. New York: W. W. Norton.

Foucault, M. (1979). *Discipline and Punish*. A. Sheridan, trans. New York: Random House.

Grumet, M. R. (1988). *Bitter Milk: Women and Teaching*. Amherst, MA: University of Massachusetts Press.

Halliday, M. (1978). *Language as Social Semiotic*. Baltimore: University Park Press.

Heller, A. (1984). *Everyday Life*. G. L. Campbell, trans. London: Routledge and Kegan Paul.

Hodge, R. and Kress, G. (1988). *Social Semiotics*. Ithaca, N.Y.: Cornell University Press.

Lacan, J. (1968). *The Language of the Self*. Anthony Wilden, trans. New York: Dell.

Rodriguez, R. (1983). *Hunger of Memory: The Education of Richard Rodriguez*. New York: Bantam Books.

Winnicott, D. W. (1971). *Playing and Reality*. New York: Basic Books.

The Irony of Gender[1]

Richard J. Altenbaugh

Introduction

Any consideration of the politics of educators must encompass gender, examining how gender affects educators' lives and work and how they have, in turn, responded to it. As I use it in this chapter, gender represents a broad term, "which includes not only physiological characteristics but also learned cultural behaviors and understandings" (Bennett and LeCompte 1990, p. 224). This socialization process for both males and females results in the latter being treated like a minority. Women, like any other ethnic and racial minority, appear identifiable, suffer from "differential power" and "differentiated treatment," and maintain a "group awareness" (Bennett and LeCompte 1990, p. 225). The irony here is that while they have been treated like a minority, women in the United States constitute a majority in society in general, and among classroom instructors in particular.[2]

Teaching became a feminized occupation in the United States with the common-school movement of the early nineteenth century, with women becoming classroom instructors in increasing numbers especially after the Civil War in the 1860s. This formalized common-school system, with its age-grading and credentialed instructors, was seen to require economy, since it was subsidized by tax revenue instead of private-school tuition fees. Women too were viewed as possessing the inherent maternal qualities required to nurture young children. Horace Mann, first Secretary of Education for the state of Massachusetts, proclaimed in his 1843 annual report that the female instructor "holds her commission from nature" (quoted in Altenbaugh 1992c, p. 8). Mann and others defined the "school as a continuation of the family" (Altenbaugh 1992c, p. 8). "The child," Weiler (1989, p. 17) adds, "was viewed as developing first within the context of maternal care in the family, and then moved naturally to the care of the woman teacher." Boston's Board of Education clearly articulated this process in 1841, celebrating the feminization of teaching:

> It is gratifying to observe that a change is rapidly taking place, both in public sentiment and action, in regard to the employment of female teachers. . . . That females are incomparably better teachers for young children than males, cannot admit of a doubt. Their manners are more mild and gentle, and hence more in consonance with the tenderness of childhood. They are endowed by nature with stronger parental impulses, and this makes the society of children delightful, and turns duty into pleasure. . . . They are also of purer morals. (quoted in Elsbree 1939, p. 201)

As Weiler (1989, p. 18) concludes, "instead of seeing women teachers as wage workers, which would have threatened the separate sphere ideology, the work of teaching itself was redefined to be part of the private sphere."

Finally, because of their subordinate social roles and perceived submissive tendencies, women appeared to fit perfectly into the emerging school hierarchy:

> Any disciplinary problems that women teachers might have could be solved easily; the teachers would simply send difficult children to resident male principals. The promoters of graded schools also thought that women were likely to be willing participants in a substantial bureaucratization of the school curriculum. While teachers in the nongraded schools had made largely autonomous decisions about curriculum, teachers in graded schools were expected to conform to the curriculum goals of school superintendents. Officials believed that women teachers would be more compliant in carrying out

centralized directives. (Strober and Lanford 1986, pp. 218–219)

Teaching, while serving the domestic sphere, also gave women new opportunities. Late nineteenth-century Colorado teachers appeared to be better educated, married later, and traveled more than their noneducator female peers; some even remained single all of their lives—a possibility stemming from the economic independence afforded by school work. Classroom instruction at the very least gave these women enough flexibility in their lives to shift from work responsibilities to domestic obligations and back again because of marriage, family illness, or childbearing and rearing. "Teaching often meant a life course for women that was both more diversified and complex than that of their peers." However, because it conformed to "nineteenth-century domestic ideology," it failed to "revolutionize women's lives; the decisions they made frequently were shaped by the social and familial context within which they lived" (Underwood 1986, pp. 517 and 530).

The growing professionalization, or formalization, of teaching, at the same time, discouraged men from pursuing that occupation.[3] Until the early nineteenth century, males had previously approached teaching in a casual, almost informal manner, using the classroom to supplement their regular income, such as a farmer teaching during the winter months or as a stepping-stone to other more lucrative and higher status occupations, such as law or politics (Altenbaugh 1992c, p. 9). As Strober and Lanford (1986, p. 219) summarize it:

> In urban areas, where teaching was first formalized, and then in rural areas, most men found that the disadvantages of teaching began to outweigh the advantages—that is, the "opportunity cost" of teaching was too great. Indeed, even though earnings increased once standards were raised and the school term was lengthened, the average teaching salary remained inadequate to support a family. Women, on the other hand—who often, though not always, were responsible for their own support and who found other occupations closed to them—were attracted to the higher annual salaries. They flocked to schooling in increasing numbers.

Women, by 1888, represented 62 percent of all classroom instructors nationwide and 90 percent of city teachers.

This chapter examines the role of gender in teachers' lives and work by tracing their rural, small-town, and urban experiences in the United States through the lens of twentieth-century social history. It first treats these women's personal lives both in schools and in their families and homes, and second focuses on the structure of their work and organizations. This essay is synthetic, drawing upon some recent scholarship in a collection of essays I edited (Altenbaugh 1992b) and a range of other sources, and stresses that female instructors have long struggled to overcome the historical context of gendered politics in an occupation in which they numerically dominated. Women have not been "hapless victims." They have often resisted, and created their own meanings (Weiler 1989).

Personal Lives

Grumet (1988) analyzes the contradictions of teaching for women. Teaching, as women's work, has been sandwiched somewhere between the "so-called private and public worlds" of women's lives, between the experiences of the home and classroom (pp. xi–xii). Teachers "go back and forth between the experience of domesticity and the experience of teaching, between being with one's own children and being with the children of others, between being the child of one's own mother and the teacher of another mother's child, between feeling and form, family and colleagues" (p. xv).

Teaching, although feminized, has functioned within a rigid patriarchal setting.

> The feminization of teaching and the cult of maternal nurturance did little to introduce the atmosphere of home or the integrity and specificity of the mother/child relationship into the schools. Dominated by kits and dittos, increasingly mechanized and impersonal, most of our classrooms cannot sustain human relationships of sufficient intimacy to support the risks, the trust, and the expression that learning requires. (Grumet 1988, p. 56)

Patriarchal culture—its forms, knowledge, and values—has permeated schooling; inflexible teaching schedules, large class sizes, and the twin emphases on curricula and authority have superseded the aesthetic, nurturing, and caring so necessary to learning (Altenbaugh 1992b; Grumet 1988).

Female instructors have responded to these contradictions in many ways. This is best illustrated by Courtney Vaughn-Roberson's analysis of 325 white, mixed-blood Indian and African-American female teachers on the Oklahoma frontier. Her thesis stresses the dual roles they balanced:

> While many of these women struggled for independence and economic equality with men, they also looked upon teaching as an extension of a woman's domestic role in which the classroom and school building were her family, and they continued to shrink from jobs that competed with their perception of themselves as females. (Vaughn-Roberson 1984, p. 39)

"Sometimes independent but never equal," in Vaughn-Roberson's judgement, these female teachers assumed assertive and leadership roles at their schools. The rough and tumble Oklahoma territory supplied many dangers and challenges:

> Rowdy, drunken men were Lottie Ross's occupational hazard. The scalawags harassed her and the pupils during the first few days on the job until she began carrying a gun. "Armed with my pistol . . . I felt like I could handle any situation," declared Ross, who described herself as a "Pistol Packing Mama." (Vaughn-Roberson 1984, p. 46)

These same poised women, who coped with crude conditions and confronted constant dangers at work, returned to their homes and became subordinate and dependent, performing traditional female roles in the family. Vaughn-Roberson argues that "married women of both races [blacks and whites] believed that their careers were secondary to those of their husbands" (p. 54). One teacher, Francis Curb, abruptly halted the completion of her dissertation and ultimately her doctoral degree because "she realized that she could not be called 'doctor' and her husband 'mister'" (p. 55). Their often fervent belief in Christianity reinforced the submissiveness of women to men. Domestic ideology, therefore, prevailed on the early twentieth-century Oklahoma frontier.

In her examination of rural Vermont teachers between 1915 and 1950, Nelson (1992) analyzed the intersection of home and work, yet found a great deal of continuity rather than disjuncture. These female instructors often drew parallels between the structures of their family and school lives, referring to schools or classrooms as big, happy families. They easily transferred rules governing behavior from one setting to another, like table manners during lunch. Skills likewise extended from home to school. The key aspect here appeared to be working with children, as one woman summarized it: "I always knew that I wanted to be a teacher because I always loved to be with children" (quoted in Nelson 1992, p. 29). These female instructors faced many of the same roles and demands in the classroom as they did at home to ensure the physical well-being of the children as well as their intellectual and moral development. Finally, domestic and work lives physically overlapped, with family members present in the workplace. In the absence of formal child-care institutions and arrangements, these teachers brought their toddlers to school with them. Mothers and daughters substituted or helped each other during illnesses, pregnancies, injuries, or staff shortages. Husbands as well assisted their teacher-wives during field trips, special programs, or projects (Nelson 1992).

Home and school lives in rural Vermont clashed at times. Spousal demands could curtail a female teacher's career. At the very least, childbearing interrupted a career, and often ended it altogether.

More importantly, all of these female instructors had to function in a highly paternalistic environment in school (as well as at home and in the community): "One teacher reported that following a conflict with her superintendent she was told that she would 'never get another job in [his] district.' And, she said, 'I never did'" (Nelson, 1992, p. 35). Nevertheless, Nelson sees an analogy between school and personal lives for these female teachers. "To a great extent, the value of their work, and the pride that they took in doing it, emerged from their sense that they were fully and appropriately engaged in fulfilling a woman's mission" (p. 35).

Quantz's (1992) interviews of small-town Ohio teachers from the 1930s reveals several metaphors which, on the surface, appear remarkably similar to Nelson's analysis of rural Vermont instructors. Two of the metaphors, "The School as Family" and "The Natural Female Avocation," touch on school as a domestic setting. The former encompasses the "sisterlike" and "mother-daughter-like" relationships prevalent in the schools. As one teacher expressed it: "Everybody was sort of a close family" (p. 145). The latter, while conforming to the narrow ideal of domesticity, dovetailed with the former. Teaching, though not necessarily a career for these women, insulated them from the real world by providing a familylike cocoon until they married. As Quantz (1992, pp. 147–148) notes:

> Teaching was one way for women to bide their time until marriage and to improve their skills as mothers. Perhaps the family and mother images placed on the schools made teaching a most inviting profession. Teachers were respected, in their way, even if also clearly subordinate. Women could learn how to order and organize their world, while remaining, at the same time, dependent on others and ignorant of the world outside their realm. In many ways, these teachers reflected the self-sacrifice and dedication which marked teaching in particular and women's social roles in general.

Their recollections reveal another side as well; idealism, which has been often attributed to teachers, did not play a key role in the job selection process. Social norms and pragmatism guided their decisions. One teacher's parents selected her occupation for her: "I guess I never really decided to be a teacher. My parents decided for me" (quoted in Quantz 1992, p. 147). Teaching long conformed to social norms as an acceptable job for women (Lortie 1975). Many instructors entered classrooms simply because they needed jobs. Still other women discovered that teaching was all they could do with their college degrees. Thus, unlike the conflicts between school and family that Vaughn-Roberson (1984) found among Oklahoma's teachers and the synchrony of those two worlds that Nelson (1992) illustrated among Vermont's instructors, Quantz (1992) locates his sample of Ohio teachers somewhere on the spectrum between these two positions. Quantz's study reports superficial harmony, but disjuncture nevertheless seeps through, revealing some tensions between, as well as within, teachers' lives and work.

Urban female instructors saw the classroom as a workplace, and, between 1900 and 1917, confronted attempts to mix their domestic and work lives. Many fought for equal pay, the right to marry, and maternity leave. In New York City's high-profile efforts, they used the Interborough Association of Women Teachers, enlisted the help of women's clubs and urban organizations, and publicized their causes through their press. "Women's increasingly marginalized position within the teaching profession," Carter (1992, p. 43) contends, "necessitated their interdependence with outside women's groups." They achieved mixed results, however. Aggressive lobbying efforts produced an equal pay bill, signed by the New York State Legislature in 1911. In California, Kate Ames led the 1908 drive "against the Male Schoolmasters' Association" (Weiler 1989, p. 21). The New York City campaign for the right to marry ended with an abiguous settlement. Protests by female teachers and the general public as well as judicial appeals resulted in no "clear guarantee of their rights" (Carter 1992, p. 53). They resorted to a clandestine strategy as an alternative.

> Some chose to enter "secret marriages" in which they hid their new status from the public, and more importantly from school administrators. Close friends and teaching colleagues took a collective vow of silence to protect these women from dismissal. There were others, as well, who succeeded in keeping their marriages secret only to have an untimely pregnancy expose their deception. (Carter 1992, p. 53)

Pittsburgh's female instructors exploited the same tactic, that is, covert collective resistance, to circumvent a similar restriction (Altenbaugh 1992a). Finally, the New York City campaign for maternity leave culminated in 1914 with a harsh school board compromise of a "two-year absence without pay," but the First World War changed all of this, "when dire teacher shortages necessitated reevaluation of the policies against married wormen teachers" (Carter 1992, p. 57).

Human agency assumed many forms, and a variety of responses characterized female teachers' lives and work. Women carefully navigated between both settings. On the western frontier, disjuncture existed, but women gave precedence to their domestic lives. In rural Vermont, the values, routines, and demands of teaching and domesticity often corresponded. In small town Ohio, no such problems existed, since domesticity prevailed. In cities, the domestic sphere for teachers often became formal and codified, sharply restricting their working lives; women addressed these obstacles in different ways— sometimes circumventing and sometimes challenging them. In all cases, women taught, preserving their individual occupational goals.

Structure of Work and Organizations

The segmented labor market, based on a gendered division of labor, as Strober and Tyack (1980) argue, appears central to any analysis of teaching; that is, gender created a stratified work environment. Men, serving as superintendents, assistant superintendents, principals, vice principals, and secondary teachers, generally occupied positions of administrative and intellectual authority in the urban schools, while women usually toiled as instructors in the lower, often primary, grades. In San Francisco's schools in 1879, men comprised 8 percent of all personnel, yet dominated that system at best and achieved disproportionate representation at worst of the power, high status, and better paid positions. Men represented

> 40 percent of all high school teachers. . . . In grammar [i.e., elementary] schools, men were two-thirds of all principals and both high school principalships (including the one at the girl's high school) were held by men. While half (52 percent) of all women personnel in the city were teachers in primary schools, only 4 percent of male personnel were so employed. (Strober and Best 1979, p. 226)

Women in this patriarchal setting faced close supervision of their adherence to strict rules, clear authority, and a "rigidly prescribed curriculum" (Strober and Best 1979, pp. 220–221).

This segmented work structure reflected a broader trend, extending to recent times. Beginning male instructors typically see education as a lifelong career, but not classroom teaching; new female teachers rarely focus on anything but "classroom work." "Teaching, it appears, is institutionalized as temporary employment for men and continuing employment for women" (Lortie 1975, p. 9). Males, conforming to historical tradition, view classroom instruction as a mere stepping-stone to more powerful, lucrative, and visible positions in educational administration (or in fields outside of education). Teaching, as women's work, has held little prestige, and men in general have responded accordingly.

The professional socialization of female instructors, which appeared to begin with their training, actually represented a process sandwiched between traditional social expectations and the structural realities of the workplace. Vaughn-Roberson (1992) found in her study of 547 women teachers, in early twentieth-century rural Oklahoma, Texas, and Colorado, that their college programs appeared to be preselected, conforming to domestic culture. Letha Campbell, a former teacher, recalled her unconscious career choice: "Who ever heard of a man taking primary teaching courses or a woman majoring in engineering?" Ruth Marshall, another retired instructor, echoed Campbell's recollection: "In those days I did not know that [a woman] went to college for any other purpose except to become a teacher" (quoted in Vaughn-Roberson 1992, p. 20).

Normal school programs—whether at the high school or college level—sought to ingrain a deep respect for administrative authority, drilling "young women to teach in a specified manner." "Pictures of normal students in Washington, D.C. . . . show women students performing precisely the same activities prescribed for their future pupils, even to the mid-morning 'yawning and stretching' session. Given this purpose of tight control, women were ideal employees." (Strober and Tyack 1980, p. 500). Teachers in rural mid-twentieth-century Vermont reflected the results of this training and socialization. Nelson's

(1992, pp. 28–29) interviews of retired female instructors found many who unconsciously transferred domestic attitudes into the classroom:

> Many of the teachers referred to the individual in charge of hiring and firing them as "My Superintendent." This use of the possessive "my" in reference to a superintendent is much like the "my" used by people to refer to other family members: my husband . . . my father. And, in fact, the structure of authority relations between a teacher and "her" superintendent seemed very much like the relations between a wife and her husband.

These female teachers, largely autonomous in their daily routine, had to defer to their superintendents and, ultimtely, to male dominated school boards for important decisions.

Although women numerically dominated the teaching force, as we have seen, salary differentiation prevailed until the 1960s, when unionization equalized male and female pay scales. In 1841, rural male teachers in the United States earned $4.15 per week compared to $2.51 for females, with $11.93 and $4.44, respectively, being paid to their counterparts working in the cities. In other words, that year rural female instructors earned 60 percent and urban female teachers made 37 percent of their male colleagues' salaries. Women never closed the gap, for the most part, because by 1865 they only collected 61 percent of men's salaries. A similar, if not worse, situation applied to male and female administrators. In mid-nineteenth-century Cincinnati, Ohio, the common-school "principals of the male department" received $85.00 a month while the "principals of the female department," with the same qualifications as their male counterparts, earned $42.00 per month, only 49 percent of what men received (Elsbree 1970).

Several explanations exist for these disparities. First, men established careers in urban schools while women worked for short periods. Coffman's (1911) classic survey of teachers found that, regardless of location and grade level, women instructors taught a median of four years compared to seven for men. Women at this time seldom made teaching a career, since most departed, "voluntarily" or involuntarily, when they married (see Altenbaugh 1992c). This pattern continued through the 1960s, when 65 percent of new female instructors planned to leave their jobs within the first five years (Lortie 1975). Higher salaries for male teachers, therefore, often, but not perfectly, reflected compensation for experience.

Second, as we have just seen, male instructors dominated the secondary grades; teaching these advanced grades resulted in a "salary premium," which also reflected a reward for a higher education investment as well as a budget consideration (Strober and Lanford 1986). In the former case, most elementary teachers only completed a normal-school program, while high school instructors typically claimed a college education. In the latter situation, school districts had the luxury of being generous when paying fewer and more prestigious, and often male, secondary teachers (Murphy 1990). This pay differential in the late 1800s appeared significant, as Marjorie Murphy (1990, p. 89) points out: "Teachers in high schools often earned a third more than elementary teachers. In Chicago, teachers in high schools earned from twelve hundred to sixteen hundred dollars a year whereas the highest elementary scale was eight hundred dollars."

Third, and after 1900, as more elementary teachers earned college degrees, such explanations failed to apply, since gender simply superseded educational credentials.

> When high school teachers had a college degree, elementary teachers with the same or higher qualifications were not given more compensation. There was an incentive for high school teachers to complete a masters degree or doctorate, but for elementary school teachers an advanced degree did not change their compensation. (Murphy 1990, p. 89)

The elementary school, a female-dominated workplace, simply held little prestige. "The elementary school teacher, if she had higher education, often transferred to a high school assignment, but she was not given compensation for her elementary teaching experience" (p. 89). Race reinforced these gender inequities in Oklahoma. "White women always earned less than the [white] men in their schools, receiving about the same as black men. Black women made the least of all" (Vaughn-Roberson 1984, p. 48).

Female instructors numerically dominated teacher organizations, like the American Federation of Teachers (AFT), but this historical experience too proved to be filled with irony. Murphy (1990) deftly chronicles how the AFT moved from a female union created for progressive social reform in general and teachers' needs in particular to a male organization focused solely on narrow bread-and-butter goals.

The Chicago Teachers' Federation (CTF), organized in 1897, attempted to bring teachers' benefits to the foreground. Catherine Goggin, a primary level instructor, and Margaret Haley, a sixth-grade teacher, won the Federation's leadership and called on teachers to become more political and active (Murphy, 1990). The CTF, after it failed to launch a national teachers' union in 1901, tried to reform the National Education Association (NEA) from within. When this endeavor proved unsuccessful, Goggin and Haley assisted teachers in many other cities to organize locals which eventually formed the AFT's nucleus (Murphy 1990).

These early organizational efforts assumed high visibility when Chicago's schoolteachers, led by Haley, successfully defeated the 1899 Harper Bill, that city's centralization measure. The bill's sexist language proved particularly offensive: "Filled with fears that feminization of schools would destroy the minds of bright young men, the authors conveyed the sense that masculine authority would cure the schools of all ills" (Murphy 1990, p. 29). This represented a nationwide concern, that is, the feminization of the schools, through the numerical domination of female teachers, would encourage docility and gentleness that would ultimately contribute to this nation's downfall. One speaker at the 1903 NEA annual meeting reported the results of his survey that indicated that male instructors "did the most good. Women were cited, he said, for "personal kindness, self-reliance, and social help," exemplifying purity, refinement, and the "ladylike" qualities, whereas men teachers embodied "masterful strength and masterfulness in relation to vitally significant things—courage, vigor, and the ability to lead" (Tyack and Hansot 1990, pp. 157 & 161; Weiler 1989, pp. 22–24). Teachers repeatedly defeated Chicago's Harper Bill in 1901, 1903, and 1909, yet it finally passed in 1917, "after the [Chicago] Board of Education had outlawed the teachers' unions and the state supreme court had upheld the untrammeled power of the Board of Education to hire and fire" (Murphy 1990, p. 31).

This drive toward the centralized control of schooling also included measures to further "professionalize" teachers, requiring higher education standards and state licensing. "Feminine virtues were not only no longer praised but were seen as qualities emasculating education" (Murphy 1990, p. 43). Female teachers became even more subordinated in this growing bureaucratic structure and lost what little autonomy they had possessed.

Professionalism, however, was not only associated with reformist calls for more training and control, it also stimulated teacher demands for a salary commensurate with this new status and, for women, equal pay. As Murphy (1990, pp. 44–45) explains:

> Women schoolteachers had been told that their demands for higher wages were unfeminine, that they had to perform their jobs selflessly, and that it was their feminine behavior more than their scholarly merit that was valued in the classroom. Professionalism negated that ideology; instead, professionalism promised that scholarly achievement would be rewarded financially, thus making the demands for higher wages no longer a question of stepping out of socially determined sex roles.

Female instructors in Chicago, as well as St. Paul and New York City, began to express their demands through political activism, specifically through their own unions (Carter 1992; Urban 1982).

Professionalism also proved to be a two-edged sword. By conferring a middle-class mantle on teaching, it acted to deflect social reformism; professionals, it was claimed, because of their higher status, simply refused to stoop to such "vulgar" goals. The AFT, like the NEA during the Progressive Era, accepted professionalism during the interwar years. Two factions developed within the Federation: "a very conservative wing consisting mainly of vocational-education men who admired Gompers and bread-and-butter unionism and a decidedly radical wing of Progressive men and women who embraced municipal socialism and remained critical of Gompers's labor programs" (Murphy 1990, p. 101).

The former leaned towards professionalism, and the conservative wing's male leadership increasingly asserted itself. "Professionalism evoked male leadership and invariably excluded women" (Murphy 1990, p. 172). By the end of the Great Depression, the union, now firmly in the hands of men, shed its "feminist and gadfly" image and goals. As a result of the radical purges of the late 1930s and further harassment of radicals during the Cold War, the AFT emerged in the early 1960s as a simple bread-and-butter union (Murphy 1990). With Albert Shanker as Federation president since 1974, male trade unionism remains firmly entrenched, substituting pragmatic issues for social idealism; the Federation no longer accommodates the "old radical politics of the union" (p. 266). This transformation towards teacher conservatism, Murphy concludes, represents "a historic process rooted in the struggles of the past" (p. 271).

Conclusion

The historical context of this feminized occupation appears clear and consistent: gender relations were tied to power differentials in American society and among its teachers, and conflicts resulted. Women numerically dominated teaching, yet men (and some women) treated them as a minority in terms of power and influence. The domestic sphere impeded female instructors' careers in some cases, while it corresponded to the classroom in other cases. Female teachers created a union for themselves, but males gained control of it, carefully crafting it to avoid progressive social reform issues that would have advanced women's (and other subordinated groups') rights.

What are the consequences? Although teaching remains a feminized occupation and school functions as a feminized workplace, male power ensures a masculine culture. This guarantees the subordination of female teachers. It also continues the traditional socialization process for men and women, because it sees to it that, in schools, competition assumes precedence over cooperation, that teaching supersedes learning, and that testing prevails over nurturing. This ultimately affects the quality of the educational process, because gender represents an integral part of teaching and learning (Brophy 1985). Female teachers, as in the past, must resist this process (Weiler 1990).

NOTES

1. Bruce Nelson, Department of History, Northwestern University, read an earlier version of this chapter. His comments, as always, proved insightful and useful. He, however, is neither responsible for the views expressed in this chapter nor for any mistakes that may appear in it.

2. Women also comprise the majority of teachers, especially at the preschool and primary levels, in many countries around the world (see Dove 1986; Schmuck 1987).

3. Some men, of course, remained in education, but, as we shall see, seldom as teachers.

REFERENCES

Altenbaugh, R. J. (Ed.). (1992a). "Teachers and the Workplace." In *The Teacher's Voice: A Social History of Teaching in Twentieth-Century America*, pp. 157–171. London: Falmer Press.

———. (Ed.). (1992b). *The Teacher's Voice: A Social History of Teaching in Twentieth-Century America*. London: Falmer Press.

———. (Ed.). (1992c). "Women's Work—Introduction." In *The Teacher's Voice: A Social History of Teaching in Twentieth-Century America*, pp. 8–12. London: Falmer Press.

Bennett, K. P., and LeCompte, M. D. (1990). *The Way Schools Work: A Sociological Analysis of Education*. New York: Longman.

Brophy, J. (1985). "Interactions of Male and Female Students with Male and Female Teachers." In *Gender Influences in Classroom Interaction*, edited by L. C. Wilkinson and C. Merrett, pp. 115–142. Orlando, FL: Academic Press.

Carter, P. (1992). "Becoming the 'New Women': The Equal Rights Campaigns of New York City Schoolteachers, 1900–1920." In *The Teacher's Voice: A Social History of Teaching in Twentieth-Century America*, edited by Richard J. Altenbaugh, pp. 40–58. London: Falmer Press.

Coffman, L. D. (1911). *The Social Composition of the Teaching Profession.* New York: Teachers College Press.

Dove, L. (1986). *Teachers and Teacher Education in Developing Countries.* London: Croom Helm.

Elsbree, W. S. (1939, 1970). *The American Teacher: Evolution of a Profession in a Democracy.* Westport, CT: Greenwood Press.

Grumet, M. R. (1988). *Bitter Milk: Women and Teaching.* Amherst: University of Massachusetts Press.

Lortie, D. C. (1975). *Schoolteacher: A Sociological Analysis.* Chicago: University of Chicago Press.

Murphy, M. (1990). *Blackboard Unions: The AFT and The NEA, 1900–1980.* Ithaca: Cornell University Press.

Nelson, M. K. (1992). "The Intersection of Home and Work: Rural Vermont Schoolteachers, 1915–1950." In *The Teacher's Voice: A Social History of Teaching in Twentieth-Century America*, edited by Richard J. Altenbaugh, pp. 26–39. London: Falmer Press.

Quantz, R. A. (1992). "The Complex Visions of Female Teachers and the Failure of Unionization in the 1930s: An Oral History." In *The Teacher's Voice: A Social History of Teaching in Twentieth-Century America*, edited by Richard J. Altenbaugh, pp. 139–156. London: Falmer Press.

Schmuck, P. (Ed). (1987). *Women Educators: Employees of Schools in Western Countries.* Albany, NY: State University of New York Press.

Strober, M. H., and Best, L. (1979). "The Female/Male Salary Differential in Public Schools: Some Lessons from San Francisco, 1879." *Economic Inquiry* 17(2): 218–236.

Strober, M. H., and Lanford, A. G. (1986). "The Feminization of Public School Teaching: Cross-sectional Analysis, 1850–1880." *Signs: Journal of Women in Culture and Society* 11(2): 212–234.

Strober, M. H., and Tyack, D. (1980). "Why Do Women Teach and Men Manage? A Report on Research on Schools." *Signs: Journal of Women in Culture and Society* 5(3): 494–503.

Tyack, D., and Hansot, E. (1990). *Learning Together: A History of Coeducation in American Public Schools*. New Haven: Yale University Press.

Underwood, K. (1986). "The Pace of Their Own Lives: Teacher Training and the Life Course of Western Women." *Pacific Historical Review* 55(4): 513–530.

Urban, W. J. (1982). *Why Teachers Organized*. Detroit, MI: Wayne State University Press.

Vaughn-Roberson, C. A. (1984). "Sometimes Independent But Never Equal—Women Teachers, 1900–1950: The Oklahoma Example." *Pacific Historical Review* 53(1): 39–58.

———. (1992). "Having a Purpose in Life: Western Women Teachers in the Twentieth Century." In *The Teacher's Voice: A Social History of Teaching in Twentieth-Century America*, edited by Richard J. Altenbaugh, pp. 13–25. London: Falmer Press.

Weiler, K. (1989). "Women's History and the History of Women Teachers." *Journal of Education* 171(3): 9–30.

———. (1990). "You've Got to Stay There and Fight: Sex Equity, Schooling, and Work." In *Changing Education: Women as Radicals and Conservators*, edited by J. Antler and S. K. Biklen, pp. 217–236. Albany: State University of New York Press.

Transformative Labour: Theorizing the Politics of Teachers' Work

Robert W. Connell

Teachers in Social Theory

Teachers have occupied at best an ambiguous position, and generally a marginal position, in social theories of education. This is clear in the social reproduction theories which swept the sociology of education two decades ago, transforming the field from a hodgepodge of surveys and unfocussed cultural debates into the domain of powerful theoretical systems. When teachers were noticed in social reproduction theories, they were generally seen as the agents of a system far beyond their control.

Bourdieu's (1966) original essay "L' École Conservatrice" ("The school as a conservative force"), for instance, noted the role of teachers and their language in social selection. However, this did not follow from teachers' agency, their capacity to produce an intended result. Quite the contrary, teachers were seen to be selecting on behalf of a class power not their own: a power manifest in the cultural capital of the upper classes of French society, which became effective through the institutional arrangements of an education system privileging an aristocratic culture.

This argument is typical of the way teachers were understood in analyses of social reproduction, whether the emphasis was laid on culture and ideology (e.g., Althusser 1971), political economy (e.g., Bowles and Gintis 1976), school-level social control (e.g., Sharp and Green 1975), or the eclectic mixture of class and gender stratification common in discussions by the end of the 1970s (e.g., Branson and Miller 1979; Arnot 1980).

Teachers were presented, basically, as the agents of a larger system, as operating under structural constraints, and as having no independent power to change the consequences of their work. Their work was not *praxis*, to use the old term for action infused by reason and political purpose. Teachers' work could even be seen as counterpraxis, an ironic negation of the possibility of social transformation through educational action.

It is not surprising that teacher activists, when they encountered this writing, were taken aback. They could respond to the social radicalism that underlay social reproduction theory, the protest against social injustice conveyed by this powerful image of the conservative school in an unequal society. But the theory gave them nowhere to go *as teachers*. So far as acting for social justice was concerned, they might as well jump off a cliff as engage in their classroom work.

This political dilemma led a number of theorists in the early 1980s to fret at the concept of *reproduction*, coupling it with cultural *production* or emphasising that it always came in a package with *resistance*. In discussions of teachers this might mean a search for signs of resistance (e.g., Bullough, Gitlin, and Goldstein, 1984), for allies in resistance (e.g., Harris 1982), or for contradictions in teachers' class situation which made them less predictable as agents of the system (e.g., Harp and Betcherman 1980). Such moves certainly lightened the burden of theoretically informed teachers, who now at least had room to wriggle; but it did not change the fundamental logic of their situation.

Reasons to change the underlying images of reproduction theory, however, were accumulating. Looking further back into the course of events, and looking further across the twentieth-century world, one sees a much more jagged history, a more contingent relationship with the structural imperatives of capitalism (e.g., W. Connell 1980). Looking more closely at the recent economic and cultural history of the rich countries, one observes the expansion of semiprofessions and intellectually trained labour, the growth of credentialized labour markets, and the increasing weight of technology—the changes often theorized as postindustrial society. All this gives education systems a weightier role in social change than reproduction theory allowed. Moreover, the concept of the *new class* advanced by Gouldner (1979), influential in recent discussions of intellectuals and classes, centred on the social dynamic of the education system.

Down at the chalkface, research on teachers showed that the social control presupposed by reproduction theory is difficult to guarantee. Wexler's (1987) pungent critique of reproduction theory called attention to the rise of the new right. In the 1980s new-right movements in North America and Europe put a great deal of energy into disciplining teachers and schools. Even with state power and a ruthless disregard of childrens' interests (as shown in the Thatcher government's abolition of the Inner London Education Authority), they had only partial success. An important reason is suggested by Gouldner (1979): The internal culture of education systems provides a basis for public definitions of the social good, and for social action, which cannot be reduced to the imperatives of capital.

Another reason is the multiplicity of social struggles in and around education. The rise of second-wave feminism placed gender issues in education firmly on the agenda. In the aftermath of postwar labour migration, issues about migrant disadvantage and multicultural education became unavoidable. Issues of race, in curriculum and workforce, were increasingly debated in the industrial countries, as they had long been in the colonial world.

On a global scale, education aid, international agencies, and the role of schools in postcolonial state formation were increasingly debated. Resistance to the simple export of Western education deepened, for instance, in the Islamic world. The history of postcolonial education and the role of international agencies such as UNESCO makes little sense in reproductionist terms. It requires us to recognize the fundamental sense in which education is a culture transformer.

With structuralist theories of society (on which reproduction theory mainly depended) in retreat across the social sciences, social analyses of education shifted ground. No new paradigm has gained the authority that reproduction theory once had, but we can identify three theoretical tendencies (rational choice or human capital theory, poststructuralism or postmodernism, and labour process or structuration theory) which lead to distinctive views of teachers.

The first is the theoretical arm of the new right itself—a movement often openly hostile to the social sciences, yet at the same time the bearer of conceptions of society and the individual which can function as an intellectual framework. This is mainly expressed in social theory as *rational choice* theory, in social and economic policy as *economic rationalism* or market-driven policy, and in education as an updated *human capital* theory. The school system is seen as the producer of the human capital needed by the economy, in the form of a trained and differentiated workforce. Teachers are then readily seen as the specialized workforce producing the larger workforce. If they do it badly, for instance, by equipping future workers with unrealistic expectations or unsaleable skills, they have to be managed differently—with controls and incentives restructured so that they produce the workforce the global market demands.

In terms of public policy, this is unquestionably the most influential theory of teachers in the advanced capitalist world at present. It underpins the British government's current attempt to reconstruct teacher education to produce a cheaper and more controllable teaching workforce. It fits with the new right's wider push in the United States to expand market mechanisms in education such as "parental choice," voucher schemes, higher fees, national testing, and so on, and thus dismantle public education as a bureaucratically coordinated public service.

Despite its influence on policy, this view has had little impact on research or theorizing about teachers; social researchers can see through it too easily. More influential is the approach that builds on the versions of reproduction theory which emphasised the sphere of culture and ideology, while repudiating their structural framework. This is exactly the theoretical trajectory of poststructuralism in social theory and postmodernism in literary and cultural studies. So it is not accidental that this route away from the dilemmas of reproduction theory in education has been taken by educational theorists most influenced by poststructuralist and postmodernist thinking.

This approach leads to a view of teachers that emphasises their similarities to other *cultural workers,* a view recently spelt out by Aronowitz and Giroux (1991) and Giroux (1992). What is political about teachers' work is their share in the contestation, subversion, and shifting of cultural codes, a process which is equally found in cultural forms such as television and popular music. The postmodern pedagogy praised by Giroux mainly involves leading students across cultural borders and resisting totalizing discourses, whether radical or establishment.

Wexler (1992) does not share Giroux's enthusiasm for floating signifiers, but his argument is certainly on the same terrain. To Wexler the social analysis of schooling centrally concerns identity formation in the students, with teachers' practices helping or hindering this. In postmodern society, Wexler thinks, teachers' defensive practices mainly tend to empty the social relations of education of meaning and trust, and thus reinforce, or even lead, a wider cultural crisis.

The third approach develops a point loosely acknowledged in some reproduction analyses, that teachers are employees and their situation resembles that of other groups of employees. Deploying ideas from industrial sociology in the field of education proved very fruitful, leading to studies of workplace supervision and autonomy, teacher unionism, the labour process of teaching, and teachers' occupational culture (e.g., Lawn and Ozga 1981, Gitlin 1983, R. Connell 1985, Lawn and Grace 1987).

This yields a messier view of the politics of teachers' work. What happens in education is the result of partly intersecting, partly independent struggles around industrial and economic issues over the curriculum, and over the institutional shape of education. Changes in the labour force, such as the "feminisation of teaching," respond to the same mixture of social forces as changes in the industrial labour force or in office work.

This approach, though more eclectic than the other two, is not quite innocent of theory. Its work is typically done with some notion of an interplay between structure and agency reminiscent of Giddens's (1984) *structuration* theory, an important alternative in social theory to poststructuralism. The agency of teachers is firmly asserted by Apple (1986), for instance, within the framework of "a political economy of class and gender relations in education."

Yet the formulae of structuration theory do not give, any more than the formulae of poststructuralism, the basis for a theory of *education*. A striking illustration is provided by Giddens. His analysis of Willis's well-known school ethnography, *Learning to Labour* (Giddens 1984: 289–304) treats it as a fine illustration of the knowledgeability of actors and the duality of structure, but there is nothing in the analysis that depends on this happening in a *school*. A factory or a bureaucracy would have done as well. Ironically, it is human capital theory, the least sociological of the theoretical frameworks now in use, that has the clearest view of the specificity of teachers' social labour.

Teaching as a Form of Work

In developing the social analysis of teaching, then, I would argue that we need an account of the specificity of education as a social process. This should start with the explicit recognition, in the recent research literature about teachers, of the old point that teaching is a kind of work (Seddon, forthcoming). The state, or some other association, employs teachers, on a wage, to work for specified hours with specified pupils in a specified place. Each of those conditions can be modified: some teachers are on a contract; some work indeterminate hours; some teach whomever shows up, and some adult literacy teachers never use a classroom. Yet this is the paradigm of teaching in Western education systems. It is carried over into contexts of Third-World poverty even when, as Avalos (1992) argues, it is profoundly irrelevant.

Students also say they are working—and they are right. Freire's (1971) critique of the *banking* concept of education, not to mention progressive educators' insights into the need for the pupil to be active in learning, are perfectly valid. Education requires work by the learners (cf. Everhart 1983).

Not only that; to the extent an educational process is going on, the teachers and pupils are working together. There is a degree of coordination and interconnecting purposes between their labour. Descriptions of this coordination can be found in almost any account of a lively classroom, such as Shor's *Empowering Education* (1992). It is a cliché that education is a social process. The specific form of the social nature of education, the one thing that remains when all other conditions vary, is that education involves the joint labour of teachers and pupils.

This conception does not imply a rose-tinted view of schools as abodes of harmony. We cannot exclude by definition the horrible situations documented in school ethnographies by Walker (1989) and Fine (1991), where working-class and ethnic-minority pupils are very roughly handled by the schools. Joint labour may be conflict-ridden to a marked degree. People may be working at cross-purposes. And the results may be far from what anyone intended. All this is true of joint labour of other kinds, and in other settings such as factories and offices.

All labour involves the transformation of some object of labour, which begins in one state and at the end of the labour process is in a new state. We can draw a broad distinction between the labour processes in which a society transforms its environment (e.g., physical objects such as lumps of iron ore, or relationships and processes, as in genetic engineering), and the labour processes in which a society transforms itself and its members. The second category includes body-reflexive practices, such as healing and clothing; operations on social relations, such as political practice; and practices that transform members' and groups' capacities to engage in other practices. This is where education comes in. It can be defined socially as the organized labour whose object is the capacity for social practice.

We can be more specific. The crucial human characteristic involved is not the capacity to learn, which is shared with a range of other species, but the socially sustained capacity to acquire learning strategies—in a familiar education-trade expression, "learning how to learn." At the core of education is the creation of a network of workers and practices that sustains this second-order learning capacity *both for the individual members and for the collectivity*. I emphasise "for the collectivity" since educators' talk mainly locates "learning how to learn" in the development of the individual. But this means nothing if it is not sustained also as a collective property of the social world that the individual is entering.

The specification of this labour process is the curriculum. The curriculum is both a definition of the pupil's learning and of the teacher's work (R. Connell 1985), a point that readily follows from a recognition of the joint labour involved. Very closely linked to the definition of the work is the definition of the criteria it is socially required to meet—that is to say, the system of assessment. Assessment and curriculum are so closely interwoven that for all practical purposes they must be analyzed together: A type of curriculum is to a large extent defined through its assessment system, and vice versa.

The labour process of education, in this conception, is a strategic component of any large-scale process of social change. (Social reproduction theory was not categorically wrong. It correctly described a particular strategic situation, and mistakenly took this to be the general case.)

Educational institutions, being large and powerful social institutions, have many social effects beyond the educational ones. For instance, they have considerable economic effects simply because they are large employers. Since they are mostly public-sector institutions they have second-order effects on taxation, public sector borrowing, and so on. The political practice of education managers and teachers' unions always has to take account of these dimensions, and so should social theory. They affect what is specific to education, the joint labour process of teaching and learning, by changing the conditions in which this work has to be carried on. A striking example is the current deterioration in the public education system in California, a long-term consequence of struggles over property and taxation which I will describe shortly.

To speak of the "capacity for social practice" is to speak at a very high level of abstraction. To arrive at a framework for understanding the political contours of teachers' work we must become more specific. In the remainder of this section I will outline a reasonably familiar classification of types of practice, suggesting the domain of teachers' labour process; and in the following section I will define the forms of politics that arise from the labour of forming capacities for practice.

First, labour itself is a type of practice, and it is an utterly familiar point that education involves developing the capacity to labour. This is the whole basis of the human capital analysis. Its significance is indicated by the habit, in conservative-agenda debates on whether the schools are teaching "The Basics" enough, of making employers' opinions of new employees the test of schools' performance. But *capacity to labour* is itself a cultural construct, not a purely technical question. A clear indication is that employers' opinions of new employees are often expressed in terms of their ability to spell—which is a technical requirement of almost no entry-level job in the economy. This point has acquired, however, a symbolic meaning of diligence, orderliness, and obedience to rules. If employers collectively manage to impose this definition of the capacity to labour on the schools, they have won a certain victory in establishing their cultural power over the workforce. (The complexity of the issues is suggested by the fact that most teachers also want their pupils to learn to spell, though for other reasons than the employers').

Second, if we follow Habermas's (1979) distinction between labour and interaction as fundamental types of practice, then a major category of educational effects concerns capacities for interaction. This is the core of Giroux's (1992) and Wexler's (1992) analyses of education, as a process operating on the terrain of culture, identity formation, and communication. This is also the traditional domain of socialization theory. It is worth recalling that in functionalist sociologies of education before reproduction theory, the functional requirement of socialization was the basis of the whole analysis. The flaw in the argument was not only in the teleological structure of functionalist theory, but in the analysis of socialization as essentially a process of social control.

In defining education as producing capacities for interaction, I would emphasise the point that social interaction (such as the use of language) inherently involves creativity. A generative grammar may specify the rules that make the creation possible, but cannot specify what use will be made of them. The capacity for an *infinite* generation of intelligible utterances is involved, in principle, in the capacity to speak any natural language. A similar argument might be derived from Derrida's semantics (Wood and Bernasconi 1988). If meaning is constituted in an open-ended play of difference, with final determinations of meaning always deferred, then the capacity to handle an open-ended, constantly evolving system of meaning is involved in education as a cultural process.

Third, if we recognize power as another broad category of practice, we can define a third broad category of educational effects. Recall that the Althusserian school (Althusser 1971) added a *political* instance to the economic and the ideological and Foucault (1980) added the dimension of power to that of symbolism to produce his evocative concept of *power/knowledge* (Fraser 1989). To speak of developing a *capacity for power* is not a usual way of speaking; it is even a troubling one. Is it the business of schools to train up potential Hitlers? Obviously not. Yet the example is relevant; Hitler succeeded because a significant number of the German people did not have the capacity to oppose him effectively. A worried literature in the 1930s and 1940s debated what it meant to "educate for democracy." This was not entirely nonsense, though the idea became corrupted during the Cold War. A progressive movement needs to develop a *culture of power*, a collective capacity to exercise political responsibility, if it is not to condemn itself to permanent opposition (Mathews 1988).

This may seem a little exotic, but it is essentially the same issue that was raised in discussions of the "hidden curriculum" in schooling. When students live and work in an authoritarian institution that gives them no real responsibility, formal exhortations to autonomy and participation are subverted.

The significance of the issue can be seen in that central theme of peer group life, the construction of masculinity and femininity. The power structure of schools is involved as antagonist in the production of a potentially violent protest masculinity in certain working-class settings (R. Connell 1989). The significance of schools as venues for asserting and contesting the gendered power of boys over girls is undeniable (Thorne 1993; Yates 1993). In high schools, teachers' work routinely includes attempts to manage (often to mitigate) gendered power relations among the students, a familiar observation in school ethnographies and interview studies (Grant and Sleeter 1986; Kessler et al. 1985).

We may argue, then, that the development of capacities for power is an unavoidable aspect of the work done in education. Whether it is made explicit, and addressed consciously as an aspect of the curriculum, is another matter.

Foci of the Politics of Teachers' Work

The politics of education can best be understood as the struggle to control the production of capacities for practice, and thus to limit or shape the social capacities that emerge and the society they in turn generate. These effects are, in a sense, universal; the capacity for practice has no institutional limits. So educators are right to be suspicious of conventional cost/benefit analyses of educational investment, confined to the capacity for labour (and ignoring labour which is not for wages). This does miss out on much of what is important in education. But educators are wrong if they assume that teachers' work should therefore be exempt from all policy analysis.

The stakes in the politics of education are high, though generally long-term. For instance, the social production of capacities for labour is deeply involved in the accumulation of wealth. This is the issue picked up in economists' discussions of the long-term benefits of having an educated workforce. We might add that the social production of capacities for power is just as deeply implicated in the distribution of the wealth produced. The level of inequality in a country is as important a determinant of its quality of life as the average income is.

By "politics" I mean, conventionally enough, the mobilization and deployment of power to affect the social distribution of resources. Given the analysis of the teaching labour process already made, there is a sense in which virtually everything about teaching is political. As Ginsburg et al. observe in the first chapter of this volume, teachers cannot choose to be nonpolitical. To identify this general condition, however, tells us little about the shape of the politics involved.

I will now outline a way of thinking about this question, starting from the characterization of teaching as a kind of labour. We can use the techniques and concepts of industrial sociology to define the foci of the politics that centre on this work. These are: the control of the labour process; the political order of the workplace; the character of the workforce; and the allocation of resources used in the work of teaching. I will sketch the general character of the politics involved, and briefly discuss an illustrative case for each issue.

Control of the Labour Process

The labour process of teaching in the most immediate sense, the curriculum-as-realized in the classroom, is the least obvious site of politics. When education is supposed to be *non-political*, it is the classroom above all that is being *protected* from politics. But the protection is imaginary. A political process invests even the most limited definition of the content of teaching and learning in the classroom, through the curriculum. The social struggles that have gone into the making of each subject of the conventional subject curriculum are now being traced in a fascinating historical literature (e.g., Goodson 1987). Apple (1993) has recently shown the complex politics among and within American states involved in the production of school textbooks of the most conventional kind.

A wider politics was involved in the shaping of the hegemonic curriculum in the wealthy capitalist countries. Its historical roots lie in the classical and literary curriculum for European ruling-class boys in the eighteenth and nineteenth centuries. As mass elementary-schooling systems developed in the nineteenth century, and especially as mass secondary systems developed in the twentieth century, a modified version of this curriculum was installed at the core of the larger system. Science gradually displaced the classics, but the hierarchichal organization of knowledge and the abstract pedagogy linked to it were carried forward. Key elements of this curriculum were exported, along with the social technology of bureaucratically controlled schooling, to the rest of the world, though the way in which this technology was adopted varied with the history of colonialism.

The competitive academic curriculum's definition of learning as the individual appropriation of elements of a hierarchically organized body of authoritative knowledge, tested competitively, with educational selection depending on the outcomes of the tests, has profoundly shaped the practice of teachers in their daily work. The control of curriculum is closely bound up with the assessment system. This has been clear from the earliest days of mass education. Her Majesty's Inspectors of Schools carried out their surveillance of teachers, not by sitting for hours as observers in classrooms, but by testing the pupils. In current education politics the attempt to set up an impersonal surveillance system by means of mass-testing programs is an important issue. The political right makes no bones about their intention to use such assessments as a way of controlling teachers and enforcing a conventional curriculum ("The Basics") and a top-down pedagogy. The capacity to change assessment practices is thus a key political issue about teachers' labour.

This curriculum and the related system of assessment are central to the formidable class selectivity of Western education systems, the issue which drove reproduction theory (for its continuing importance, see Whitty 1985). The hegemonic curriculum has therefore become a major issue for teachers in disadvantaged schools wishing to make education work for children in poverty. These teachers are well aware that this curriculum and its competitive assessment technology are a key part of what is producing educational failure for their pupils. They have often sought alternatives. The Disadvantaged Schools Program in Australia, for instance, has seen a range of experiments with alternative assessment systems (Connell, Johnston and White 1992). Most involve some attempt to increase the relevance of the process by individualizing it, through dossiers of work, teachers' daily observations, and so on.

This gives greater leeway for curriculum enrichment than do conventional grading systems. But it runs into problems. If carried very far, it means intensification of teachers' work. An individualising strategy is not likely to be a good long-term answer to a collective problem like class inequalities in education. And where schools' assessment practices intersect with employers' demands for credentials, reform runs the risk of disadvantaging economically the very students it is trying culturally to serve.

The issue of credentials thus becomes a focus of politics. This has to be tackled at a system-wide level: Individual schools cannot sustain a credentialling system, since credentials operate at the interface between schools and much wider labour markets. Some systems have launched innovations to make the credentialling process more responsive to the demands of social justice. An important example is the "Record of Achievement" negotiated credential developed by the Inner London Education Authority—shortly before its abolition by the Thatcher government. Another is the "Victorian Certificate of Education" recently introduced by the state government of Victoria in Australia—immediately the target of fierce attacks from neoconservatives (R. Connell 1993). As these examples show, the reconstruction of credentials is not a technical process; it is immediately, and rightly, perceived as affecting broad social interests.

The Political Order of the Workplace

Like any other workplace the school has a political order. By this I mean the structure of authority in the school; the powers and resources brought to bear on decision making by the different players; the alliances, mobilizations, and divisions currently existing in the workplace. Familiar elements of the political order are the relations between departments of a school, the relations between rank-and-file teachers and school administrators (principal, deputy principal, etc.), the effectiveness of local teacher unions, and social divisions among the school's staff, such as gender and ethnic divisions. All of these affect the way teachers' work is done.

A significant part of this political order is the legal constitution of the school in relation to the state. It matters, as we argued in *Making the Difference* (R. Connell et al. 1982), that working-class families confront state power and compulsion in their public-sector schools; while ruling-class families confront a market mechanism, in their private (or semiprivatised public) schools, through which they call the tune. Teachers are placed in a fundamentally different situation vis-à-vis their students in the two cases. In one, they are the bearers of state power; in the other, they are—at only a slight remove—skilled employees of the students' families. Ruling-class pupils can drive the point home. In one elite school we studied, the young ladies locked the classroom door against a teacher who was late for class, and called out through the door that the teacher now owed them ten minutes' worth of their fees.

The political order of the school is never fixed for good. It is subject to change under pressures from outside, and it is subject to challenge from within. An important case of both is the feminist challenge to the gender order in school authority. Women as teachers have long been subordinated in school systems (Acker 1983). In the last two decades women teachers, with a certain amount of support among the men, have widely challenged the concentration of authority in the hands of male administrators. Pressure for wage justice, for equal opportunity in promotion, and for an equal share in decision making has gone together with pressure for gender desegregation for the pupils and attention to girls' curricular, social, and security needs.

This combined political strategy has not always been straightforward. For instance, the gender desegregation of (most) schools in New South Wales, Australia, reduced promotion opportunities for women teachers as it abolished the list of girls' schools reserved for headmistresses, without altering the promotion criteria that gave men an institutionalized advantage in the general list.

Gender desegregation, in the form of coeducational classes, has commonly been pursued as an organizational reform without introducing means of contesting sexism in the desegregated classes. This can make girls' learning vulnerable to sexual harassment, in a wide variety of forms. It can also make girls' learning vulnerable to the pressure of a peer culture that emphasises romance and sexual desirability, as shown in the striking ethnography of undergraduate culture by Holland and Eisenhart (1990). For such reasons, an influential current of thought in feminism turned back toward endorsing separate classes or schools for girls (Deem 1984). This strategy of resegregation has problems, especially when seen in relation to class and race inequalities in education. It is by no means clear that a strategy that helps the academic ascent of girls from advantaged backgrounds is good for the majority of girls in working-class communities or oppressed ethnic groups. Curiously, the discourse of resegregation in the United States has now been turned to the interests of *boys*, especially African-American boys, who are supposed to be disadvantaged in coeducational schooling because of the lack of strong masculine role models.

These debates could not have happened without the growth of a broad feminist movement and its concern with the way education advantaged or disadvantaged women. In this and other respects, the political order of the school is not insulated from the wider society; it is, inevitably, part of a broader pattern of social struggle.

Character of the Workforce

The character of the workforce in teaching is, on the face of it, specified by the job description and required training. There is a labour market for teachers, an interplay of demand and supply. During periods of rapid expansion of demand, training requirements may be diluted. Over the long run, however, training requirements have risen as teaching itself has become more credentialized.

This does not necessarily mean that all the training is technically necessary. Teachers' own narratives of their "First Year Out" often emphasise how different their training was from the actual requirements of the job. But the training provides an important social definition of the job as a profession; and as Lawn (1987) emphasises, professionalization has provided a key means of indirect control over teachers.

Training and job specifications, however, are far from settling the character of the workforce as a functioning social unit. It takes a complex social process to turn these general technical capacities into a specific set of practices. Most of this occurs on the job and most of it is inexplicit. Sometimes, however, it is made explicit.

Compensatory education programs, for instance, draw on the general labour intake to the school system. For the most part, the staffing of disadvantaged schools is governed by the rules and practices of the larger systems they are parts of, and their administrative and teaching practices are orthodox (for evidence see R. Connell, White and Johnston 1991). As we see in the Disadvantaged Schools Program (DSP) in Australia, however, something more can happen. In this case a network of teachers formed in DSP schools took the lead in the remaking of curricula and pedagogy, in the creation of participatory structures for the program, and in the defence of the program when it was in political trouble. Experienced teachers in DSP schools would try to pass on this specific experience to newcomers. Some of them remained long-term in schools usually marked by high teacher turnover, providing a committed core for the workforce. The "DSP ethos" (much commented on locally) is to a large extent the expression of this teacher activism, intersecting at times with parent activism and often with teacher unionism (White and Johnston 1993).

The teaching workforce, then, is not fixed in its political character by the structures that produced it as an economic category. Its capacities for action can be developed by social mobilization and the development of a political consciousness about the labour in which it is engaged.

Struggle for Resources

Governments exert power over educational practice partly by legislation and regulation, partly by promoting ideologies, but above all by the power of the purse. Contemporary education as a practical enterprise requires resources on a very large scale.

The most important resource deployed is teachers' labour itself. The bulk of education systems' budgets goes into salaries, and the largest category of salaries is for the teaching staff. How this resource is distributed among the various groups of pupils is a crucial issue about how an education system functions. Kozol's *Savage Inequalities* (1991) vividly describes the effects of unjust distribution of funding for schools within the United States. An enquiry sponsored by a congressional committee found ratios of 2½ or 3 to 1 in per-pupil spending between richer and poorer local educational authorities in many American states (Taylor and Piché 1991). On a world scale the inequalities dwarf these.

The kind of politics involved in producing such inequalities is illustrated by the recent economic history of public schools in California. Like most U.S. systems they were primarily funded by local taxation, and in the 1960s had been funded at per-pupil levels above the U.S. average. (Figures from California Department of Education, reported in the *San Francisco Chronicle*, November 16, 1992.)

A period of conservative political hegemony (Ronald Reagan being state governor) brought funding levels down to the national average. In 1978 a new-right political initiative, Proposition 13, was passed in a referendum and immediately limited local property taxation. For a time the state government made up the difference and held overall school funding constant. But when California's financial reserves ran out and the recession deepened in the 1990s, public-school funding fell sharply below the national average. Class sizes jumped, and the condition of schools deteriorated.

None of these constraints applied to private schools, which serve principally the economically advantaged class that most benefited by reduced property taxation. The funding of a class-divided school system thus became part of a circuit of redistribution, indirect enough not to have stirred a strong political reaction, but potent in its long-term educational effects.

The decline of the public school system by 1993 had produced enough anxiety to drive another new-right referendum initiative. This would push the redistribution further, through a voucher scheme to divert a proportion of public-education funding to private schools according to "parental choice." Teachers' unions and the state political establishment combined to defeat this initiative. It is clear, however, that the political struggle is not over.

Concluding Thoughts on
Democracy and Education

To identify a field of politics is to identify possibilities for democracy. In this case they are as important as the distinction between a participatory democracy and a fake democracy, if we take seriously Dewey's (1916) vision of democracy as the creation of an informed, active citizenry, supported by an informative, activated public school.

Some false hopes are embedded in the belief that more education, or better education, in itself produces a democratic politics. One need only recall that it was the better-educated part of German society that provided most of the money and the votes for Hitler. In our day, the better-educated countries of the world are those which are profiting from the global power of multinational corporations and from the international arms trade.

So teachers, for better or for worse, are not the messengers of a better world, the advance guard of the good society. The main effect of educational labour is not the direct shaping of practice. As I argued earlier, it is the formation and transformation of capacities for practice. This inevitably means more indirect, more circuitous effects on social relations than teachers might like and reformers might hope. But the transformation of capacities for practice is a real and important effect. The contemporary state is not being stupid in putting large resources into education. Nor was Dewey (1916) being starry-eyed in connecting the character of education with the chances of democracy.

Capacities for practice affect the possibilities that can emerge in the social process. Without an informed and active working-class citizenry, no constitutional magic can make your system democratic. A striking example is the contemporary United States: formally democratic, in fact dominated by corporate and property-owning interests, with a working class that generally does not vote and has very little presence in policy making.

To point to the way schooling transforms capacities for practice is to show that the politics of teaching involves a real politics, not just symbolic stances and gestures. This is a domain where struggle really does affect outcomes. Given the massive scale and internal complexity of the education system, only parts of which have been traversed in this chapter, it is obvious that large-scale change in this domain is likely to be slow. Sometimes the pace of change is mortally frustrating, sometimes the direction of change is dire. "But," as Galileo said of another ponderous object, "it does move."

Teachers make up a significant part of the world intelligentsia, and are, it may be argued, a key group in the making of a world culture. The global expansion of Western-style schooling has both created teachers as an international workforce and placed them at the centre of battles to impose, appropriate, and resist the culture produced in the core states of the world economy. If this analysis is correct, teachers are likely to be strategic participants in the emerging global struggle either to democratise the world system or to maintain it as a structure of inequality. A new order of complexity in educational politics, and a new range of possibilities, open up when we consider the meaning of global citizenship and the ways it can be brought into being. (For an introduction to this global politics, see Brecher, Childs, and Cutler 1993.)

The way these possibilities are taken up depends to a considerable degree on teachers' capacities for reflection and strategic thinking about their work. If we take seriously the familiar arguments about the growing weight of organized knowledge in modern economies and political systems, then teachers' capacity to operate as designers and producers of knowledge is important to the vitality of education. And if it is true, as I have argued through this paper, that school systems have a major though indirect role in social change through the transformation of capacities for practice, then the capacity of teachers to steer that transforming process depends on the growth of their capacity to reflect on their practice.

It follows that attempts to de-skill teachers or to impose new systems of surveillance over their work, and the struggle of teachers' organizations against such control, have more than local industrial significance. Such questions bear on the larger possibilities of education in a world where democratic outcomes are very much in doubt.

REFERENCES

Acker, S. (1983). "Women and Teaching: A Semi-Detached Sociology of a Semi-Profession." In *Gender, Class and Education*, edited by S. Walker and L. Barton, pp. 123–139. Lewes: Falmer Press.

Althusser, L. (1971). *Lenin and Philosophy, and Other Essays*. London: New Left Books.

Apple, M. W. (1986). *Teachers and Texts: A Political Economy of Class and Gender Relations in Education*. New York: Routledge.

———. (1993). *Official Knowledge: Democratic Education in a Conservative Age*. New York: Routledge.

Arnot, M. (1980). "Schooling and the Reproduction of Class and Gender Relations." In *Schooling, Ideology and the Curriculum*, edited by L. Barton, R. Meighan and S. Walker, pp. 29–49. Lewes: Falmer Press.

Aronowitz, S., and Giroux, H. A. (1991). *Postmodern Education: Politics, Culture and Social Criticism*. Minneapolis: University of Minnesota Press.

Avalos, B. (1992). "Education for the Poor: Quality or Relevance?" *British Journal of Sociology of Education 13(4)*: 419–436.

Bourdieu, P. (1966). "L'École Conservatrice." *Revue Française de Sociologie 7*: 325–347.

Bowles, S., and Gintis, H. (1976). *Schooling in Capitalist America: Educational Reform and the Contradictions of Economic Life*. New York: Basic Books.

Branson, J., and Miller, D. B. (1979). *Class, Sex and Education in Capitalist Society: Culture, Ideology and the Reproduction of Inequality in Australia*. Malvern: Sorrett.

Brecher, J., Childs, J. B., and Cutler, J. (Eds.). (1993). *Global Visions: Beyond the New World Order*. Boston: South End Press.

Bullough, R. V., Gitlin, A. D., and Goldstein, S. L. (1984). "Ideology, Teacher Role, and Resistance." *Teachers College Record 86(2)*: 339–358.

Connell, R. W. (1985). *Teachers' Work*. Sydney: Allen and Unwin.

———. (1989). "Cool Guys, Swots and Wimps: The Interplay of Masculinity and Education." *Oxford Review of Education 15(3)*: 291–303.

———. (1993). *Schools and Social Justice*. Philadelphia: Temple University Press and Toronto: Our Schools Ourselves.

Connell, R. W., Ashenden, D. J., Kessler, S., and Dowsett, G. W. (1982). *Making the Difference: Schools, Families and Social Division*. Sydney: Allen and Unwin.

Connell, R. W., Johnston, K. M., and White, V. M. (1992). *Measuring Up: Assessment, Evaluation and Educational Disadvantage*. Canberra: Australian Curriculum Studies Association.

Connell, R. W., White, V. M., and Johnston, K. M. (1991). *Running Twice as Hard: The Disadvantaged Schools P,rogram in Australia*. Geelong: Deakin University Press.

Connell, W. F. (1980). *A History of Education in the Twentieth Century World*. New York: Teachers College Press.

Deem, R. (1984). *Co-Education Reconsidered*. Milton Keynes: Open University Press.

Dewey, J. (1916). *Democracy and Education*. New York: Macmillan.

Everhart, R. B. (1983). *Reading, Writing, and Resistance: Adolescence and Labor in a Junior High School*. Boston: Routledge and Kegan Paul.

Fine, M. (1991). *Framing Dropouts: Notes on the Politics of an Urban Public High School*. Albany: State University of New York Press.

Foucault, M. (1980). *Knowledge/Power*. New York: Pantheon.

Fraser, N. (1989). *Unruly Practices: Power, Discourse, and Gender in Contemporary Social Theory*. Minneapolis: University of Minnesota Press.

Freire, P. (1971) *Pedagogy of the Oppressed*. New York: Seabury.

Giddens, A. (1984). *The Constitution of Society*. Cambridge, England: Polity Press.

Giroux, H. A. (1992). *Border Crossings: Cultural Workers and the Politics of Education*. New York: Routledge.

Gitlin, A. (1983). "School Structure and Teachers' Work." In *Ideology and Practice in Schooling*, edited by M. W. Apple and L. Weis, pp. 193–212. Philadelphia: Temple University Press.

Goodson, I. (Ed). (1987). *International Perspectives in Curriculum History*. London: Croom Helm.

Gouldner, A. W. (1979). *The Future of Intellectuals and the Rise of the New Class*. New York: Seabury.

Grant, C. A., and Sleeter, C. E. (1986). *After the School Bell Rings*. Philadelphia: Falmer Press.

Habermas, J. (1979). *Communication and the Evolution of Society*. London: Heinemann.

Harp, J., and Betcherman, G. (1980). "Contradictory Class Locations and Class Action: The Case of School Teachers' Organizations in Ontario and Quebec." *Canadian Journal of Sociology 5(2)*: 145–162.

Harris, K. (1982). *Teachers and Classes: A Marxist Analysis*. London: Routledge and Kegan Paul.

Holland, D. C., and Eisenhart, M. A. (1990). *Educated in Romance: Women, Achievement, and College Culture*. Chicago: University of Chicago Press.

Kessler, S., Ashenden, D. J., Connell, R. W., and Dowsett, G. W. (1985). "Gender Relations in Secondary Schooling." *Sociology of Education, 58*: 34–48.

Kozol, J. (1991). *Savage Inequalities: Children in America's Schools*. New York: Crown.

Lawn, M. (1987). *Servants of the State: The Contested Control of Teaching, 1900–1930*. London: Falmer Press.

Lawn, M., and Grace, G. (Eds.). (1987). *Teachers: The Culture and Politics of Work*. London: Falmer Press.

Lawn, M., and Ozga, J. (1981). "The Educational Worker? A Reassessment of Teachers." In *Schools, Teachers and Teaching*, edited by L. Barton and S. Walker, pp. 45–64. Lewes: Falmer Press.

Mathews, J. (1988). *A Culture of Power: Rethinking Labour Movement Goals for the 1990s*. Melbourne: Pluto.

Seddon, T. (1994). "Teachers' Work and Political Action." In *International Encyclopedia of Educational Research*, edited by T. Husen and N. Postlethwaite, Volume 10, pp. 6132–6139. Oxford: Pergamon.

Sharp, R., and Green, A. (1975). *Education and Social Control: A Study in Progressive Primary Education*. London: Routledge and Kegan Paul.

Shor, I. (1992). *Empowering Education: Critical Teaching For Social Change*. Chicago: University of Chicago Press.

Taylor, W. L., and Piché, D. M. (1991). *A Report on Shortchanging Children: The Impact of Fiscal Inequity on the Education of Students at Risk*. Washington, DC: U.S. House of Representatives Committee on Education and Labor.

Thorne, B. (1993). *Gender Play: Girls and Boys in School*. New Brunswick, N.J.: Rutgers University Press.

Walker, L. (1989). "Australian Maid." Unpublished doctoral dissertation, Sociology. Sydney, New South Wales: Macquarie University.

Wexler, P. (1987). *Social Analysis of Education: After the New Sociology*. New York: Routledge.

————. (1992). *Becoming Somebody: Toward a Social Psychology of School*. London: Falmer Press.

White, V., and Johnston, K. (1993). "Inside the Disadvantaged Schools Program: The Politics of Practical Policy-Making." In *Education, Inequality and Social Identity*, edited by L. Angus, pp. 104–127. London: Falmer Press.

Whitty, G. (1985). *Sociology and School Knowledge*. London: Methuen.

Wood, D., and Bernasconi, R. (Eds.). (1988). *Derrida and Différance*. Evanston, IL: Northwestern University Press.

Yates, L. (1993). *The Education of Girls: Policy, Research and the Question of Gender*. Hawthorn: Australian Council for Educational Research.

The Political Nature of Teaching: Arguments Around Schoolwork

Martin Lawn

In this chapter, I begin by explaining my use of the terms, *politics* and *teachers*, in relation to each other and in particular with regard to the study of teachers' work *as work*, the creation of policy related to the conditions and contexts of work, and the right of teachers to be involved in the creation and maintenance of that policy. Second, I describe the early formation in the modern period of a distinctive way of managing teachers, their work, and their politics by their incorporation into the education system (using the ideas of Sydney Webb 1918) and the management of their "independence" under indirect rule. The consequence of these congruent processes was the paradox for the politics of teaching that teachers had to be nonpolitical. Third, I raise another related issue about teachers' politics, which was the social danger the teaching workforce represented to the modern state. Even though this danger might be symbolic, it had consequences for the political relations between teachers and the state. The social danger of an organised teachers' workforce wasn't necessarily based on what teachers did; it was what they represented. However, while the danger might be symbolic, the means to deal with the collective of political teachers also included a method of policing the boundaries of teaching so that they became separated and coerced. Fourth, I explore the continuing politics of teaching in the modern period as a war of position, based around the double-edged ideology of professionalism, around schoolwork disputes, and around images of the "good" teacher. Finally, I want to look at a further and related aspect of the relations between the state and teachers. Each party had to win support politically over time, in periods of change. Teachers might work within teaching as part of their membership in new social movements. They work, inside and outside of their unions, in a discrete public politics that involves the policies of the state and contemporary ideas about work, citizenship, and society, and which is affected by different periods in the development of the modern state.

Politics and Work

I should begin by explaining my use of the term political with regard to teachers' beliefs and actions. I am interested in the way teachers act politically within education, acting within their teachers' associations and making alliances with other groups or using a language of politics drawn from outside teaching to explore their roles, relations, and work.[1] I am also interested in the way the modern state (using England and Wales as an example of the modern social democratic state in the twentieth century) deals with its workforce of teachers politically.

My argument about teachers and politics is based on the assumption that teachers have certain legitimate interests that flow out of their conditions of work: these interests seem to cross all kinds of societies if they employ a distinct group of people in a system of schooling. Teaching is organised in the modern state within particular forms of production, containing labor processes that determine many aspects of the content, skills, speed, and work relations of teaching. This is not a socially neutral process to be excluded from our understanding of what teaching is; without a knowledge of the work context of teaching, their collective actions in their various forms tend to make little sense or are excluded by nature of their lack of fit to the "real" teaching. As the school is a site of struggle over the nature of teaching so is the history of the relations between the teachers and their employers; in one form or another this means the state in modern democratic societies. As has been argued before,

> The study of teachers' work as work should remain at the
> centre of research in this area. Like other forms of work,
> teaching should be properly served by a thorough study
> of its practices, struggles, lived experience and
> contradictions. Such an approach can range from studies
> of relations at work or the politics of skill control through
> to local and national policymaking involving organised
> teachers and their arguments on the nature of their
> industry. Most importantly, this study should be
> historical, recognising the movement of teachers in and
> out of teaching, and change in schools, in local authorities
> and in central and local educational policies. (Lawn and
> Ozga 1988, p. 334)

Obviously the concerns of the collective of teachers are
expressed within their organised deliberations, as is their
relationship with their employer and management. Another
feature of their work is their interest in the policies reflected in
the schooling system, namely its funding, expansion or decline,
resources, and current ideologies. Yet when teachers involve
themselves in these policy areas it can be regarded by their local
and national employers as an usurpation of "democratic"
processes or the management's right to manage. Teachers can be
seen as both main agents of social reproduction *and* low status
operatives in the education system: This is the source of the
contradiction that the phrase "the political nature of teaching"
describes. It is revealed in different ways, for example, in the gap
between their actions and the way these actions are seen by the
state. Alternatively, this tension in their work and their relations
with the state is seen in contemporary English history within
debates on professionalism, following a strike or an outbreak of
moral panic or a political crisis. While this tension may very well
take different forms in other societies, it will always be there in
one form or another. So *politics* means, in this context, the
achievement of policy related to the conditions and contexts of
work *and* the right to be involved in policy making.

However, this right to be involved in policy making leads
into a further dimension of teachers' politics. Teachers are not
neutral in society or just defenders of their labour process. They
may enter into teaching with a particular view of society and
education, expressed within contemporary politics or social

movements. They may develop a social/education project that leads them into a party or movement membership or into public alliances through their collective associations.

When a new group or class is beginning to move toward power, it must develop support and then win hegemony. In the twentieth century in particular, teachers are important, locally and nationally, as key members of the community and/or workers in a key public service. In this situation teachers are both the audience (the potential support) and often part of the new group attempting to win power, and so are often politically involved. They may be divided sometimes by gender, race or school sector (elementary and secondary) in their attraction to this form of politics and its solutions to their problems.

In Nazi Germany, for example, many teachers moved into the Nazi party when they were faced with a deprofessionalization process that attacked their standard of living and their role as cultural agents. Using Nazi arguments about women and Jews in their profession, they tried to exclude them. Moreover, "they facilitated the erosion of Weimar democracy and turned youths towards illiberalism" (Jarausch 1985, p. 394). In Britain, a decade earlier, the early rise of the Labour Party attracted teachers as voters or members, partly because it offered a new professionalism, a role in policy making and better pay.[2] Teachers may also be used by groups hoping to retain hegemony. Both the Left and the Right may view teachers as possible agents in the creation of a new society: In effect this always meant that certain groups of teachers were favored, while others were expelled.

There are also permanent political tensions around the job of teaching that surface in times of crisis or when a radical government is organised. A statement like this one, made by a Prefect in Vichy France, can echo around any society:

> The National Revolution will never really penetrate the countryside except through the teachers: if the Government has at its disposal a body of primary schoolteachers who are attached to the regime and who are the leading propagandists of its doctrine, the rural masses will be all but won over. (Kedward and Austin 1985, p. 16)

The Vichy question is always there, expressed in different ways in different places, and its result is that teachers find out that trying to change their work or even just keeping quiet involves politics. If they are not trying to alter their work, somebody else will: There is no stasis in the policy and management of education and teaching!

These elements, such as the language of confrontation or responsibility, the greater or lesser concern with social and political loyalty, the generally low status and high social responsibility, the changing idea of the state with its major restructuring or creation of new education sectors may vary at different times in different societies. What is consistent is the tension between teachers and their employers revealed in the working out of these elements and the social/education projects, expressed within party or movement membership. This is the source of the public politics of teaching.

Four examples reveal the complexity of this public politics. First, Nikkyoso, the main teachers' organisation in Japan has a constitution that defines the teacher as a labourer, albeit one who defends freedom, equal opportunity, and proper government. This is a reflection of its opposition to the old imperial idea of the teacher and the influence of the postwar U.S. administration. This idea, deeply embedded in its definition of its own unionised "good teachers," has now to be persistently defended against a state that has moved conservatively to absorb the older ideas of the imperial state and to reject the Nikkyoso model. Interestingly, divisions occurred in the union when the Socialist Party faction opposed the suggestion (from the Communist Party) that the older definition of the teacher as part of a "sacred profession," associated with the proscription of strikes and political activity among teachers, should be reintroduced. So, again, professionalism is introduced and, in this case, is used to divide teachers and is expressed within different party allegiances or factions which, presumably, follow a party line in the union. As one of its tactics for defence, Nikkyoso sponsors a large annual research conference to further its foundation aims to establish a democratic education system and freedom of research, and it tries to make alliances with groups of educationalists or citizens in the wider society (Ota 1985).

Second, in Portugal the postrevolutionary teachers' unions began to use the idea of professionalism to defend teachers from attacks by a conservative government wishing to "normalize" schooling, though unions attached to either the communist or socialist/social democratic party used this term in different ways. Indeed different unions organize themselves around key political and educational ideas that distinguish them from the other unions and take them nearer or further away from the government. These ideas are fundamental and represent the teachers' own views and involvement in a changing Portugal, allying them with other groups of workers in their associations (Stoer 1985).

Third, the Maltese teachers' union was influenced by the Catholic church and opposed to the secular independence leaders, the Labour Party (Darmanin 1985). It found itself on political and cultural grounds unable to work with an independent labour government which, in turn, was unable to develop any strategies to win hegemony in education without teachers.

Fourth, in Jamaica, both teachers' unions supported political independence, partly to increase their influence over policy making and paticularly to encourage the "nationalization" of the elementary schools, though they did not affiliate directly to the new parties (Goulbourne 1988). Anticolonial independence movements may cause difficulties for unions created as a reflection of a colonial system of education.

The Making of Modern Teachers in Britain

In the modern period of state education in Britain, which in my view extends from the early 1920s to the late 1970s, a dependable corps of teachers was important to the state and its parties in the creation of a new, mass education system. This political concern with dependability translated itself into a practical philosophy of teacher management and an ideology of professionalism that shaped what teachers should *or* would be doing in their social behavior and work relations. The modern British state, this century, was influenced, first, by a social democratic labour party which saw teachers as a crucial part of the government of education. This view of the essentially political nature of teaching has its roots in in a paper written in 1918 by Sydney Webb, the Fabian theorist, at a time when popular education was expanding and the Labour Party was trying to encourage teachers to join. Webb (1918, p. 3) argued that

> as systematic education is now more and more predominantly a Government function, and the bulk of the teaching profession is enrolled in one or other form of public service, we have necessarily to treat all educational projects as being, in the strictest sense of the word, politics, and as politics of the highest national importance.... [The teaching profession] has consequently a claim to exercise a professional judgement, to formulate distinctive opinions upon its own and upon cognate services, and to enjoy its own appropriate share in the corporate government of its own working life.

In policy terms Webb (1918, pp. 4–6) argued that teachers should "advise and warn, to initiate and criticise, but not decide." The claim to a political role for teachers then was based on a new claim to professional service for all the community, regardless of the "affluence or status of the persons in need," and the means and organisation for this to be achieved. It should instruct those who "move for educational reform what exactly it is that they should demand and press for." This was an invitation to policy making by the front door and was the herald of a shift in state policy toward teachers and a bid to win teachers over to a new hegemony by Labour.

The second influence on the state in its relation to its teachers was the generation of a distinctive way of managing teachers, drawn from British colonial practice, which depended on the discreet use of power, control of finance, and a dominant ideology of self-government. At the same time as Webb was developing his view on the essentially political nature of teaching, an important Minister of Education, Eustace Percy, argued with members of his own Conservative Party that the leftward drift of the teachers (in the 1920s) should not be met with an overt attack upon them by means of oaths of allegiance to the state, but that "the best safeguard against [the drift of teachers towards the Labour Party etc.] is to give teachers a sense of reasonable independence and not to subordinate them too much either to a central or to a local authority" (Lawn 1988, p. 119).

This idea of a "reasonable independence" soon developed into a major political myth, coming to characterise the distinctly British, democratic way of governance, particularly in the education service, against totalitarian systems in the 1930s through to the 1960s. So, in effect, the social democratic incorporation of teachers into the management of the service and the conservative approach to managing education were homologous (although not entirely).

What is not evident in the statement by Webb is the other part of the bargain to be struck with teachers. If teaching was political, in the sense of being part of the corporate governance of the education system, then teachers had to become nonpolitical, another paradox. This paradox is present in the theory of teaching professionalism expounded by Asher Tropp in the 1950s. Tropp argued that the teachers' union was determinedly nonpolitical but operated a series of alliances, discarded at the union's convenience, with political parties or other significant groups to achieve its consistent aims. In his view, the profession of teaching

> was created by the state and in the [nineteenth century] the state was powerful enough to claim almost complete control over the teacher and to manipulate his [or her] status while at the same time disclaiming all responsibility towards him [or her]. Slowly, and as the result of prolonged effort, the organized profession has won free and has reached a position of self government and independence. (Tropp 1957, p. 4)

It may be summarised in this way: the more nonpolitical the union was, the more power it was able to achieve or was given, and as long as nonpolitical meant nonparty political, then, it was possible for the unions to talk of professionalism.

Because of the new importance of education to the state, and of teachers within the management of the education system, the politics of teaching meant that teachers had to be nonpolitical. The question in England was only how best this was to be achieved.

Policing the Boundary

One consequence of this modern definition of the teacher, as nonpolitical and as an independent professional, is the way in which the world of teaching is defined so that any attempt to view the teacher outside the frame of the classroom is seen as unnatural. While this approach places teachers at the centre of the frame, it does so by reducing the teacher; they are shorn of the political, economic, and cultural aspects of their work. This is not just a comment on the paucity of theoretical understandings about teachers, constantly separating these aspects from some version of the core teacher, but it is also a reflection of the dominant way in which teachers are managed. Paradoxically, one of the ways the political nature of teaching is dramatically acknowledged by the state is when there is a moral panic about the politics of teachers and what they may and may not do in the classroom and in society.

The history of teaching, prior to the 1920s, suggests that the fact that teachers existed as a group was enough for them to be regarded suspiciously by political leaders. It wasn't what they did; it was what they represented. Historically, they were seen as a problem when they either grew in numbers so that the guardians of the state felt they were either (1) out of control and becoming too secular (i.e., disruptive of the natural order because of their existence!); (2) expressing their opinion about their work, however discreetly, in a way that their employers found challenging; or (3) using a language or taking actions that appeared to link them to a wider labor movement. What appears to count was the *symbolic* nature of their actions, not the reality of the action itself. It was what their teachers *appeared* to be doing![3]

As their numbers grew, teachers were regarded collectively as a possible social danger. This perspective on teachers by their local employers (members of the business class, the landed class, or the church), expressed in local discussions on teachers' pay, or by contemporary observers in the national press, concerned about their political or social influence, should not be ignored. It is not that teachers' actual political views or actions were extreme, in the main, but the fear their actions caused and the symbolic power they were seen as wielding to a state concerned with control or reproduction. While the political beliefs of some teachers were regarded as a reason not to employ them, and these teachers were a numerical minority, their presence caused outrage among the ruling elite (Lawn 1988).

The modern response of an indirect control and professionalism was a sophisticated way of managing the social danger of the teaching workforce. To manage the collectivity of apolitical teachers within this corral of a limited independence, it was necessary to police the boundaries. In this operation, action was used against individuals and loudly publicised to "encourage the others!" The policing generally operated through teachers' politics scares, involving bans and proscription as well as local campaigns against individual teachers and unions. At the same time the local and national press pursued individual teachers, while statements about professionalism were made in conferences or in public meetings by Ministers to isolate radicals or freethinkers from the rest. Teachers were sacked in the 1920s for their beliefs, which in a time of teachers' unemployment must have been very effective in reducing the idea of teachers' politics to a question of private belief and quiet party membership. In the 1940s and early 1950s there was a ban on teachers' membership of the Communist Party in parts of London.

In later years, it was union membership that was regarded as a sign of external forces, symbolically and practically, intruding into the natural relations between the employer and the employee. The union officer or union lawyer arriving to help members in a dispute was always the herald for an outcry about "our teachers and outside agitators."[4] They were seen to represent an outside force that attempts to destroy the harmony of work relations locally (Ozga 1987). It is a major political act to be a school-building representative of a teachers' union and could be described, in the past, as attempting to "turn the world upside down." This suggests that a "natural" world is broken when teachers are seen as threatening the local status quo; politics and work are easily joined in this symbol of disruption.

Schoolwork: The Social Construction of the Good Teacher

The incorporation of teachers into the modern idea of the nonpolitical servant of the state needed policing at its boundaries and a regular reinforcement of the ideology. The ideology of professionalism operated at a number of levels: versions of a General Teaching Council, regular pronouncements about teacher professionalism from ministers, consultations at local and national levels, membership of advisory bodies, and so on. But professionalism is a double-edged sword. As well as being a way of controlling teachers, it can be used to protect the space around the labour process in the arena of policy and politics. Professionalism becomes part of the politics of the labor process, a political notion that teachers and their unions have drawn upon to defend schoolwork or to demand access to change. Professionalism was a major weapon in their tactics but it is a sensitive one; the state is capable of using it itself, of dividing teachers by it and of restructuring education so that it is of reduced value. The use of professionalism by teachers and the state is one arena for political manoeuvering around the politics of teaching in England and Wales. An example of this is the way that a strike or a dispute could be regarded as a professional action by some teachers, and unprofessional by other teachers as well as by the government.

Another arena is schoolwork, the labor process of teaching in which teachers, like other people, try to determine the nature of their work through individual and collective action to structure work relations at the school site in the context of national and local policies.

> The social construction of skill is a powerful tool, but it comes from a particular "kit," and needs to be located in labour process theory. . . . Labour process theory provides the theoretical framework, and the social construction of

> skill is a key component of the labour process of teaching.
> This emphasis puts the politics of the production process
> in schools—something recognised by current gov-
> ernments—in higher profile. In teaching, active agency
> and therefore teacher politics are key elements of the
> labour process. . . . The labour process perspective
> outlined here clarifies the intentions of the state in
> controlling its educational workforce, but also permits us
> to more fully understand individual teachers' tactical and
> strategic actions. (Lawn & Ozga 1988, p. 334)

Schoolwork is not just an internal school process or a
union one. One of the ways this war of position is seen is
through the definition of the "good teacher,"[5] that is the image of
the teacher on which educational policy makers or managers
base their expectations. Teaching quality is seen here as a social
construction, an attempt to make visible and explicit the practical
and ideological management imperatives in any given period.
There tend to be competing definitions of the "good teacher."
The social construction of teacher quality is a contested process;
initiatives are taken in response to shortages or emerge out of
particular political and social conjunctions which are then
responded to by teachers. In turn, teachers produce their own
versions of the "good teacher," using the contradictions of
particular times and places, and influenced by wider ideas
moving through society. Generations of teachers are themselves
divided, containing as they do, competing practices, favored
"good teacher" models, and biographically ordered work
experience around which teachers organise or group.

So, this version of politics has to be seen contextually. It
reflects a particular shift in the place of education versus the
state. The role of the teacher differs from society to society and
from period to period. The definition of the "good teacher" must
then differ as the state decides the role the employed teacher
should take through a training, management, or inspection
process. For example, the "good teacher" was defined as an
active citizen and the educator of other active citizens-to-be in
Britain after the Second World War; the reconstruction of the
new society was seen, in part, as the responsibility of the teacher
and so the "good teacher union" was expected to play a major
role in the new system (Lawn 1987). Indeed, these definitions of

the "good teacher" and the "good teacher union" were an extension of the "reasonable independence" teacher, a symbol of the organising myths of the modern period, given some actuality in the period of postwar reconstruction under a Labour Government.

Teacher unionism has political aspects when it is actively engaging with the labour process in school (schoolwork). In England today this could mean defending pedagogy, questioning curriculum content, and opposing performance appraisal and the dismantling of teacher training. In the past, it meant campaigning for child-welfare policies and a comprehensive schooling system. Teacher unionism is political when it seeks alliances to achieve major policy changes in national programs or structures—for example, on vocational education—with employers or other unions.

The current English definition of the "good teacher," a 1980s postmodern definition in my terms, is nearer to that of competent employee, trying to meet production or efficiency targets, decided nationally and rewarded locally. In this case the "good teacher union" has an impossible role, expected to be active by its members and inactive by the state. Far from an encouragement to be active citizens, restrictions are now operating on their civil liberties with regard to standing for school governorships and local councils. So, what is viewed as political by the employee or the employer will vary according to the dominant definition of the "good teacher" of the particular period.

Social Movements and the Politics of Teaching

There is a further expression of the teachers and politics question. When a new group or class is beginning to move toward power, it must develop support and then win hegemony. In the twentieth century in particular, teachers are important, locally and nationally, as key members of the community and/or workers in a key public service. In this situation teachers are both the audience (the potential support) and often part of the new group attempting to win power, and so are often politically involved. They may be divided sometimes by gender, race or school sector (elementary and secondary) in their attraction to this form of politics and its solutions to their problems. Both the Left and the Right may view teachers as possible agents in the creation of a new society. In effect, this has always meant that some groups of teachers were favored while others were made outsiders.

In England, there have been, historically, at least two examples of the connection between teachers and social movements. One is the relation between teachers and the labor movement in the early decades of the century, when it is clear that teachers acted as resources for local movements of socialists of various kinds and for emerging unions. The early rise of the Labour Party attracted teachers as voters or members, partly because it offered a new professionalism, a role in policy making, and better pay. Teachers may also be used by groups hoping to retain hegemony. "The Drift of Teachers to the Labour Party," as the political police (the Special Branch) called it, occurred in the early 1920s and there are cases recorded of waves of disgruntled teachers working hard at election time for Labour Party candidates (Lawn 1988). In rural areas teachers had been involved with the organisation of farm workers' unions. This connection grew over the years so that significant groups of teachers were active in left-wing causes in the following decades.

The second significant link is between women teachers and the first wave feminism of the suffragettes. This resulted in the creation of a new union, the National Union of Women Teachers, in the early 1920s, which united the feminist teachers of the period, many of whom had been in the suffrage movement (Lawn 1988). They were described recently as subjugating themselves to the cause of feminism. "Their identity as feminists was forged through an adherence to the greater political cause, of which each individual was a part. This concept of feminist identity also helped them make sense of their role as educators inside—and outside—the classroom" (Kean 1990, p. 45). Another writer described these teachers as being part of a "vigorous, optimistic feminist network" (King 1987, p. 32). So, the relation between teachers and wider social movements is complex, suggesting an interplay between politics, social movements, and teachers' work, which is possibly more interesting than organized alliances.

Recent debates about the emergence of new social movements (NSMs) in Britain, such as feminism, the peace movement, and the green alliance, have raised questions about the role of the service class and, in particular, professional public service employees in their formation. In summary, it is suggested that the growth of the service class is related to the rise of new political agendas and organizations and the restructuring of old class relations. A part of this argument, which may illuminate the political role of teachers, suggests that public employees "facilitate the emergence of new social movements through the application of their skills as producers and organizers of knowledge" (Bagguley 1992, p. 39). The same author suggests that this class has two areas of political practice: the first is a form of professional trade unionism, often involving the state as employer; and the second is in civil society, locally based, where they act as a resource for social movements, conservative or progressive. This then suggests that teachers may be seen as political actors more clearly elsewhere than in their unions *and* that a union may act as a vehicle to express these wider social and political activities. When teachers were the only educated members of the community and were working in the public service, they had an influence in other ways (in Britain and elsewhere).

> [Teachers] could use their cultural capital locally by acting as "experts" in different fields, such as hygiene, vaccination, gardening, local administration, etc.; and their training also gave them cultural competence to lead choirs, theatricals, to form associations and lead courses. Teachers occupied a key position in local communities. (Florin 1987, p. 196)

Political action, built on a local cultural role, is a powerful one. From the turn of the century, in England, there was a growing concern among the elite about the political and social effect of teachers acting as political agents. When the Labour Party grew and began to attract teachers with its educational and social policies, concern was palpable in the ruling elite. Teachers were not and are not a homogenous group; they are recruited from different social classes, for different school sectors, in different periods. It is not surprising, therefore, that their political action should take different forms or that the state should operate in awareness of their role both as agents and resisters.

Conclusion

I would suggest that teachers may be seen as political actors because of their conditions of work and their own views and actions, individually or collectively, on their work. Their role as political actors has particular meaning in a social democratic project, especially one like England's, where there is an expectation of working in and for the state as a public employee, and at the same time a particular way of managing employees of the state. The consequence of this "indirect rule" and an ideology of independence is the circumvention of teachers' political action. A sort of professional welfarism ensued in which only a favorable apoliticism by the teachers was allowed. The social danger that teachers symbolised was neutered by co-optation.

In this vacuum, politics came to be transmuted and was waged around and in the complex bureaucratic procedures of social democracy and corporatism, in the changing definitions of the "good teacher" driven by circumstance, and in the daily aspects of schoolwork. The politics of teaching became waged in a war of position, kept in place by a policing of the boundaries.

Finally, it would be an error to emphasise the politics of work and exclude the way in which teachers used and were used by social movements to extend the definition and nature of teaching, the politics and policies which contained it, and the kind of society which contained them.

NOTES

1. I am not interested (at least for the purposes of this chapter) in the micropolitical relations in schools, although the politics of the school labour process, of which micropolitics is a part, is of importance. However, the micropolitics of teachers' work and union activity is a new field that appears to reduce politics to a form of interpersonal behavior for the achievement of private or group aims, or for their resistance.

2. This move toward Labour or socialist parties by teachers appears to have been a common phenomenon in the West in the early years of this century, namely, in Canada and France. See also Lawn (1988).

3. Examples of the large and small incidents that were used to attack teachers as being "political" can be found in Lawn (1988).

4. This is not just an historical phenomenon. Rural areas and small schools in England and Wales are prone to this problem today. The position of a union representative in a school in a rural area is almost saintly. They sacrifice themselves for the sake of others, as there is no chance of promotion or an easy life. Whatever they do, they are seen by the local managers as intruders on their "natural relations" with their employees.

5. The idea of the "good teacher" is a heuristic device only; there is no intention to suggest there is a preferred version of the teacher. It is a lens to view the employer's or the teacher's version of the teacher in any one period (see Lawn 1991).

REFERENCES

Bagguley, P. (1992). "Social Change, the Middle Class and the Emergence of 'New Social Movements': A Critical Analysis." *Sociological Review* 40(1):26–48.

Darmanin, M. (1985). "Malta's Teachers and Social Change." In *Politics of Teacher Unionism*, edited by M. Lawn, pp. 158–190. London: Croom Helm.

Florin, C. (1987). *Kampen om Katedern*. Sweden: Umea University.

Goulbourne, H. (1988). *Teachers: Education and Politics in Jamaica 1892–1972*. London: Macmillan Caribbean.

Jarausch, K. H. (1985). "The Crisis of the German Professions." *Journal of Contemporary History* 20:394.

Kean, H. (1990). *Deeds Not Words*. London: Pluto Press.

Kedward, R., and Austin, R. (1985). *Vichy France and the Resistance*. London: Croom Helm,.

King, S. (1987). "Feminists in Teaching: The National Union of Women Teachers 1920–1940." In *Teachers: The Culture and Politics of Work*, edited by M. A. Lawn and G. Grace, pp. 31–49. London: Falmer Press.

Lawn, M. A. (1987). "What is the Teacher's Job? Work and Welfare in Elementary Teaching 1940–1945." In *Teachers: The Culture and Politics of Work*, edited by M. A. Lawn and G. Grace, pp. 50–64. London: Falmer Press.

————. (1988). *Servants of the State—The Contested Control of Teaching 1900–1930*. Basingstoke: Falmer Press.

———— (1991). "The Social Construction of Quality in Teaching." In *Teacher Supply and Teacher Quality*, edited by G. Grace and M. A. Lawn, pp. 87–121. Multilingual Matters.

Lawn, M. A., and Ozga, J. T. (1988). "Schoolwork: Interpreting the Labour Process in Teaching." *British Journal of Sociology of Education* 9(3):323–336.

Ota, H. (1985). "Political Teacher Unionism in Japan." In *The Politics of Teacher Unionism*, edited by M. A. Lawn, pp. 103–140. London: Croom Helm.

Ozga, J. T. (1987). "Part of the Union: School Representatives and Their Work." In *Teachers: The Culture and Politics of Work*, edited by Martin Lawn and Gerald Grace, pp. 113–144. London: Falmer Press.

Stoer, S. (1985). "The April Revolution and Teacher Trade Unionism in Portugal." In *Politics of Teacher Unionism*, edited by M. A. Lawn, pp. 40–72. London: Croom Helm.

Tropp, A. (1957). *The Schoolteachers*. London: Heinemann.

Webb, S. (1918). *The Teacher in Politics*. London: Fabian Society.

Fictional Dialogues on Teachers, Politics, and Power in Latin America

Carlos Alberto Torres

> I am not referring to an historical event. What interests me is to tell stories of interest to the reader, true stories. They are not necessarily documented accounts, but stories taken from my own lived experience. Searching, I have come to realize that reality in Latin America, the reality in which we live, in which we were raised, that reality which formed us, is confused daily with fantasy.[1]

This chapter is concerned with teachers' lives and their political action in Latin America. The chapter is divided into three parts. The first part, looking at the past and present of education in the context of the state in Latin America, provides a fundamental background to understanding teachers' lives and struggles in different societies in Latin America. The second part, looking at teachers' lives and political action or inaction, presents fictitious dialogues with three teachers, one each in Argentina, Brazil, and Mexico. The third part offers an afterthought on teachers' lives, politics and education in Latin America.

The narrative emerging from these fictitious dialogues in the second part of this chapter is informed by real, lived experiences. If I close my eyes, I can recall hundreds of hours of conversation with intellectuals, teachers, and educators in Latin America. Informal, semistructured and structured conversations provide the themes, convictions, impressions, and expressions reflected in these dialogues. Likewise, hundreds of pages of my notes of field research accumulated over the years also provide substance to these dialogues about the experiences, political practice, values, and systems of meanings of teachers.

Does it matter that, although I draw from empirical data from my field notes and from my own continued learning about education in Latin America, I shaped my narrative with explicit intentionality and self-reflective constructivism? For some, this may be just another piece of (bad?) literature, but certainly not science. However, I would concur with William Foster when he argues:

> Most readers who have any experience with contemporary writing accept that the boundaries between "literature" and other forms of cultural writing have become hopelessly blurred. It is this blurring that provides one of the most dynamic principles of contemporary cultural writing and exemplifies one of the bases for speaking of current forms of "experimental," "disruptional," or simply "innovative" writing. . . . It is for this reason that such works overlap so notably with the general sociopolitical concerns of intellectuals in Latin America as part of a continuous fabric of cultural writing.[2]

Not only cultural studies but also historical research has been affected by disruptional or innovative forms of writing, including the "thickening" of narratives by resorting to micronarratives, or the development of "histories from below," or telling stories from multiple viewpoints, that is, "multivocality," resulting in what British historian Peter Burke described in the following manner: "It looks as if historians have to develop their own fictional techniques for their factual works."[3]

Furthermore, I concur with Burke when he argues that "the point of looking for new literary forms is surely the awareness that the old forms are inadequate for one's purposes."[4] Nobel Prize recipient Gabriel García Marquez, among other Latin American writers, developed the notion of magic realism, so well expressed in his *One Hundred Years of Solitude*. In this novel, García Marquez shows how the history of a family reflects the universal history. The history of the Buendía family, from the foundation of Macondo to its demise and destruction, is the history of Latin America. Yet, we should emphasize here that this family's history is narrated through the eyes of the visionary Melquiades, who had dreamed of Macondo even before this town ever existed.[5]

García Marquez lets us know that when the first Buendía arrived at the place where Macondo was going to be, he began naming things, and in naming he was not only recognizing but creating them. This is exactly, for García Marquez, the experience of Christopher Columbus "discovering" America. García Marquez seeks to put in an imaginary perspective, a totalizing perspective, a critical perspective, the experience of Latin America. Thus, fantasy and exaggeration are integral parts of García Marquez' view of realism. The history of the Buendía family is the history of Macondo, and the history of Macondo uncovers an uprising in the coffee plantations, civil war, and even revolution, certainly not fictitious events in Latin America.

Gabriel García Marquez starts with the *a priori* assumption that to narrate is to invent, and therefore there is no distinction between the real and the unreal. Thus, magic realism is understood as a narrative that has the ability to transcend the factual nature of the historical to reveal the world of imagination, myths, and collective memory of fables. In short, Latin America, the world of García Marquez, is magic because it is real; "if it were not magic, it would be simply unreal, and his novels would simply be poetic or fantastic fictions."[6]

Therefore, while fictitious, my dialogues[7] with teachers reflect a multiplicity of voices—individual and collective—of political and pedagogical experiences in the region. Thus the imaginary is real, a claim that should not substitute for quantitative and ethnographic research, and yet, invites the reader not to dismiss the dialogue for being imaginary, or lacking documentation, or "empirical proof." The imaginary as real provides an avenue for a generic reflection on the limits and possibilities of political action in teachers' work and lives.

Past and Present

During the second half of the nineteenth century and the first three decades of this century, the predominant state model in Latin America was the oligarchical state. This form of the state consolidated the nation and generated relative political stability. In this political model, the oligarchy maintained tight control over the political process, at times by means of direct control over the state, and at other times through control of the parliament and important political parties. In order to implement this control, on occasion electoral fraud or simply open repression was employed.[8]

Public education systems in the region were all developed as part of the project of oligarchical states seeking to establish the foundations of the nation and the citizenship. The role and function of public education, the creation of a "disciplined pedagogical subject," the role, mission, ideology, and training of teachers, and the prevailing notions of curriculum and school knowledge were all deeply marked by the prevailing liberal philosophy in the oligarchical state.[9]

The oligarchical state controlled different facets of the political and cultural life of each country based upon a liberal perspective. The dissolution of the oligarchical pact opened a new political epoch in Latin America, marked by a new development model and by new models of the state—albeit, still in an embryonic stage—within different countries.

What has marked this political period and historical conjuncture, are patterns of conflict and accommodation between the state and the labor movement. The emergence of distinct forms of control and mobilization signal what R. Collier and D. Collier define as periods of incorporation, with distinct historical legacies.[10]

They point to the introduction of corporatism—a set of structures that integrate society in a vertical manner, and as such lead to the legalization and institutionalization of the workers' movement formed and controlled by the state—as the distinctive characteristic of Latin American capitalism and politics in this century. Corporatism appears as the one central and distinctive political characteristic shared by all countries in the region.[11]

The working class and the middle classes—two new sectors that evolved out of the process of modernization—began to incorporate themselves in subordinate positions within the context of an important corporatist redefinition of the role of the state in society. A transformation from the *laissez-faire* oligarchical state to a more interventionist state took place. For R. Collier and D. Collier, the common legacy of corporativism in Latin American countries is the creation of an organized labor movement and a system of industrial relations to a large extent controlled and regulated by the State. [12]

State interventionism has been the central feature of the performance of Latin American states with different political regimes during the 1940s until the 1970s. The 1980s witnessed a dramatic economic and social crisis. The 1980s have been labeled as the "lost decade" for economic development in Latin America. In this decade, the region witnessed a cycle of high inflation and recession as never before. In this context, the tenacious hammering of neoliberal economic ideologies (pursuing "free market" economies, "trickle down" economics and monetarist policies), underscoring the "demonstration effect" of the Chilean model of stabilization, indicated a common pattern of economic stabilization and structural adjustment.

This model of stabilization and adjustment has been relentlessly pursued as the economic and political recipe for the region by the International Monetary Fund (IMF) and the World Bank—policies that have been characterized as the "Washington consensus." [13] The combined pressure of the conditionalities of the IMF-World Bank loans, and the difficulties for financing created by the external debt crisis, generates new problems in the educational policies of the region. [14]

In addition, the seemingly never ending political crises in the region, the political debacle of the left in the region after experiencing authoritarian states in the 1970s, the failure of a socialist revolution in Central America in the 1980s (i.e., Nicaragua, El Salvador, Guatemala), and the collapse of the socialist economies created the "right conditions" for structural adjustment policies to be fully implemented regionwide, breaking the deadlock between the programs of the popular sectors (particularly trade unions) and the economic and political elites' political preferences.[15]

In the 1980s, the most profound changes of the Latin American societies have been associated with the processes of structural adjustment of the Latin American economies. Structural adjustment imposes a number of conditions, including the reduction of governmental expenditure, devaluations to promote exports, reduction in import tariffs, and an increase in public and private savings. Other aspects linked to the policies of structural adjustment include the reduction of the fiscal deficit at the same time that the public expenditure is reduced and strict monetary policies are applied to diminish inflation. Key aims of this model are a drastic reduction of the State sector, the liberalization of salaries and prices, and the reorientation of industrial and agricultural production toward exports.

Structural adjustment has been implemented in Latin America after the countries experienced high inflation rates or even hyperinflation. Labán and Sturzenegger, providing a rationale for the strongly conservative nature of the governments implementing structural adjustment in Latin America, argue that in economies with social conflicts, and with moderate levels of inflation, there is not likely to be popular support for adjustment

> since many individuals visualize the process as a negative sum game for them. Early attempts to stabilize are often blocked by different interest groups. As inflation reaches higher levels, the total disruption of normal economic life may generate the required political support that will be the basis of a successful stabilization program.[16]

Hyperinflation may prompt people to accept conditions for economic stabilization that, under conditions of "normal" distributional conflicts were totally unacceptable for them. As Labán and Sturzenegger observed, "financial adaptation may be beneficial in the sense that it may trigger the *economic crises* required to build up the political consensus for stabilization to be attempted."[17]

Thus, economic stabilization came about in Latin America as a response to debt crisis, fiscal crisis, industrial recession, and inflation (in some contexts, hyperinflation), but only after key social actors in the distributional conflict (working class, campesinos, and even sectors of the middle classes) relinquished, by default or purpose, their ability to challenge cuts in expenditures and the reform (reduction) of the state's interventionist role in society.

The history of the state, the type of incorporation of teachers' unions, uneven rates of growth, and inflation rates in the context of distributional conflict and structural adjustment play key roles in the political behavior of teachers, which we will explore in the next section where we will meet educators from three countries of the region: Argentina, Brazil, and Mexico.

Teachers as Agents: A Fictitious Dialogue

Tomás Agustín

A cold breeze, hundreds of dead leaves crackling under my shoes, an unnerving concert of horns, and the sweet smell of diesel oil bring together the old memories of a crepuscular autumn in Buenos Aires. When I arrived at the Regocijo del Loro, a traditional bar at the corner of Callao and Corrientes, Tomás Agustín was already waiting for me. He greeted me with a warm hug, and we start remembering the last time we had a coffee together in Buenos Aires, more than fifteen years ago in the same bar.

In his late forties, Tomás Agustín looks as energetic and enthusiastic as ever. His academic background and impeccable credentials, a large number of articles and books on democracy, political theory, and the new conditions of capitalism in Latin America, and his constant lecturing in the United States and Europe, qualify him as one of the foremost political scientists in the region. A former student of political sociologist Gino Germany, Tomás Agustín had worked in Chile during the period of the Christian Democratic Government and the beginnings of Allende's Unidad Popular.

Upon graduation from Yale, Tomás Agustín worked at two prestigious research institutions in Mexico, returning to Argentina in 1984, during the first year of the democratic regime of President Raúl Alfonsín. After creating and directing the most successful private social-science research institution in the country, the Institute of Social Research, he obtained a position as scientific researcher in the Council of Science and Technology, also securing tenure as professor of two courses, Political Philosophy I and Political Philosophy II, at the University of Buenos Aires (UBA), the largest and most prestigious public university in the country. Elected as a representative of the Faculty of Social Sciences and Philosophy to the Board of Governors of the UBA, he joined representatives of alumni and students of the university at the governing board of the university. Most recently, Tomás Agustín had been elected democratically as the President (Rector) of the UBA.

Our last conversation in Buenos Aires was at the beginning of the dictatorship of General Videla, in the Fall of 1976. Then, we couldn't talk much. Our perception was clouded by fear. Our senses were alerted, discreetly scrutinizing every person that, like us, pretended to look casual, relaxed, being reinvigorated by an expresso that on a cold day Argentines relish like the elixir of life. Fifteen years ago we discussed why we were leaving the country and where to go. Today, we discuss a different country, a democratic country, and the topic is part of our everyday experience, our work as university professors, Tomás Agustín at UBA, and I at the University of California in Los Angeles (UCLA).

After we inquired about the health and condition of our mutual families, and when we were about to drink our third expresso, I asked him about the university, about his experience as president of a university dispersed among dozens of run-down buildings throughout the city. I asked about the governability of a university with 170,000 students and about the political and pedagogical lives of professors and administrators.

Carlos, he said, while the university budget remains the same as it was thirty years ago, approximately .51 of the GNP, enrollment at the public universities has tripled from 1970 with 240,139 to 823,320 in 1987. This explosion is a result of the repression under the military dictatorship that depressed total university enrollment to 372,780 students in the whole country. With the advent of democracy, enrollment exploded while budgets were held stable or sizably cut, making the budget of the UBA today comparable to that of 1961. This is at the root of the problem of Argentine public universities. Also, expenditure in research and development that by the early 1980s was (US) $24.20 per capita, has fallen in the early 1990s to only (US) $12.60 per capita. This, of course, has serious repercussions in the ability of the university to contribute to scientific development, and to create an appropriate professional environment and working conditions for professors and researchers.

How could a young *Jefa de Trabajos Prácticos* (Practicum Associate), dedicated only part-time (working 16 hours per month), making 60 australes a month (equivalent to 60 U.S. dollars), pay for her bills? What is even more ridiculous is that a Full Professor, with twenty years of seniority, Ph.D. in hand, publications and international recognition, makes around 1,000 australes per month, equivalent to the salary of a Major Sergeant in the Army!

In these conditions, the political lives of professors in the university are deeply marked by their survival needs. There is a sense of fragmentation, traveling between universities, teaching part-time, conducting short-term research in two or three research institutions, and consulting for the private or public sector, to meet their financial obligations. Moreover, these tragic economic conditions, for a university like the UBA that expends ninety percent of its budget in salaries, brings about serious in-house battles around the appropriation of resources. While I will not press the issue that every political alliance is the result of an evolving operation to obtain more resources for a particular political faction, group, or clique within the university, I will argue that most of the political debates are clogged by the need of groups and individuals to position themselves in the pipeline of distribution of our meager resources. Thus, opportunity costs heavily determine political strategies and values.

This fragmentation of academic life, resulting from lack of resources, the need to accumulate small jobs that pay modest salaries, the lack of space in our run-down buildings, the lack of a library (let alone a good one), and the manifold demands upon the time and talent of professors, also influence policy debates.

Politics is natural to the academic life of the Argentine—and I must say, to every Latin American—university.

The university, still a bastion of Latin American middle classes, has failed to attract working-class students proportionally to their numbers in the social stratification, continues to reflect, to some extent, the macrocosm of political life in the country. Although there are some small extremist right-wing parties and groups represented, the university remains a liberal and left-wing environment. University politics follow party lines, and on occasion, pedagogical-political projects within the university reflect the disagreements or petty fights, including personality conflicts, or quarrels of factions within political parties.

Thus, the political life of a university professor does not hinge on their epistemological or broader theoretical or methodological allegiances and beliefs alone. For a competition for a specific *cátedra* (faculty position), candidates are supported by specific political groups who actively campaign for the selection of their candidates. In return, some of these professors, particularly those who are unable to create some 'breathing space' between the demands of political militancy and their academic work, find that they should reflect in their *cátedras* the positions (theoretical and/or political) that are endorsed by the groups that have supported their candidacy. This, of course, has implications at several levels. For one, the widely accepted notion of freedom of *cátedra* (the Argentine equivalent of academic freedom in autonomous universities) may be tarnished if the particular teaching of a professor reflects not so much meta-theoretical or epistemological preferences and disagreements but corporatist or political positions (diplomatic views, to use Gramsci's euphemism).[18]

This distribution of meager resources also generates intolerance and bureaucratism and deeply marks the academic and political life of the faculty. Look, I have with me a memo describing a dialogue that researchers in the Faculty of Engineering reported having just yesterday with Engineer Sorrento, the director (Chair) of the Department of Engineering in the Faculty of Engineering of UBA. After several problems between this new director and a group of full-time researchers of the department, he was asked in a meeting with the researchers if he was

> willing to aid and promote scientific research. Mr. Sorrento said that he did not agree to continue hiring researchers nor with the development of research. And he added that these premises were the ones which allowed him to rise to the position of Director of the Department. When he was questioned regarding the subject by the Deans Reznik and Consudec, his response in that sense was a determining factor in his having been offered the position of Director of the Department. Since the researchers pressed for Sorrento to give his opinion on the relationship between teaching and research, Sorrento said: "I cannot offer an opinion of what I do not know. As an engineer I worked 20 years in the street and it was never necessary for me to conduct any type of research." Sorrento, furthermore, indicated that researchers created problems for the administration, specially with their request that their private and university correspondence not be opened by the administrators. When it was made clear to him that these administrative problems should not be weighed against the existence of 15 research groups (with 35 full-time researchers and more than 15 fellowship holders) with a reasonable scholarly production related to the science of materials, physics, and pedagogy, he was asked how, as Director of the Department, he intended to orient the Department in the direction of the good universities of the world. Sorrento responded: "I don't know of any other university. It is a political problem. In Engineering there are two groups and I respond (I am accountable) to one of them.[19]

This breed of bureaucrat with a particular political agenda, in this case clearly parochial and highly detrimental to scientific research, or who uses administrative positions to crash the power of another group, makes research the greatest casualty of their disgraceful politics.

Power, I added, according to Wartenberg, "manifests itself as a complex social presence that exists in an intricate network of overlapping and contradictory relations."[20] Don't you think, Tomás Agustín, that if we view power and education relationally,[21] we will begin to reveal how teachers are embedded in, constituted through, even crossed by power relationships? Moreover, as Ginsburg has recently argued, teachers—and university professors are no exception—"they work and live within relations of power, that is, within both unequal, dominant-subordinate relations and mutually enabling connections."[22] Then, Tomás Agustin, I think you would agree with me that it is power that matters in the university?

Of course! But power takes many forms, and some are not closely related to the conceptual categories informing the specialized literature. There is an intellectual myopia, mediocrity, and even the idiocy of bureaucrats and petty politicians who articulate or materialize power in university environments. It is this set of contradictory micro- and macropower practices that makes university politics so muddy. Clearly someone like Mr. Sorrento thinks of a university that simply trains professionals without research expertise and devoid of any critical consideration of their own professional practice. This is also a political agenda, and this disgraceful politics is very difficult to reconcile with academic work. It is at odds with the idea of a university as a place to produce new knowledge or the quest for truth. Moreover, it gets in the way of a truly political debate, and deeply affects the academic and political life of university professors. It is no wonder that so many university professors find academic politics totally unacceptable, because they fail to recognize that it is not the political debate in the university but the bastardization of politics that bothers them.

Well Carlos. It is late. We shall continue this conversation soon.

Yes, Tomás Agustín, I know it is getting late, but I want to ask you one more question: What can you tell me about the politics of the leftist professors in the University? What do you think is the role of a university professor with an allegiance to Marxism, Critical Theory, or coming from a socialist persuasion like yourself?

Carlos, the Left is in total disarray. The collapse of the authoritarian regimes in the region put on the table the question of the multiple meanings of democracy, and the Left has been unable to carve out a distinct meaning and democratic practice.

The so-called crisis of Marxism, and the fall of the socialist systems in Eastern Europe darkens the perception and political project of many socialist faculty members.

The paradox is that when the Left is considering alternative meanings of democracy, and is taking democracy seriously, coming back to its liberal roots, the new international "ideological climate," as correctly defined by the Vice Chancellor of the University of Buenos Aires, political scientist Atilio Boron, is the so-called crisis of democracy and the rise of neoconservative doctrines.[23]

Let me add that the ominous condition of being an overworked, stressed-out, and underpaid faculty does little to help rethink the meaning of political resistance, critical consciousness, or alternative political and pedagogical practices in the academy. I don't want to advance a conspiracy thesis, but the conditions couldn't be worse for representatives of this post-New Left in Latin America to establish a clear political and academic presence at the universities. Many historical figures of the Left are "broken" by the experience of exile, repression, their disappearing relatives, and their present economic need. Many had given up their political and perhaps ethical principles.

Perhaps the only option for the Left in the University is to reconstitute ideas and attitudes, and understand democracy as *governing* democracy rather than, as *governed* democracy, as José Nun has suggested.[24] Since there is only a distant possibility to recreate an alliance of progressive people in the University in Argentina having some independence from the two mainstream parties, and, apparently, it is only exercised in the context of university governance, the only option is to have an impeccable ethical conduct and continue with a systematic theoretical praxis, attempting to link our action, existentially and politically, with the popular sectors.

Leftist academics should continue working, despite adverse conditions, studying and analyzing reality with their students, not for their students. They should continue to criticize the rationale and impact of these insensitive neoliberal policies advanced in the context of structural adjustment in Argentina. They should also establish the bases for a theoretical and political dialogue among themselves, the new generation, and the large number of progressive and honest people who work with the two mainstream parties in the country.[25]

Until a social representation of the Left like the *Partido dos Trabalhadores* in Brazil takes place in Argentina, the Left in Argentina can overcome its fragmentation and reconstruct its identity only with solid, rigorous, systematic, and wide-ranging research and teaching, and with honest and ethical behavior that is accountable to the broader university community, and I shall say, the country.

Well it is too late and I am philosophizing again. Chau Che.

Thinking about my conversation with Tomás Agustín while sitting in my bus going home, I thought not only of the idiocy of bureaucratic warfare, and how damaging it is for academic politics. I also thought of the notion of micropower, à la Foucault,[26] and how petty bureaucrats, in different layers of the university life, exert their influence or power, feeling good about their own political abilities. Tomás Agustín was right. This is simply another example of the bastardization of politics. All in all, Alejo Carpentier comes to mind with his reflections about the real-imaginary world of Latin America. Certainly, Carpentier's analysis could serve as a good epigraph or even a corollary of my conversation with Tomás Agustín about politics and university life:

> But many forget, disguising themselves as cheap magicians, that the marvelous manifests itself unequivocally only when it derives from an unexpected alteration of reality (the miracle), from a privileged revelation of reality, from an unaccustomed or singularly advantageous illumination of the unnoticed richness of reality, from an amplification of the registers and categories of reality, perceived with a special intensity by virtue of an exhaltation of the spirit, which it transports to a sort of "critical state." But what is the history of America if not a chronicle of the marvelous real?[27]

I was still thinking about Alejo Carpentier's famous statement about the fabulous quality of Latin America, the story about Mr. Sorrento, and Tomás Agustín's last remarks on the politics of the leftist academics in the university of Buenos Aires as I sat in the plane that took me to Brazil for my conversations with Luiza Amorosa, a teacher in the Municipal Secretariat of Education, in São Paulo.

Luiza Amorosa

I met her in 1990 in São Paulo, when I was doing research on the new policies of the Partido dos Trabalhadores (Workers Party or PT) municipal administration of Luiza Erundina. *Gaúcha*,[28] young, *bela*, and energetic, Luiza Amorosa exemplifies the new generation of teachers of the Left in São Paulo. Having worked for six years as an elementary school teacher in the periphery of São Paulo, she quickly embraced the political campaign of the PT Candidate, Luiza Erundina de Souza, for Mayor of São Paulo in 1989. Luiza Amorosa worked as one of her educational advisers, and as a tireless promoter of the PT program in the different social movements of São Paulo.

Radical in conviction and action, with strong opinions, intolerant of people who hesitate, who want to remain neutral, or change their previous leftist political position, with an ability to work twenty hours a day, and the capacity to endure marathon meetings, Luiza Amorosa is capable of summarizing a lengthy discussion in a few sentences and suggesting reasonable courses of action. Despite her talent for intellectual speculation, her pragmatism has few parallels in the discursive context of Brazilian politics. Her contribution to the educational policy of the PT in São Paulo was seen as invaluable. In fact, she wrote the educational manifesto of the party. After the triumph, she was invited to join the Secretary of Education as one of the advisers of Paulo Freire, the new Secretary of Education.

The youngest daughter of impoverished *campesinos* or peasants and the only one who achieved postsecondary education, she demonstrated very early in her life a commitment to her class origins when she studied to become a teacher. She rejected the invitation to work for the Secretariat of Municipal Education and decided to enroll, instead, at the Pontifical Catholic University of São Paulo (PUC), to learn more about educational policy and curriculum. At the same time, she returned to her post as third-grade teacher in East São Paulo, at the outskirts of the city, and one of the poorest and more violent areas.

We meet for *cachaça* in a small bar in Avenida Tiradentes, in downtown São Paulo. With the affection that only Brazilians can demonstrate, we engaged in a long conversation blessed by the Brazilian gin. Luiza Amorosa, a chain-smoker, was already halfway into her last package of cigarettes when we began discussing her experience as a teacher during the socialist democratic administration of Luiza Erundina. I asked her why she decided to turn down the offer to work at the Secretary of Municipal Education, with a higher salary than her regular salary as a teacher, and why she returned to the university. I asked her how she combines education and politics in her life and work.

Carlos, to live is to choose. I spent most of my youth fighting against policies and practices of an authoritarian capitalist state. I couldn't bring myself to work in the state apparatus. I knew that during Erundina's administration, and with the presence of Paulo Freire as Secretary of Education, the Left, and the progressive educators and militants of the PT, my party, would occupy this bureaucratic apparatus of the state, and would change its orientation and policies.

But I couldn't do it personally. I felt that I would be co-opted by the bureaucracy, that I would lose touch with the social movements, the Women's Movement in which I participate in my neighborhood, the movement of Progressive Lesbian, Gays, and Bisexuals. I am helping my best friend, Marília, who is a lesbian, to organize in Tirandentes. But above all, I wanted to continue with my work with the children of the streets, 'as meninos e meninas da rua'[29] in my school. They need me more than the state bureaucracy or the party. I also felt that earning more money would take me further away from my own roots, as a peasant, *gaúcho* women. Perhaps a better salary would corrupt me, it would buy my own soul as a militant and a committed teacher.

But, I asked with some hesitation, knowing her distaste for what she surely would consider a whimsical question, don't you think that this is an extreme position, one of "get all or nothing"?

She lit her last cigarette, asked the waiter for another package and more *cachaça* and answered: I know that academics play around with notions of objectivity, neutrality of education, tolerance, value judgments, apoliticity, but not me. I am a militant and a teacher. I cannot hesitate or doubt my own principles. This is a very difficult time for my country, for my people. As a friend of mine, Budd Hall, a professor at the Ontario Institute for Studies of Education in Canada, said in a meeting I attended in Jamaica, "if the world is on fire, I cannot understand why we are not on fire."[30] These are difficult times, and I think that your question of "getting all or nothing" is correct. I want all or nothing.

As a young woman teacher I endured sexual harassment of male senior teachers and principals. Even in the festive and liberal context of Brazilian sexuality, *o jogo bonito do sexo*, their passes at me, their constant provocations, bother me. As a peasant girl from the South, I feel very close to all the oppressed. I have been discriminated against as the Mulatto and Negroes are. I suffered too many racial slurs and derogatory comments too many times to accept just fitting into Brazil's racial democracy. I learn from Marília that no struggle is small, and I think I shall continue supporting her own struggle for sexual equality. As a leftist, in the context of the Brazilian Authoritarism, and considering the powerful cultural and economic Brazilian Right, I know who my enemy is, and I am ready for it. As a teacher, I know where my loyalty is. It is with my community, with my *meninos e meninas da rua*.

As you see Carlos, you, from your own privileged position as a professor in Los Angeles, may have the luxury to reflect on political or intellectual options in considering alternative jobs. I cannot do that. The struggle is immense, endless. The task is monumental. The demands on my time and energy cannot accept bureaucratic procedures, styles, rules, regulations, norms. That is the reason I stepped down after the campaign, and returned to my position as teacher, and continue with my multiple roles in the social movements.

We, the militants of the social movements in São Paulo, should always have one foot inside the state when there is a popular and democratic administration, and another foot inside the social movements but outside of the state structure. The idea of a partnership between state and social movements is appealing but can only work temporarily. Now that the PT candidate to succeed Erundina has been defeated by the right-wing coalition of Maluf, I know that my decision was correct. During the past three years, rather than being detached from my own bases, I solidified my commitment with the social movements and with the *escola pública popular*.[31] I knew then, and I know now, that I am right.

Going to PUC was a difficult decision for me. Not only the cost of fees, too high for my salary, but also the feeling of being "debased," of being surrounded by middle class women and men, most of whom are more concerned with their personal appearance than with a recognition of their own political practice as oppressors. But I had no choice if I wanted to go to the university.

You know that in Brazil is very difficult for someone like me, who did all her education in public schools to pass the entrance examination (*vestibular*) to attend our good public universities. The irony is that those who can enter our public universities are those who studied in the most prestigious, private high schools. The rest of us have only the option of the private universities in Brazil.

I have no reservations, and this was also a decision that I had to carry through. While I may not have agreed with all the initiatives of the Freirean administration, I do agree however with Freire's criticism of *basism*. I remember the videotape that you showed me of your dialogue with Freire when he argued that

> There is a kind of illness in the popular politics which we call grassroots movements. But it is not the grassroots movements which are wrong. It is the exacerbation of the value of the grassroots' movements. Basism means that virtue, knowledge, wisdom, and everything else, reside with the masses of the people, the bases, with the grassroots. And those who are not in sight of the grassroots are classified as elites or academics.[32]

Carlos, for me, Gramsci's notions of hegemony and organic intellectuals are important.[33] You teach Gramsci in your courses, don't you? Would you agree with my interpretation? Gramsci's notion of hegemony refers to two rather distinct phenomena. On the one hand, hegemony refers to a process of social and political domination in which the ruling classes establish their control over the class allied to them through moral and intellectual leadership. On the other hand, hegemony refers to the dual use of force and ideology to reproduce social relations between the ruling classes and the subaltern classes and groups. Hegemony is produced by organic intellectuals of the ruling classes, and is also transmitted by traditional intellectuals. In Gramsci's theory of political struggle, for the subaltern classes to achieve hegemony in society, they have to produce their own organic intellectuals, and should attain moral and intellectual influence in society (counterhegemony) before achieving political control.[34]

I told her that I agreed with her interpretation of Gramsci, and we discussed Gramsci for a while, analyzing the importance of his thinking in linking class politics with cultural politics.

Suddenly, Luiza Amorosa moved away from our theoretical discussions and said: I believe that only people like me, committed to the social movements, with a clear perception of their own contradictions of class, gender, sexual preference, race, and geographical location can become organic intellectuals, and challenge the traditional and organic intellectuals of the Brazilian Right.

And I believe that while the universities are part and parcel of the establishment, and most of the intellectuals in the universities are self-serving, privileged people, universities continue to be democratic spaces, with their own contradictions and tensions. Still some professors are valuable *companheiros* of social movements, particularly when they know how to listen, and to learn with us and from us, those of us who are up to our necks "wet" with the experience of oppression. Yes, some books and articles help us to think and to act. For me, to encounter the vibrancy of Gramsci's analyses in my university education, or the reading of *Pedagogy of the Oppressed* or *Educação e Compromiso*,[35] has been invaluable. It could be dangerous to withdraw from furthering our own knowledge and education.

Luiza Amorosa, I said, I am surprised by your passionate defense of the benefits of academic work. How would you relate the benefits of academic work to your commitment with *os meninos e meninas* in your neighborhood?

Carlos, I agree with the position of the *crítica social dos conteúdos* [the critical and social appropriation of universal knowledge], a position that started an important political debate in pedagogical circles in Brazil years ago, and very often in contradistinction to Freire's work. The critical and social appropriation of universal knowledge on behalf of the popular sectors seeks to improve the popular sectors access to and control of public schooling.

For instance, former Secretary of Education of the State of São Paulo, Giomar Namo de Melo, argues:

> I know how much the idea of a universal knowledge has been questioned, but I cannot stop asking myself if a solid general formation, based on the existent dominant knowledge, is not the best that the school can offer to the popular classes. In fact, they can criticize that knowledge and improve it. How can it be improved without passing through it?[36]

Look, Carlos, our public schools should play a key role in the socialization of the people in the systematized knowledge, in connecting people to dominant cultural capital. The school is the principal (if not exclusive) environment to guarantee the education of the people; an education that allows the popular sectors, the subaltern sectors, a more competent participation in the world of work, culture and politics.

You see, Carlos, I like to live dangerously. I have been accused many times of being a *basista*, and many times of defending the critical and social appropriation of universal knowledge. I believe there are serious tensions between putting all our belief in the people and their wisdom, and the need to use the public schools as the place where the people will find the universal knowledge that will empower them. Nobody is free of contradictions, and certainly not I, always searching for a total coherence between my words and my actions. I hope that these ideas will satisfy your question.

Carlos, I know that this interview is part of your research, of your job, but I live here, and tomorrow I have to work. I am afraid it is getting late. If I don't hurry up I may miss the last bus home. *Obrigada e boa viagem pra California.*

A conversation with Luiza Amorosa is a cultural and a spiritual experience. The next morning, while my plane to Mexico City was taking off from the São Paulo Airport, I was still confronting Luiza Amorosa's eyes, profound, sincere, fearless, inquisitive. Her voice, her smile, her corporal signs, her bold intelligence, were all challenging, bringing immense enthusiasm and energy to a conversation about politics and education—a memorable conversation.

Before I dozed off to avoid thinking that I was flying at an altitude of thirty thousand feet, aboard a mechanical bird with principles of aerodynamics I never understood and therefore are, well . . . , magical to me, and I imagine to the majority of the passengers, I thought of Luiza Amorosa's contradiction. Her faith is bold and unyielding in the wisdom and practice of the popular sectors, and her project of using public schooling to empower through universal knowledge.

Air turbulence brought me back from my own rumination. I started reading Gadotti's *Uma Só Escola para Todos* with the hope that the book would distract me from my own thoughts, and from Luiza Amorosa's challenging insights on education and politics. Then I stumbled on a page were Gadotti argues that a *crítica social dos conteúdos* privileges a depoliticizing view of educational reform. What a paradox, I thought, remembering Luiza Amorosa's comments on hegemony and education, and her political and ethical commitment. For Gadotti, the critical-social appropriation approach seeks to create the citizen through enlightenment that is in frontal opposition to a political view promoting the use of education and schooling as a tool in the struggle for hegemony.[37]

Hum!!!! Which way ahead? Is there a "correct" thinking on this issue? Is there any sure foundation, or has postmodernism destroyed them all?

By the time I was ready for dinner, the thesis of the appropriation of cultural capital based on the hope that its acquisition strengthens the dominated classes and weakens the power of the dominant classes, became even more dubious to me. This, expressed in the framework of hegemony makes no sense, given that what happens may be exactly the opposite. The more that hegemonic discourse penetrates the common sense of dominated classes, the more it saturates their world view, their moral and life world, and the more it will increase the power of dominant classes, which in that way will consolidate themselves also as hegemonic classes.[38]

A luta continua. . . . It was clear to me, however, that if there were many more Luiza Amorosas, the population of bureaucrats like Mr. Sorrento would diminish, and the conditions that facilitated Latin American fantastic realism would eventually become constrained to a novel of fantastic fiction or poetry, or indeed remain as a reflection of the feverish imagination of the writer. Teachers like Luiza Amorosa will bring about a utopian realism in teachers' lives and political action.

Lupita

Francisquito, sprinting from the corner of the modest two bedroom apartment in Copilco, at the southern end of Mexico City, stopped abruptly inches from my knees, laughing, and brandishing his plastic—and exasperatingly loud—machine gun, a gift from his mother for his seventh birthday. Leodonilda, a gracious two-year-old girl, approached me trying to keep her equilibrium while handling a bear as large as herself. She also wanted to show me her priceless toy and companion. Lupita's other children, Pablo and Santiago, are married and live outside the Federal District of Mexico.

August in Mexico City is the tail end of the rainy season. A semitropical, persevering rain was flooding the parking lot of Lupita's apartment in Copilco, mercilessly pounding the windows. I couldn't help feeling protected in a cozy environment, with the smells of food on the stove. With this weather, I thought, I hope my conversation with Lupita, my former student, will last at least for a couple of hours. In Mexico City, despite the fierce intensity of the summer rains, by 8 P.M.

the rain will almost automatically stop, and I will be able to find my way to my hotel in Paseo de la Reforma.

In her late forties, Lupita, a small Chatino Indian with dark skin, a proud and stern face, and a very strong temper hidden by her traditional and gentle mannerism, was finishing cooking the traditional, delicious chicken in mole. Born in the periphery of San Cristobal de Las Casas, in Chiapas, Southern Mexico, she learned Spanish at the age of twelve, becoming a very active member and a young leader of her community. When she was twenty-four, after completing her secondary education, she took advantage of President Echeverria's pilot program of residential teacher's college for indigenous groups in Mexico, and obtained her teaching credential for elementary education in two years in 1972. She taught elementary school in Chiapas, and completed at the same time her *normal superior* degree (teaching credential for secondary education). Given her close connection with the national teachers union, *Sindicato Nacional de Trabajadores de la Educación* (SNTE), and her demonstrated leadership, she was promoted to vice principal in 1978, and transferred to Mexico City, with an assignment in a working class school in the district of Netzahualcoyot.

I met Lupita when she enrolled at the newly created *Universidad Pedagógica Nacional* in 1979 to complete her master's degree in educational administration. Although I had ninety-eight students in my course "Education and Society in Mexico," she stood out for a number of reasons. The quality of her comments in class, her insightful papers, but above all, her natural, intuitive and sharp intelligence in discussing the political role of education in Mexico struck me. I met her again and her husband, Raúl, also a former student of mine, by pure chance while I was shopping for some religious masks at the arts and craft market of Avenida Revolución, on a grey and cold Saturday morning. They were so surprised and pleased to see me that they invited me for supper that evening, an invitation I couldn't refuse—particularly when I was trying to interview some of my former students working in elementary or secondary schools in the Federal District.

Lupita set the table, served the *pollo con mole* with warm tortillas, and we began a conversation, discretely inspired by a

much improved Mexican wine, *Castillos de la Colina*. I asked
Lupita about her pedagogical and political experiences teaching
in Mexico City during the last two decades, and her opinions on
the political role of teachers in Mexican education. Raúl, silent,
followed the conversation with a cryptic, distant look. Lupita
had already put the children in bed, and the sounds of the
machine gun toy were no longer intermittently present in our
conversation.

Maestro, she said with the ceremonial and deferential
treatment so commonly granted to teachers by former students
in Mexico, Mexico's education has been in turmoil since the
events of 1979.[39] The SNTE has always worked laboriously to
defend our rights, but those disgruntled leftists, the *democráticos*,
have undermined the authority of Don Carlos Jonguitud,[40] and
were successful in taking him out of office a few years ago.
Though Elba Esther is a good leader,[41] I am afraid we will not
have the same political clout in the party and the government
anymore. And this is, in part, the fault of the *democráticos*. Now
we are at the mercy of the decisions in the party and in the
Secretariat of Public Education. Before, with the Revolutionary
Vanguard, we had a lot to say in the policy decisions, and we
could better protect our working conditions, salaries, and
prestaciones (perks), but now the situation has changed.

Lupita, I asked, please tell me, how education has changed
in the last two or three *sexenios*,[42] and how that affects the
political actions of teachers in the system?

Maestro, you know that in Mexico education is a labor of
love. I will say this with some trepidation because of the reform
and the ideology of Mexican liberalism. For us teachers,
education is a kind of religious activity. We, the teachers, are the
missionaries of progress, and the cement of the nation. Without
the rural teachers like Luis Alvarez Barret or the heroic efforts of
pedagogues like Joaquín Baranda, José Vasconcelos, Narciso
Bassols, and, of course, Jaime Torres Bodet,[43] Mexico, the proud,
the indomitable, the Indian, Creole, and Spanish, the many
Mexicos in the words of *Maestro* Jesus Reyes Heroles,[44] would
not be one. We, the teachers, rebuilt the nation from the ashes of
the Mexican Revolution and now, we are not even recognized
anymore. The new statutes of secondary-school teachers try to

control our minds and time. The SNTE and particularly the Revolutionary Vanguard always made sure that teachers were informed, consulted, and that we participated with voice and vote in the construction of public education. It was the Revolutionary Vanguard that managed to increase the salary of the teacher in the late seventies, and got us a number of *prestaciones*, including the loan that I obtained with Raúl to buy our humble apartment. You see *Maestro* Carlos, the *democráticos* criticized the Revolutionary Vanguard because it was "corporatist," "clientelist," because it had a tight grip in the different sections of the Teachers' Union,[45] and because, they said, not everybody participated in the politics of the Union. But I say that is false. Every time they wanted to make a decision, they asked my opinion as vice principal. Every time the Secretary of Public Education (SEP) wanted to appoint a delegate to one of the SEP education delegations in the country, the SNTE would make sure that the appointment went to a prestigious *normalista* who had spent all his or her life working for Mexico, for its children, for its people. So, I don't understand why the *democráticos* politicize the Union and undermined the will of Don Carlos Jonguitud, our spiritual leader.

The *democráticos* said that the Union was corrupt. Well, let me tell you this, corruption is not to take advantage of a position to gain influence, power, or some wealth. Corruption is a way of life in Mexico. Everybody in the government is corrupt; the police that ask you for a *mordida*[46] are corrupt. I don't mind that some people in the Union make themselves rich. What matters for me is that they defend my interests, my so hard-won position in the system, and not, as the *democráticos* say, the possibility for everybody to argue, to say what they want, to influence decisions. This only brings chaos, disorganization, anarchy. This kind of Swiss type of direct democracy does not reflect the feeling of the Mexicans, the basic social personality of the Mexicans. We Mexicans know what a revolution is, and what is the price a country and its people paid for social change. We teachers paid the price to forge a new country after the Revolution. As long as the country recognized our efforts, we never minded the sacrifice.

As an Indian woman, I also know how difficult it is to prosper. Without the Union, and without the help of the *maestros normalistas* that worked for the SEP, I don't think I could have ever had the success I have had as a teacher in Mexico. We have to play politics the way it is. We shall simply accept the rules of the game, and try to advance our own interests; that is what corporatism is all about. Corporatism may not be the best social system, but it gave us stability and growth for more than sixty years. Moreover, corporatism gave to the teachers more power than we could ever have had. When the *democráticos* with their silly destabilization tactics, undermined the Revolutionary Vanguard, this simply gave an opportunity to these *universitarios* (university graduates), the technocrats controlling the upper posts in the SEP, to implement their ridiculous planning, their number crunching, and their simulation models! What do they know about teaching? They have not been in front of a classroom, trying to establish discipline, trying to teach poor and hungry children that they have to do their homework, that they have to learn their arithmetic tables and ABCs?

At least with the Revolutionary Vanguard we were able to press upon these people not to change the roots of our postrevolutionary education, and to have the teacher—the central protagonist of our daily education drama—becoming a central actor in educational policy making. Now with the process of decentralization, and the higher profile offered to private education in this country, including changing the third article of the Constitution that kept education under strict control of the Mexican State, the government is eroding the power of teachers and the teachers' union. They want to create a system like that in the United States, where unions have little influence or power. *Maestro*, this is the tragic political situation of teachers in Mexico. We have come a long way to find that our professional gains, our organizational gains, and our political clout in the system, are being affected by the new process of modernization of the Mexican State, and by the action of these *democráticos* who don't realize they have created a lack of unity among teachers' ranks, and have handed to the technocrats in the government a weaker and less efficient teachers' union.

I am very skeptical for the future. I am also very demoralized. I just want to continue working until I reach retirement age, and just leave the system without making waves.[47] I spent too many years doing community work, professional work, and work within the union. Now, I am tired, and I have very little energy left. I just want to look after my own family, especially my youngest children."

Lupita served the coffee. The smell of the traditional *café de olla*—a mixture of strong coffee with cinnamon and sugar cane—reminded me of the poor taste of the indescribable American coffee. Supper was coming to an end, and I felt I had the chance and time for one more question. I asked Lupita why she defended the union so much. After all, in so many years as vice principal, she could not get promoted to principal in any school in the Federal District.

Maestro, she said with a smile, in Mexico the majority of principals are males, and it is difficult to break that tradition. I understand the limitations of my own actions, and I feel that, for someone like myself, a full-blooded Indian who did not speak Spanish until her adolescence, my professional career has been very successful, and I should not be overly ambitious. Now, however, with a woman like Elba Esther in charge of the union, the rights of women will be achieved at a speedier pace than ever expected. We were always invisible for a union dominated by males.

Now, we are not invisible anymore. For me, it is too late, but not for my children. I sincerely hope that the union activities, with more women activists in it, will be more sensitive to the needs and demands of the rank and file. And remember that the majority of the women like myself, women who come from a humble status, have to work doubly hard to achieve professional recognition, while raising a family and doing the domestic chores as well. I don't have the luxury of the women who teach at the university. They have maids, but I cannot afford one.

Mexico City at night is a different city. Only dozens, not thousands, of cars circulate, and the *pesero*[48] that took me to my hotel in Paseo de la Reforma was half full. I had room to think. I was wondering about Lupita's political perception of her role as teacher, and her proud assessment of her many accomplishments, considering her own upbringing. I was thinking about the powerful combination of a woman and a Chatino Indian who understood the rules of the political game in the teaching profession. Lupita knew how to take advantage of the game, without challenging the rules or protesting its faults.

She is not cynical about her experience; quite the contrary. She will reassert her own values as a teacher, especially her patriotism and her commitment to education as a religious activity, as she puts it. She may understand that the teachers' union is not perfect; even more, that it may have been riddled with corruption. For her, however, corruption was political currency in Mexico and there was no point in fighting it. It was important for her to take the union as the principle of organization for the teachers, as the institution that will defend her own corporate interests, but, at the same time, as the corporate institution that, in a dialectic of collaboration and conflict, will challenge the state. For Lupita SNTE was an indispensable instrument—albeit not a perfect one—to represent the aspirations of teachers in policy formation.

Her comments on the heavy legacy of patriarchy in Mexican labor relations resonated with me. I don't think she gave up her struggle for a different presence of women teachers in Mexico's education system. She was simply too tired to continue her struggle. Reviewing some of my own notes from that conversation before falling asleep, I couldn't help remembering Michael Apple's reference to a woman teacher in the South of the United States who said: "We have to go slow in the South. . . . We may not at first do very big things and we are perfectly certain not to do spectacular things, but . . . we are not dead."[49] This could have certainly applied to the large number of anonymous women teachers, like Lupita, who are not dead in the Latin American educational settings. They are simply subjected to processes of power that construct their identity as women and men teachers through "mechanisms that censor the self; that is, the choice of one set of practices over its alternatives as a component in the production of identity.[50]

My final entry in my notebook that day reads as follows:

I should resist the temptation to compare analytically Tomás Agustin's, Lupita's and Luiza Amorosa's self-consciousness of race, gender, and class. Existential and structural rules and historical processes create the conditions for the development of gender, class, and race. The interrelation of class, gender, and race is historically and socially conditioned. They are not "given" biological facts but historical ones. They are created through social relationships that are historical and interact through multiple determinations. I must know much more about the relationships between education, power, and personal biography in Tomás Agustin's, Luiza Amorosa's, and Lupita's experience, before I attempt to understand their own claims to truth, education, and the politics of race, class, and gender.

Afterthoughts

This chapter has attempted to show some flashes, a sequence of static photographs in the lives and political action of teachers in Latin America. I sought to show the life and political action of teachers that, although subject to structural and symbolic rules, are neither marionettes of structures or rules, nor eminent and calculating agents following rational choice theory. I tried to show them as social agents, as flesh and bones drenched with historicity and full-of-life stories.

If the history of America is nothing but a chronicle of the marvelous-real, as Alejo Carpentier has so stubbornly defended in his literary work challenging surrealist perspectives, then teachers' narratives can transcend the factual nature of the historical, and in so doing, the construction of these narratives invites us to reveal the world of imagination and myths, and the ever-present life of structures, rules, and regulations of power. That teachers are apolitical and their actions are politically neutral are two such myths. While the real is the product of multiple determinations, alternative narratives exploring border crossings[51] of teachers' lives and political action contribute to blurring fictitious distinctions in cultural and historical writing.

In so doing, these narrative also play with the notion that the real acquires new imaginary dimensions in teachers' lives.

Ginsburg et al.,[52] discussing the relationships between teachers, politics, and education, argue that every domain of educational policy and practice is crossed by ideological and political decisions. The above narratives confirm this assessment. Curriculum decision making entails political work. How educators organize their classrooms and how they relate to different groups of students, that is, teachers' pedagogy, is also a form of political activity. Students' evaluation, insofar as it contributes to the distribution of power and material and symbolic resources through sorting students, implies political work and so does research, although it is not exclusively part and parcel of political work. From the decision to study a particular problem, to discuss the empistemological implications and research framework, to select a method for data collection and data analysis, to the treatment of the "subjects" of the research, to the production and analysis of data, to the use of research findings and their policy implications, all of this is crossed by and embedded in political decisions, values, and actions. Teachers' labor relations, demands, salaries, and the like, fall neatly within the notion of political action. Particularly teachers unions, so prominent in Latin America, clearly show the connections between politics and education, and more specifically how institutional politics intervene in teachers lives and action. Finally, the work, thinking, and action of teachers as members of families and communities entail political action.

Not only the political nature of education impacts teachers' lives and actions. Historical-structural aspects cut across virtually all the domains of teachers lives and action. Two very meaningful dimensions, teachers' salaries and labor conditions, and how they relate to politics and power; and teachers' unions, their political work, and the possible linkages to educational reform and democracy have proven very relevant in my dialogues with three teachers in the region.

There is unity in the diversity of these three teachers' short stories: teaching is a political activity. When Tomás Agustín complains about the material conditions of university teachers in Argentina and the bastardization of university politics; when

Luiza Amorosa struggles with keeping her party commitments and her commitments to social movements and, especially, her students; or when Lupita passionately defends the union as an instrument for teachers to sustain their salaries and labor conditions, and to influence public policy; these stories let thousand of anonymous teachers speak with a single voice.

NOTES

1. Gabriel García Márquez cited by Roger M. Peel, "Los cuentos de García Márquez," in Enrique Pupo-Walker (editor) *El cuento hispanoamericano ante la crítica* (Madrid: Editorial Castalia, 1973, p. 240). Translated by María del Pilar O'Cadiz.

2. David William Foster, *Alternative Voices in the Contemporary Latin American Narrative* (Columbia: University of Missouri Press, 1985, pp. 147–148).

3. Peter Burke, "History of Events and the Revival of Narrative," in Peter Burke (editor), *New Perspectives in Historical Writing* (University Park: Pennsylvania University Press, 1991, p. 241).

4. *Ibid.*, p. 238.

5. I would like to thank María Cristina Pons for bringing this to my attention. Analysis of Gabriel García Marquez's work, and particularly *One Hundred Years of Solitude*, can be found in Donald L. Shaw, *Nueva Narrativa Hispanoamericana* (Madrid: Ediciones Cátedra, 1981); and John S. Brushwood, *The Spanish American Novel: A Twentieth-Century Survey* (Austin: University of Texas Press, 1975).

6. Fernando Alegría, *Historia de la Novela Hispanoamericana* (Mexico: Ediciones de Andrea, 1974, pp. 300–301).

7. I will follow Bakhtin here, and argue that an imperative for a dialogue is that there can be no actual monologue. Dialogism "is the characteristic epistemological mode of a world dominated by heteroglossia. Everything means, is understood, as part of a greater whole." M. M. Bakhtin, *The Dialogic Imagination: Four Essays*, edited by M. Holquist, translated by C. Emerson and M. Holquist (Austin: University of Texas Press, 1981, p. 427). In fact, my dialogues with fictitious teachers are based on heteroglossia. This implies that a word

uttered in a place and a time will have a specific and unique meaning given the set of conditions—social, historical, physiological, etc.,—that constitute a matrix of forces that insures the primacy of context over text. In this respect, the text I am proposing to the reader is heteroglossic because it is dialogic and not merely monologic.

8. Ruth Berins Collier and David Collier, *Shaping the Political Arena: Critical Junctures, the Labor Movement, and Regime Dynamics in Latin America* (Princeton, N.J.: Princeton University Press, 1991).

9. Adriana Puiggrós, *Sujetos, disciplina y curriculum en los orígenes del sistema educativo argentino* (Buenos Aires: Editorial Galerna, 1990).

10. R. Collier and D. Collier, *Shaping the Political Arena* (see Note 8).

11. For a discussion on corporativism and education see Daniel A. Morales-Gómez and Carlos Alberto Torres, *The State, Corporatist Politics, and Educational Policy-Making in Mexico* (New York: Praeger, 1990); Neidson Rodrigues, *Estado, educação e desenvolvimento econômico* (São Paulo: Autores Asociados e Cortez, 1982); Joe Foweraker and Ann L. Craig, *Popular Movements and Political Change in Mexico*. (Boulder and London: Lynne Rienner Publishers, 1990); and Matilde Luna and Ricardo Pozas Horcasitas (editors), *Relaciones Corporativas en un Período de Transición* (Mexico: Instituto de Investigaciones Sociales-UNAM, 1992).

12. The argument is based upon the notion of relative political autonomy, and the presence of a "political logic," which is, in a sense, analogous to that of the "logic of capital" which has dominated many analyses in the social sciences. Another salient aspect of R. Collier and D. Collier's analysis is their study of the form of legitimation of the new model of the state and the manner of incorporation of an organized labor movement. Notwithstanding the political residues of the distinct historical legacies and different strategies employed in the search for legitimization, the authors argue that an understanding of interest groups, costs, and institutional rigidities illuminates the state corporatist project in all Latin American nations. The general model, based upon the logic of politics, conceptualizes social change as the occurrence of profound discontinuity within structural, institutional, and political arenas.

13. Atilio Alberto Boron, *Estado, Capitalismo y Democracia en América Latina* (Buenos Aires: Imago Mundi, 1991); Luis Carlos Bresser Pereira, "La Crisis de América Latina. "Consenso de Washington o Crisis Fiscal" (*Pensamiento Iberoamericano*, No. 19, 1991); José Maria Fanelli, Roberto Frenkel and Guillermo Rozenwurcel. "Growth and

Structural Reform in Latin America: Where We Stand" (Buenos Aires: Documento CEDES 67, 1990.)

14. Sylvain Lourié. "Impact of Recession and Adjustment on Education" (Paper submitted to the round-table "Development: The Human Dimension," Salzburg, September 7–9, 1986); Fernando Reimers, "Deuda Externa y Desarrollo: Implications para el Financiamiento de la Educación en América Latina" (*Revista Brasileira de Estudos Pedagógicos*, Vol. 71(169), 1990:195–277); Fernando Reimers, "The Impact of the Debt Crisis on Education in Latin America: Implications for Educational Planning" (*Prospects*, Vol. XX, No. 4, 1990:539–554).

15. Raúl Labán and Federico Sturzenegger, "Fiscal Conservatism as a Response to the Debt Crisis" (Los Angeles and Santiago de Chile: manuscript, 1992).

16. Labán and Sturzenegger, "Fiscal Conservatism," pp. 3–4.

17. Labán and Sturzenegger, "Fiscal Conservatism," p. 6.

18. See Antonio Gramsci, *Selections from the Prison Notebooks*. Quintin Hoare and Geoffrey Nowell Smith, editors and translators. New York: International Publishers, 1971.

19. Edited dialogue transcribed in a Argentine news service produced by the Faculty of Physics of the University of Buenos Aires and disseminanted by different channels, including Bitnet, throughout the world. Names are fictitious.

20. Thomas Wartenberg, (editor) *Rethinking Power* (New York: State University of New York Press, 1992, p. xix).

21. Michael W. Apple and Lois Weis, "Seeing Education Relationally: The Stratification of Culture and People in the Sociology of School Knowledge," *Journal of Education, 168(1)*, 1986.

22. Mark B. Ginsburg, "Contradictions, Resistance and Incorporation in the Political Socialization of Educators in Mexico" in M. Ginsburg and B. Lindsay (eds.) *The Political Dimension in Teacher Education* (New York: Falmer Press, 1995).

23. Atilio Alberto Boron, "Transition toward democracy in Latin America: Problems and prospects" (Buenos Aires: EURAL, manuscript, 1992).

24. José Nun, *La rebelión del cor: Estudio sobre la racionalidad política y el sentido común* (Buenos Aires: Nueva Visión, 1989).

25. He is referring to the Peronist Party, the ruling party under President Carlos Saúl Menem's administration, and the Radical party, the main opposition party.

26. See Michel Foucault, *Power/Knowledge*, edited by C. Gordon (Sussex: Hassocks, 1980); Mark Philp, "Michel Foucault" in Quentin Skinner (editor) *The Return of Grand Theory in the Human Sciences*. (Cambridge and New York: Cambridge University Press, 1985).

27. Cited by David William Foster, "Latin American Documentary Narrative." *PMLA*, 99(1), 1984, p. 41.

28. People who were born in the southern part of Brazil.

29. Children of the street.

30. Budd Hall, "Social Movements and Higher Education" (Paper presented to the Comparative International Education Society Annual Meeting, Kingston, Jamaica, March 16–19, 1993).

31. For a description of the movement of *escola pública popular* (public popular schooling) see Carlos Alberto Torres, "Paulo Freire as Secretary of Education in the Municipality of São Paulo," *Comparative Education Review*, 38(2): 181–214; Moacir Gadotti , Paulo Freire, and Sérgio Guimarães, *Pedagogia: Diálogo e Conflicto* (São Paulo: Cortez Editora-Editora Autores Associados, 1986).

32. Conversation with Paulo Freire, São Paulo, Brazil, videotaped, May 1990.

33. Niuvenius Junqueira Paoli, *Ideologia e hegemonia. As condições de produção da educação* (São Paulo: Cortez editora-autores associados, 1981); Antonio Tavares de Jesus. *Educação e hegemonia no pensamento de Antonio Gramsci* (São Paulo: Editora Unicamp-Cortez Editora, 1989); Walter L. Adamson. "Beyond 'Reform or Revolution': Notes on Political Education in Gramsci, Habermas and Arendt," *Theory and Society*, 6(3), 1978: 429–460; Walter L. Adamson, *Hegemony and Revolution: A Study of Antonio Gramsci's Political and Cultural Theory* (Berkeley, Los Angeles, and London: University of California Press, 1980).

34. See, e.g., Mario Manacorda, *Il principio educativo in Gramsci* (Cagliari: Armando Editore, 1970); Antonio Gramsci, *Selections from the Prison Notebooks* (Edited and translated by Quintin Hoare and Geoffrey Nowell Smith, New York: International Publishers, 1971); Harold Entwistle, *Antonio Gramsci: Conservative Schooling for Radical Politics* (London and Boston: Routledge and Kegan Paul, 1979); Walter Adamson, *Gramsci, Hegemony and Revolution: A Study of Antonio Gramsci's Political and Cultural Theory* (Berkeley and Los Angeles: University of California Press, 1980); and Rafael Díaz-Salazar, *El proyecto de Gramsci*, foreword by Francisco Fernández Buey (Madrid: Editorial Anthropos-Ediciones HOAC, 1991).

35. Moacir Gadotti, *Educação e Compromiso* (Campinas, Papirus, 1986).

36. Giomar Namo de Melo, "Las clases populares y la institución escolar: Una interacción contradictoria." In *Educación y clases sociales en América Latina* (Mexico, Departamento de Investigaciones Educativas-Centro de Estudios Avanzados del Instituto Politécnico Nacional, 1985, p. 58).

37. Moacir Gadotti. *Uma só escola para todos: Caminos da autonomía escolar* (Petrópolis, Rio de Janeiro: Vozes, 1990, p. 161).

38. José Tamarit, "El dilema de la educación popular: Entre la utopía y la resignación," *Revista Argentina de Educación*, VIII, No. 13, 1990, p. 37.

39. Traditionally, the conflict in Mexico's public education is viewed as the contradiction between technocrats (i.e., people with university degrees in charge of policy planning and operation) and *normalistas* (graduates from Normal Schools who controlled the teachers union, SNTE, by means of clientelistic practices). In the late seventies, a new group emerged characterized as *"democráticos"* or "the democratic teachers," according to Susan Street, *Maestros en Movimiento. Transformaciones en la Burocracia Estatal (1978–1982)* (Mexico: CIESAS-SEP, 1992). Thus, "the growing opposition to the Revolutionary Vanguard, the political group that controlled the SNTE for the last two decades, was successful in overthowing the leader of the Revolutionary Vanguard, Carlos Jonguitud Barrios, and the democratic teachers through mobilizations and strikes in the spring of 1989 succeeded in obtaining a salary increase of 25 percent—well above the ceiling imposed by the government's social pact between workers and capital" (Morales-Gómez and Torres, 1990, p. 53).

40. She refers to Maestro Carlos Jonguitud Barrios, leader of the Revolutionary Vanguard, the hegemonic faction that controlled the SNTE from 1972 until its demise as a political organized group within the SNTE on April 23, 1989. See José Angel Pescador Osuna and Carlos Alberto Torres, *Poder Político y Educación en México* (Mexico: UTHEA, 1985); Beatriz Calvo Ponton, *Educación Normal y Control Político* (Mexico: Ediciones de la casa chata, CIESAS-SEP, 1989); María Eulalia Benavides and Guillermo Velasco (coordinators) *Sindicato Magisterial en México* (Mexico: Instituto de Proposiciones Estratégicas, 1992); and Aurora Loyo Brambila, "De las Virtudes y Vicios de las Formas Corporativas de Intermediación: El Caso de los Maestros" in Matilde Luna and Ricardo Pozas Horcasitas (editors) *Relaciones Corporativas en un Período de Transición* (Mexico: Instituto de Investigaciones Sociales-UNAM, 1992, pp. 245–259).

41. She refers to Elba Esther Morales Gordillo, current General Secretary of the SNTE.

42. Refers to the Mexican presidential period of six years.

43. For reference to these historical figures of Mexican education see Fernando Solana, Raúl Cardiel Reyes, and Raúl Bolaños Martínez, *Historia de la Educación Pública en México*, 2 vols. (Mexico City: 1981).

44. The late Jesús Reyes Heroles occupied several positions in the Mexican government, including Secretary of Interior (Governación) and Secretary of Education.

45. The SNTE was created December 30, 1943, combining several large and small teachers organizations. It is organized in a National Council with an Executive Council of the National Council—with the figure of the general secretary as the most powerful position in the structure—and 32 regional councils.

46. Demand of a bribe to forgive or overlook a traffic violation.

47. Her exact expression in Spanish was "sin hacer olas."

48. Collective taxi cab.

49. Michael W. Apple, *Official Knowledge: Democratic Education in a Conservative Age* (New York and London: Routledge, 1993, p. 85).

50. Thomas S. Popkewitz, *A Political Sociology of Educational Reform. Power/Knowledge in Teaching, Teacher Education, and Research* (New York and London: Teachers College Press, Columbia University, 1991, p. 43).

51. Henry Giroux. *Border Crossings: Cultural Workers and the Politics of Education* (London and New York: Routledge, 1992).

52. Mark B. Ginsburg, Sangeeta Kamat, Rajeshwari Raghu, and John Weaver, "Education and Politics: Interpretations, Involvement, and Implications" in this volume.

The Work of Schoolteachers as Political Actors in Developing Countries

Linda A. Dove

The Intrinsic Political Work of Teachers

In developing countries, by definition, contexts of scarcity, "modern" knowledge, and educational qualifications are prized political goods. This is true for the state and the individual. From the point of view of the state, the school is a source of political and economic capital—an important instrument for forging nationhood out of diversity, socializing youth as future citizens, preparing the future labor force, and through maximizing human capital, encouraging economic development. From the point of view of the individual pupil and family, success in school brings enhanced social status and at least the hope of jobs and increased income.

Because school places, modern sector employment, and income earning opportunities are severely rationed, schoolteachers have inevitable and critical roles as political actors. In schools and in society, they determine "Who Gets What, When and How" (Lasswell 1936). They communicate to their pupils values, knowledge, and skills as defined in official curricula, evaluate educational performance for the purpose of grade promotion or repetition, tracking, credentialling and job eligibility, and sometimes act as spokespersons for the community's and children's interests or as intermediaries for parents with school authorities.

Teachers have always been informally involved in politics because of their roles in helping determine pupils' educational and occupational destinations. They have long been charged with providing their pupils with income-earning skills. In many countries they have been responsible for training pupils in prevocational subjects and for making links with local firms which might employ the school leavers. Parents, communities, teachers, and even governments, however, have sometimes resisted teachers' "dilution" of academic education with vocational training because they perceive the school's role as fitting children for wider and better opportunities (Foster 1965; Foster and Sheffield 1974; Middleton, Ziderman, and Van Adams 1993).

The case of Sri Lanka is a contemporary example of how, whether they like it or not, teachers are involved in a highly charged political process. Government jobs in the country are held by earlier generations of educated folk and jobs in the small, private, nonagricultural sector are few. Secondary schools try to offer a wide range of prevocational and technical subjects as well as general education. Because there are no school fees, pupils prefer to repeat the secondary school examination two or three times in the slender hope of qualifying for university places, rather than leave school to seek elusive jobs or to chance self-employment. In the early 1990s, competition for top marks in the terminal examination at the end of high school was so intense that some 40 percent of candidates were repeating the year in the hope of doing better next time. Even so, the government still symbolically upholds the role of the school in extending opportunities to youth. Teachers are not allowed to engage formally in electoral politics but, nevertheless, they are in the political spotlight when school examination time comes round because the results are so critically important to pupils' life chances. Teachers are, understandably, subjected to a great deal of lobbying by anxious parents. If their pupils succeed, they are viewed as political patrons. If pupils fail, they are scapegoats.

Teachers in Politics in the Colonial and Independence Eras[1]

Teachers' overt engagement in political life outside the school in past generations is not widely remembered today. However, this history merits being recorded because of the valuable support teachers have given in various ways to their countries, helping in nation building and participating in efforts to free subjugated countries from colonial rule (Dove 1979).

Teachers' political involvement was at a peak during the preindependence era in colonized countries and in the immediate postindependence years. For some thirty years, from the 1920s, conditions were ripe for the rise of the village schoolteacher to national political status in the fledgling national institutions that would provide the framework for independent statehood. Some teachers led nationalist movements and inherited the leadership of postindependence governments. Many prominent national leaders who became heads of state, prime ministers, cabinet members or parliamentary representatives, started out as village schoolteachers. This was the case in Sub-Saharan Africa particularly, but also to some extent in the Caribbean and South and Southeast Asia.

Teachers' Community Roles

Since the mid-nineteenth century, teachers have involved themselves in community activities and community development, either through individual inclination or with official encouragement (Sinclair and Lillis 1980; Thompson 1983). Community involvement is intrinsically political, influencing "Who Gets What" in terms of educational and other social goods. During the independence period, attempts to move away from "colonial" and "imperialist" models of schooling prompted indigenous programs for "peoples' schools," Gandhi's "basic" education, for example, Tanzania's Community Schools for "Self-Reliance," the Cuban "Schools in the Countryside," the Philippine's Baranguay (Village) Schools and the Nuclear Schools of Peru and other Latin American countries. In all of these teachers were a vital community resource (Dove 1980a, 1980b, 1986).

Under colonial and independent regimes alike, teachers were charged with extending government ideology and control into the community. In the contemporary world, teachers may still be direct agents of the state in the community, purveying political messages or carrying out duties as government functionaries. Acting as intermediaries between local folk and the administration is still an important political role in remote, disadvantaged, and illiterate communities, but less so than in the past.

Sometimes, as grassroots agents of government—colonial or independent—teachers' community work has included being electoral officers or census-data collectors. Sometimes, alongside agricultural extension agents and health-care personnel, they have supported "integrated rural development" as "animateurs." Sometimes, they have been responsible for literacy training for adults and out-of-school youth. After the Second World War, UNESCO championed this movement but few pilot projects survived due to lack of funds, teacher incentives, technical know-how, and public interest in nonformal education.

Very frequently, teachers have been responsible for fostering economic development by imparting skills relevant to the locality. In the nineteenth century, this meant introducing crafts into the curriculum alongside the three R's and Bible study (Batten 1953). In its report on "adapted" education the 1920s, British Phelps-Stokes Reports on *Education in Africa* (Lewis 1962) declared that teachers should participate in

> a clearly defined programme of school and community activities for the improvement of African villages. In addition to the training of the individual, it is important that the school shall be organised so that its activities also extend out into the home and institutions of the community.

In part, because of the local community roles they performed, teachers came to play larger political roles, including that of heads of state, legislators, and extraconstitutional radical activists.

Teachers as Government Officials

From independence through the 1970s, at least a dozen heads of state in Africa were former schoolteachers (Hodgkin 1961; Cole 1975). In ex-British Africa these included Julius Nyerere of Tanzania, Kenneth Kaunda of Zambia, El-Azhari of Sudan, Sir Abubakar Tafawa Balewa, Prime Minister of Nigeria, Kwame Nkrumah, president of Ghana, and the military heads of state after him, Generals Ankrah and Acheampong. In ex-French colonial West Africa there was Senghor of Senegal (Senegambia), Dacko of the Central African Republic, Diori of Niger, Tomalbaye of Chad, and Maga of Dahomey (Benin). Kayibanda of Rwanda had also been a teacher. In the Caribbean, teacher Eric Williams of Trinidad, and in Papua New Guinea, teacher Michael Somare, became first heads of state in their respective countries.

Apart from those who became leaders, teachers worldwide became involved in independence-era politics in colonized countries. In parts of the Caribbean, for example, teachers were in the vanguard of the campaign for independence. In 1944, 15 percent of the legislators elected under the new Jamaican constitution were teachers. The first Jamaican Governor-General, Sir Clifford Campbell, had been an elementary schoolteacher. In Trinidad, cabinet members who were ex-teachers included Hamilton Morris, president of the Senate, Cuthbert Joseph, Carlton Gomes, and Frank Stevens. Even in South Asia where lawyers and medical doctors, in particular, migrated to politics, teachers were also represented. In India, for example, 8 percent of the legislators in the first postindependence parliament had teaching backgrounds and by 1956 they constituted 12 percent of the Council of Ministers (Morris-Jones 1957). In Ceylon (Sri Lanka), the proportion of intellectuals (teachers or journalists) rose from under 10 percent between 1931–1947 to 30 percent in the third parliament in 1960.

Africa, however, provides the most striking examples of widespread teacher engagement in electoral politics during the decolonization period. In the 1950s, between a fifth and a third of the French West African House of Assembly were teachers.

In British West Africa, Gambia had two ex-teachers among its ministers. In the Gold Coast (Ghana), teacher involvement increased over the years, with two teachers among the country's eight-member national delegation to the preindependence Congress of British West Africa in 1918. By 1950 teachers constituted 3 percent of the members of the Legislative Council, rising to 12 percent in the new 1951 Assembly, and 29 percent in 1954. In the early 1950s, secondary teachers and lawyers predominated in political life, but as Nkrumah's party, the Congress People's Party, gained mass appeal, it attracted more elementary teachers.

In southern Africa teachers gained prominence in national politics as elected representatives or government ministers. For example, teachers constituted 12 percent of elected officials in Swaziland, about 20 percent in Northern Rhodesia (Zambia) and Bechuanaland (Botswana), and 33 percent in Nyasaland (Malawi).

In East Africa nearly 30 percent of representatives in Tanganika (Tanzania) had teaching backgrounds. In Uganda many teachers attained high political office, while in Kenya, where many teachers were party activists and nominees for the African elections, they constituted about half of the entire legislature. President Daniel Arap Moi, who succeeded Jomo Kenyatta in 1978, was formerly a teacher.

Even in Sierra Leone, where the highly educated, professional Creole population dominated preindependence politics, seven teachers were nominated as candidates in the 1957 election and two were elected. In Nigeria, African representation on the Legislative Council in the interwar years was increased in an attempt to defuse the grievances of elites who were still largely excluded from posts in the administration. Among this group were schoolteachers, clergy and local employees of British firms.

Teachers and Extra-Constitutional Radical Action

The Nigerian case is an important example of how teachers engaged in radical fringe politics—what the colonial powers often perceived initially as subversive activities (Abernathy and

Coombe 1965; Abernathy 1969). These activities later helped teachers into constitutional office. From the 1930s until independence in 1959, teachers were activists in the tribal unions in towns, which were the grassroots basis for nationwide political parties after the war (Zolberg 1966). By 1951, there were a fair number of teachers in the new Houses of Assembly, a quarter of the representatives in the Western Region, and nearly a third in the East. By 1958, teachers featured prominently in the leadership of the four major parties, and in the 1959 federal elections educators constituted nearly 30 percent of candidates in the East, West, and Lagos. At the local level at that time, one fifth of the Action Group in the East, West, and Lagos were teachers.

Even in the Muslim North, where secular and Christian mission schooling were less widespread, teachers were still politically active. Sir Ahmadu Bello, premier of the Northern Region, 1946–1966, provided a role model, starting his career as a middle-school teacher in his home town. Nearly 10 percent of the Northern Nigeria Consultative Council (NNCC) were teachers and 5 percent were candidates for the 1959 elections. Between 1959 and 1964, five out of nine ministers of the Federal Government of the North and 8 percent of the members of the Northern House of Assembly were teachers, of whom six also later became ministers.

In Asia too, teachers' involvement in radical and quasi-constitutional politics has long traditions. They often led movements of cultural survival and revival in countries where indigenous cultures were threatened by colonization. In Vietnam, for example, teachers strenuously resisted curricular and language policies imposed by the French (Kelly 1978a, 1978b).

In India, politics and education were very early entwined. In the 1830s, for example, the schoolteachers of South Behar were informally involved in political life through their dissemination of controversial language policies—in this case, in their dissemination of Hindi, the language of administration, or in their support for the many local languages, including the important minority language, Urdu (Dibona 1983). In the 1880s, the nationalists, Tilak and Gokhale, formed the Deccan Education Society to found colleges for future national leaders.

College teachers were drawn to such groups by a sense of mission that became passionate in the Gandhian 1920s when many "national universities" were set up. Educators did not limit themselves to "moderate" nationalist activity. In Bengal, for example, teachers and their students were in the forefront of extremist opposition movements, a tradition of politicization in educational institutions that still continues.

In Indonesia schoolteachers had long been involved in "subversive" and "constitutional" politics. In the early years of the twentieth century, teachers in the "wild schools" aimed to reconcile the best of "western culture" with traditional Islam. The radical Sarekat Islam movement, 1900–1922, led by Muslim teachers in rural areas, and later the 1950s Masjumi Islamic Modernization Party in Java, aimed to fuse Islam and the secular educational benefits introduced by the colonial regime. The *Taman Siswa* school system, founded in 1922 by Dewantara, aimed officially at cultural harmonization. But teachers in these schools were often at risk of official sanctions for suspected opposition to the Dutch colonizers. In addition, village teachers, working in three-grade "bush" schools for "natives," were attracted by the nationalist youth organization before independence and participated in guerrilla groups in the unstable years of early statehood and communist opposition. Sitanggang, for example, a prominent leader in the interwar period, was a product of Christian mission school and by 1957 he had risen to be the first secretary of the Indonesian Communist Party (PKI) in North Sumatra. With the 1960s postindependence expansion of secular elementary schools, a new class of young teachers, reared on the politics of nationalism and regionalism, were funded by the PKI to spread antigovernment sentiment amongst rural populations who felt keenly their renewed domination by the Javanese political elite (Thomas 1970).

In contrast, some Indonesian teachers believed constitutionalism was the way forward (Soemardi 1956). In 1939 teachers made up 10 percent of parliamentarians and some were even in the cabinet. Today, the 1.3 million teachers are a considerable political group because of their large number. Their political inputs are guided through the government-sponsored teachers' union, which represents many different religious and cultural interests on the presidential consultative council for education.

Conditions Underlying Teachers' Political Activism

What factors contributed to the rise of the teacher-politician in the independence era? First, the expansion of elementary education in Christian mission or public schools, prior to independence, supplied many more local, educated youth looking for modern sector work than were previously available under the restricted, colonial-elite schooling. Most school-teachers were products of elementary schools. They had not usually come from independently wealthy families, like the sons of traditional rulers or the few legal and medical professionals in politics. They had few alternatives to teaching among white-collar jobs as avenues of upward mobility because colonial regimes restricted the range of public-service occupations for which colonial subjects were eligible, and because the private, commercial, and trade sectors were small and less socially valued.

Second, teacher training was usually free and trainees were given a stipend. This meant that the equivalent of secondary education was made available to many children of poor colonial families and these teachers became the first generation of a "Western" educated, new middle class. Being an educated minority, their social status was respected and, thus, many easily became leaders in their communities, participating in political life.

Third, through their training in the three Rs, narrow, formalistic and culturally alien though the school curriculum was, these teachers learned to use the language of the colonizers and gained insight into their sociocultural values. Some unconditionally adopted these values, as in the case of the West African "Black Englishmen," especially the "Been To's." Others became oppositional, challenging the colonialists and developing nationalistic ideals. The point, though, is that the very experience of having succeeded in school meant that these schoolteachers had learned perseverance and application and could relate to an achievement ethic and the wider world as well as to particularistic, local values (Inkeles 1974; Holsinger and Theisen 1977). All of this was good political training. The result was that they were able to penetrate colonial administration and act as brokers with colonial regimes on behalf of local community members.

Fourth, and of great importance, teacher-politicians were able to exert political patronage through winning resources to build schools and provide teachers and books. This patronage was possible because local parents prized modern education. Social status and political clout was especially high for teachers in rural areas where schools were scarce and illiteracy was high. But even in cities and towns, teachers commanded considerable respect and influence.

Explaining the Decline in Teachers' Political Activism

Teachers were prominent, then, in political negotiation and agitation during the struggles for independence and the early period of state-building. After independence, some activists even rose to high political office in fledgling democracies. But by the 1970s, although teachers continued to play roles in informal politics in classrooms and communities, they no longer played roles in the national political arena. Why is this so? What conditions underlay this decline in prominence? We can better understand the decline in teachers' political activism if we examine structural and ideological changes (consolidation of state power, nationalization of educational systems, bureaucratization of schools, and teachers' status decline) that have occurred.

Consolidation of State Power

Political power has gradually consolidated within a small group of professional politicians from which the ranks of the teaching force have mainly found themselves excluded (Robins 1976). After the few heady years of free political association, newly established and brittle democracies began to shatter, with one-party or military regimes taking over, often backed by former colonial powers and multinational companies. Political resources and channels of communication became restricted. There is still, of course, a minority of politically active teachers in some countries. They spend a lot of time participating, with official blessing, in teachers' union activity, serving as brokers between government and rank-and-file teachers (Morris 1977; ILO/UNESCO 1977). But the overall effect of the consolidation of state power is to reduce legitimate political activism by schoolteachers. Teachers' political activity is not usually condoned by contemporary developing country governments, who are fearful that their fragile legitimacy could be undermined at the grassroots level.

Nationalization of Education Systems

As private schools were nationalized and the state took over mass public-school systems, the linkages between teachers and local communities changed, with a consequent deflation of their local political leverage. Private schools were taken into government control as weak governments sought to get a grip on key state institutions. This happened mainly in Africa but also in other continents. In the Asian nation of Sri Lanka, for instance, independent schools run by religious bodies (Christian, Muslim, Buddhist) were taken over by the state or heavily subsidized and regulated under state control. The extensive Buddhist school system received public grants and in return partially secularized its program. Large, urban, Christian denominational schools were taken over by the government. In parallel, the teaching force was nationalized. Teachers became government servants with pay and benefits provided from the public purse and conditions of service regulated by the state's Education Services Committee.

With nationalization and the extension of state control, teachers' reliance on local communities for their livelihood declined, and, concomitantly, their need to be so strictly responsive to local communities. They began to be deployed nationwide, often far away from their homes. The majority would hesitate before engaging in what might be construed as "political" activity. Their first concern would be not to be bypassed for promotion, or to avoid official "punishment," such as being transferred to a school further away from their homes.[2]

In summary, extension of state control over teachers reduced their local influence and deflated the respect in which they were held by local communities, thus weakening their base for involvement in formal politics.

Bureaucratization of Schools

With industrialization and modernization, small community schools largely gave way to public schools in large-scale, bureaucratized, mass school systems (Inkeles 1974). Bureaucratized schools tend to be impersonal, with much division of labor and specialization. Schools in large bureaucracies are, ideally, efficient, hierarchical, rule-governed and clock-watching. Teachers, according to this model, become apolitical functionaries.

The way bureaucratic organizations operate is said to have a powerful influence on political learning—for teachers and for pupils (Dreeben 1968; Shipman 1972). Bureaucratic settings are assumed to mould teachers and pupils into passive, obedient subjects and to inhibit development of their sense of political efficacy, which would enable them to bargain, negotiate, and compromise in an open, democratic way (Oppenheim et al. 1975). Perhaps, a closer approximation to the truth is that, in practice, school systems work imperfectly as bureaucracies and not all teachers are malleable.

Imperfect bureaucracies lead to unequal treatment and such conditions may well encourage free-spirited individuals to "fight the system," forcing them to become politically active within the bureaucratic school organization (and perhaps more generally). Absenteeism, lack of punctuality, and even strikes may become commonplace as they try to win resources for themselves and use school time to lobby officials. Harber (1984) shows, for example, that bureaucracy works very inefficiently in Nigerian schools and teachers behave accordingly. In such situations teachers need to find political patrons and protectors among school officials and other influentials. This explains the common experience all over the developing world where teachers have to spend many long hours travelling to the Education Office and waiting in line to lobby officials in search of favors—better pay, promotion, transfer to attractive schools, or places in good schools for their own children.

One certain effect of educational bureaucracies is that classroom teachers have very little in the way of a career ladder. In large bureaucratic systems, diversification out of classroom teaching is possible but rare. *Ambition* means distancing oneself from ordinary schoolteacher colleagues and moving into advisory work, school administration, inspection, or out of primary into secondary teaching, or even out of secondary teaching into primary teacher training. There is not much room at the top. Thus, most teachers are not exposed to a variety of management or supervisory experiences that would sensitize them to wider political perspectives. This also has the effect of diminishing, in the eyes of the community, the occupational and political status of the majority of teachers who stay at classroom level.

Decline in Teachers' Economic and Social Status

Status decline for teachers occurred at the same time as countries were striving for universal primary education and as school systems were developing explosively. As school systems expanded, the number of teachers also grew and the communities that they served became more literate. The result was that teachers lost their capacity for fast upward social mobility and scarcity value as political brokers. The status of teaching also declined as a variety of other administrative and professional job opportunities opened up with better pay and conditions of service. The result has been to deflate teachers' political influence in society.

In the early days after independence, teachers' pay, benefits, and secure tenure were an attractive aspect of the job and contributed to the respect teachers were accorded. But, over time, pay and benefits became less attractive, especially relative to the private sector. In most of Sub-Saharan Africa even primary teachers used to be relatively well-off. But in recent times, especially during the harsh economic conditions of the 1980s, relentless inflation (and structural adjustment and related policies) eroded salaries (Edwards 1993; Zymelman 1993). Moreover, salaries often arrive late, forcing teachers to demean themselves asking for credit to meet their personal needs for cash.

In addition, as school systems have penetrated more deeply into disadvantaged and underserved areas, teachers' working conditions have generally deteriorated. They endure dismal, crowded classrooms with few books and teaching aids. They often live in substandard accommodations or have to lodge with local people. Many governments try to subsidize them with housing and other incentives, especially in more remote areas. But efforts to upgrade working and living conditions have limited impact through lack of operating funds and weak managerial capacity.

Furthermore, many teachers have to moonlight to try and make ends meet, taking second or third jobs or running small farms or shops. This activity sits uncomfortably with their dignity as high-status, local influentials. A poor social image, in turn, deters the most academically successful graduates from entering teaching. Parents see less competent individuals recruited, and many uncommitted individuals leave the schools as soon as they find jobs with better prospects. The public perception of schoolteaching as a noble, dedicated vocation has virtually disappeared and, with it, teachers' status as important and respected members of society.

Especially in English-speaking societies the question of teachers' status is articulated as whether they are professionals or technicians.[3] In developing countries, there are, of course, many trained and skilled teachers, but to refer to *the teaching profession* in these contexts is hardly at all appropriate,[4] given their relatively low occupational status, poor working conditions, lack of unity,[5] autonomy,[6] and self-regulation, the low "price" they can exact for their services.[7]

Some governments have introduced deliberate measures to "deprofessionalize" teaching, for example, by using the "barefoot doctor" model of China and Tanzania requiring teachers to work with unqualified community members as classroom aides. The same consequence, albeit perhaps unintended, followed from countries' adopting the prevailing mode of centralized planning and national curriculum development in pursuing the goal of "development" and "modernization" (Hawes 1979; Dove 1980c, 1983). Teachers were regarded by most planners as mere technicians, helping meet national educational goals by routinely transmitting the required curriculum content to pupils through the medium of the standard textbook. National examinations, used as selection mechanisms for the fortunate few to win a place in secondary schools or universities, further reinforced the role of teachers as mere technicians by forcing them to concentrate on routinely coaching their pupils.[8] When national curricular schemes failed to get implemented in classrooms and pupils' test scores and examination results remained poor, new instructional materials were developed in the false expectation that these would be more effective because they were "teacher-proof." Innovative delivery systems were devised, such as educational TV and radio schools. These appeared to reduce teachers to semicompetent aides in contrast to the experts at the center, who provided the technology and the content.[9]

Trends and Issues for the Future

Schoolteachers, then, have recently become much less involved in overt political action in contrast to the periods preceding and following independence in colonized developing countries. This has happened to the extent that they have suffered status decline, become servants of national-level bureaucracies of states in which power has been consolidated, and failed to create for themselves the conditions of autonomy and political influence that professionals enjoy. Though teachers' numbers have increased many times as a result of the expansion of school systems, they have not achieved their potential political influence in the wider society or in the educational process.

But what about the future? It is likely that civic and occupational policies will continue to discourage political activity in the wider society, both by individual teachers and by the teaching force as an occupational group. In the classroom, in contrast, teachers will continue to have political impact, in one way or another, and whether or not they intend to do so.

The new factors likely to reduce political activity by teachers include tighter screening of new recruits, feminization of the teaching force, and decentralization and privatization of school systems.

Screening

In countries where teacher supply exceeds requirements, the authorities have more control, in principle, over who becomes a teacher than in places where there are dire shortages. This gives more scope for the state to screen applicants for teacher training or teaching positions, to determine their political correctness, and to exclude those with undesirable political views.

In many countries teachers' salaries are such a burden on the public purse that the authorities cannot contemplate further expansion of the teaching force, even when local shortages exist. Therefore, the scope for tight screening is increased. In African countries that endured economic adjustment in the 1980s, Ghana for example, further expansion of the school system toward universal basic education has given way to consolidation and rationalization of the existing school system and a consequent reappraisal of teacher requirements. Guinea exemplifies a common situation where there has long been a massive oversupply of teachers in towns. In recent years, however, the authorities have managed partly to redress the imbalance without employing more teachers. They have attracted some 1,200 administrators and senior primary-trained teachers to the countryside by guaranteeing their current salaries, which are above the level paid to new primary-trained teachers.[10] In the process of negotiating redeployment, officials and parents were able to screen the teachers for their suitability to teach in particular localities.

Conditions in Indonesia, a much wealthier country, also now favor tighter screening of entry into teaching. The country has too many teachers overall, with major imbalances—large, overcrowded classes in popular, urban schools and very small classes in remote, sparsely populated rural areas and in inefficiently managed subdistricts in densely populated Java. The Indonesian government used revenues from the 1970s oil bonanza to give education to every child on all its thousands of islands. By the late 1980s, 27 million children were in school. Throughout the 1970s and 1980s, the policy had been to increase the number of teachers in preservice training in line with expansion. By 1990, primary-school enrollments had declined by about two million.[11] But some 250,000 surplus teachers had emerged from the training colleges and were unable to find teaching jobs, at least in favored locations. A serious problem of mismatch between total teacher supply and demand had emerged.[12] The government took advantage of the breathing space allowed by stabilized enrollment to change policies. It raised the entry requirements for primary-teacher training from secondary to college level. This had the effect of delaying by two years the output of qualified teachers. It also cut back the number of recruits into primary-teacher training from tens of thousands to only seven thousand. This sharp reduction in recruitment enabled the provincial authorities to screen applicants much more rigorously.[13] Teaching positions in government schools have always been allotted on the basis of further selection criteria at the provincial level, including knowledge of *Pancasila*, the five politico-ethical principles on which the Republic of Indonesia is established. By reducing the numbers of teacher trainees to only seven thousand a year, the authorities can now more efficiently screen out undesirable candidates, including free-floating political activists.

Conditions of teacher surplus alone, however, are not enough to allow the authorities to discourage, stifle, or stamp out political activism in the teaching force whenever they wish to do so. Cutting back on recruitment affects only new recruits, not those teachers already on the payroll. If most teachers are young, as in Indonesia, natural attrition is usually no higher than 4–6 percent annually. Serving teachers cannot be fired without cumbersome red tape, even if the state views them as politically undesirable.

Moreover, in countries where teachers are in surplus and underemployed, time is available for political activism outside the schools. Sri Lanka, for instance, has a long and proud tradition of public education, which people regard as their birthright. It is extremely unpopular to close even the smallest all-grade village school. The government is firmly committed to keeping schools open and so village schools often have as many as half a dozen teachers for only a handful of pupils. The government has also used teaching to absorb chronic youth unemployment and to reward political clients, a common practice across the developing world. These measures do little to enhance educational services because youths recruited off the streets and political appointees are rarely committed to the classroom. An unintended outcome is that political activists engage in communal politics under the umbrella of a teacher's salary and the teaching force is further politicized. The disruption can be serious in a poor country, such as Sri Lanka, suffering from communal conflict and sensitivity at grassroots level.

Nepal's case is similar in that many teachers are recruited through political patronage and are underemployed. In the country's remote areas, tiny schools continue to exist because the government wants to give basic education to all its dispersed and remote peoples. In these contexts throughout the developing world, teachers are left unsupervised for months, even years at a time, and political activists can use their time unfettered by the administrative requirements of being on the job in the classroom. Transfer to remote areas or denial of promotion as an administrative sanction to encourage conformity exists in theory but, as in Nepal, inspection and supervision are usually too costly, too labor-intensive, and too arduous to effectively ensure that all teachers are on the job throughout the school day, let alone that they are not involved in antiestablishment political activity.

Feminization

Teaching in developing countries outside Latin America and parts of Africa has traditionally been a male occupation, just as it was in earlier times in the industrialized world. So far this chapter has reflected reality by referring to teachers in the masculine. Indeed, in many countries, the term *schoolmaster* is still commonly used instead of a gender-neutral term. Politics, at least in the public sphere,[14] has also traditionally been a male pursuit. If teaching becomes increasingly feminized as is likely in many countries, will fewer teachers be involved in public arena forms of political activity?

In the 1970s and 1980s only one in three teachers at primary and secondary levels in Asia and Africa were women. As recently as 1985 women still comprised, respectively, only between 20 percent and 40 percent of the teaching force across the developing world (Herz et al. 1991).

Typically, officials still tend to view women teachers as administrative problems, complaining that they cluster in schools in urban centers, that they are often reluctant to serve in remote or rural areas away from parents or spouses, and that they are more frequently absent due to home and childrearing responsibilities. This is the case in Malaysia where the limited mobility of female teachers has led to shortages in rural schools. The country faces major teacher shortages, needing nearly 100,000 teachers over the next seven years in order to fill gaps created by expanding enrollments. Beginning in 1994 the government is doubling its intake of teacher trainees and is requiring that 40 percent should be men. The teachers' unions are against this quota, claiming that many male applicants are of inferior ability (Parkins 1993).

Malaysia is probably an exceptional case. Most other countries have policies to encourage women into schools. Women are entering the teaching force in increasing numbers, especially at primary level. Teaching has traditionally been one of the few modern occupations that is respectable for girls before marriage. And after marriage, the job suits wives and mothers with home responsibilities. In Nepal, for example, where cultural constraints on women have kept them from the classrooms, only one in three pupils are girls and only one in ten of the 100,000 teachers is female. With the recent drive toward universal basic education, a more adequate pool of qualified girls is now forming and government policies encourage recruitment into teaching.

Even in Muslim cultures, where women have been traditionally secluded, teaching is often open to women before other modern-sector occupations. In Bangladesh, until recently, primary teaching was almost exclusively for men. Many of them had been rewarded with a teaching or teacher-training position for their part in the liberation struggles nearly three decades earlier. They are now retiring and teaching vacancies exist. In the thrust to enroll more girls in school, the government is encouraging women recruits because parents are less anxious about the safety and reputation of their female children if teachers are women. Scholarships are awarded to qualified girls from poor homes to continue through secondary school. This widens the pool of educated girls available for selection into teacher training. In Pakistan similar policies are in place, but there is still a long way to go. Schoolteaching still has very low prestige among elite groups. Educated men prefer the military, police, and banking to teaching, and educated career women prefer medicine.

In some circumstances, the authorities may even prefer women teachers over men. In Sri Lanka between 60 and 70 percent of the teachers today are women, and there is equal gender participation in school. Officials tend to view the best qualified young male graduate teachers as a liability. This is because they tend to be fly-by-nights. They have a very high rate of attrition, leaving the classroom as soon as better prospects appear. This is a common occurrence with economic and social diversification. Men use teaching as a bridging occupation, while women, in general, have lower aspirations and expectations.

Sri Lanka's policy to recruit female teachers is mainly to improve the qualifications and quality of the teaching force in poorly served rural schools. The government has recently begun a scheme of preservice teacher training through six prestigious colleges of education. Most of the trainees are female secondary-school graduates. The intention is that, after qualifying, these high fliers will teach science or English for two years in a rural community. They are expected to become model teachers, setting an example of professionalism for their colleagues. There is some evidence that these young women recruits are startled and dismayed by the sharp difference in culture and environment between their own experience of good schools and the poor classrooms to which they are sent. Whether this will deter them from teaching as a career remains in balance, as does the question of whether, when exposed to gross inequalities in the physical condition of the country's schools and unconscionable differences in educational quality, they may become more engaged politically in order to change this situation.

Is it reasonable, then, to suggest that, as more women enter teaching, they will play less active political roles (in the public sphere) than men have done? In the short run, the answer is, probably yes. Women will still have main responsibility for home and children and, therefore, less time for other activities, just as working women in developed countries do. But in the longer term this may change over the years as younger women teachers become more senior.

Today's recruitment will mean more qualified and experienced women available for future promotion. Currently, women do not occupy managerial and supervisory positions in proportion to their numbers in the classroom (Davies 1987). In Indonesia, for example, over half the primary teaching force is female. In some provinces, such as Aceh, the vast majority of teachers are women. Except, however, in a few prestigious urban schools, women are rarely promoted to headships or supervisory and administrative positions. Overall, less than one in five primary school heads are women. If there is no glass ceiling and younger women teachers have ambition for positions of responsibility, the proportion of women managers with political savvy should grow. It is arguable that management experience could merely encourage bureaucratic conformism, just as it does for some men. Alternatively, it is just as likely that it could sensitize and train women in the politics of "Who Gets What,

When and How" in the school system and thereby give them a taste for community and national politics.

Decentralization

School system decentralization is a worldwide trend aimed at increasing educational quality, efficiency, affordability, and responsiveness to local needs and cultures (*The Forum* 1993). The question to be addressed here is whether it has an influence on teachers as political actors.

Certainly, the process of moving from centralization to decentralization is a political process *par excellence*, because it is about who is going to be in control and make critical decisions affecting the delivery of educational services—the school staff, a community, a provincial or regional bureaucracy, or a central administration. Decentralization tends to energize national and local interest groups to lobby for their share of the action and stirs hopes and fears among stakeholders and parents. Teachers' unions are just one of the interest groups that may become more active (as chapters in this volume by Ginsburg et al. and Lawn illustrate).

The configuration of control usually varies. It may mean that a central authority, such as a Ministry of Education, deconcentrates decision-making powers nearer to the school level of its own bureaucracy, say, to the school-district level. In this case, local administrators and school personnel report to the regional line-ministry officials. This has been happening gradually in the Philippines in recent years. Or it may be that autonomous local bodies, such as local governments, have prime responsibility for education, with school personnel reporting to local governments. This is the case for countries as far apart as India, Nigeria, and Mexico. It may be that nongovernmental organizations (NGOs) are given wider powers at local level, as, for example, in Botswana. In this case, teachers report to the NGO authorities—in Botswana, a church administration.

Powers are usually shared between center and locality. Central, or state authorities in a federal system, usually retain the right to a wide range of activities—to set national policies and plans, regulate, inspect and audit, and provide compensatory funding to prevent gross inequities in educational provision between rich and poor localities. Quite often the central or state government pays teachers and regulates their conditions of service, develops national curricula guidelines, national assessments and examinations, and manages teacher training. Local units usually have responsibility for school organization and day-to-day operations, curriculum implementation, selection of textbooks, pupil testing, grade promotion, and parental outreach.[15]

So what does all this mean for teachers' political lives? Decentralization is sometimes equated with "teacher power." If teachers are willing to assume responsibility for school and classroom activities, such as curricula, instructional materials, evaluation, and relations with parents, they are politically empowered because their role as purveyors of culture and as controllers of who climbs the educational ladder is more immediate and direct than when they merely carry out instructions from the center. Recent experience in the Colombian Escuela Nueva, where groups of schools and communities worked together to upgrade teaching and learning, showed how administrators and teachers could enhance the quality of educational services through decentralized powers of decision making (Schiefelbein 1992). But such empowerment seems to depend on whether school heads and teachers are well trained, confident, supplied with adequate funds for operations and maintenance, and have community support (Tangyong, Wahyudi, and Hawes 1989).

In contrast, if these conditions do not hold, teachers may feel less empowered to make vital decisions. This is especially so when clear principles and guidelines are lacking, which central supervision and accountability previously provided. Such principles and guidelines protect schools when they have to make difficult decisions about "Who Gets What." In any case, decentralization means teachers are more vulnerable to direct, local pressures and patronage. This is especially the case if they are paid, evaluated, promoted, and transferred by local administrators.

Recent experience in Paraguay shows that teachers felt disempowered and discouraged because decentralization was implemented too quickly without adequate preparation. Government officials endorsed the process as a means of making the education system more responsive to regional differences but it was implemented before the local administration had been set up. Teachers were fearful that they would have even more problems in receiving their paychecks than under the centralized system.

Private Schools[16]

Common sense would suggest that private-school systems provide more opportunities than public schools for teachers to engage in political activity. Why? Because, *prima facie*, private schools would have fewer bureaucratic regulations and more freedom. But is this so?

For an answer, some context is essential. In most developing countries outside Latin America, primary and secondary education is largely public. It has either been taken over by the state from religious foundations since independence, as in most of Sub-Saharan Africa, or has always been more or less a state monopoly by virtue of its importance for colonial powers or for independent governments using the schools for nation building. Public schools are an enormous burden on public resources, with teachers' compensation comprising 80–90 percent of the total recurrent budget in many cases. Privatization of the construction, financing, or management of public schools is now again being cautiously encouraged by governments and international funding agencies as a potentially effective means of increasing the affordability and sustainability of school systems or to enhance efficiency and responsiveness to human resource development needs.

Given this context, private schoolteachers, and, in particular, principals and heads, are likely to engage in political work in response, first, to their clients on whom their survival depends. Second, their focus is likely to be lobbying for resources and support from their own administrative system, the Catholic Church, for example, rather than from the Ministry of Education office. Third, they are likely to be absorbed in interschool rivalries over "Who Gets What." Such rivalries are likely to be more intense in a small, encapsulated, private school system than in a large, public system.

But are private schoolteachers likely to be more political in the society at large? The answer is probably not. First, private schools rarely provide the autonomy that their nongovernment status implies. In most countries they are heavily regulated by the state. Governments tend to bind them in regulation, supervision, and inspection. In the Philippines, for example, the government has recognized that private schools are more regulated than public schools. Red tape has frustrated attempts to increase the efficiency of private school administration, and so the government has begun to give these schools more autonomy. It is as yet too early to assess the impact on teachers.

In general—and this is counterintuitive—private-school status is likely to discourage individual teachers' political activity in the wider society. In most private schools they do not have secure tenure and may be averse to taking risks that would lose them their jobs. In addition, they need to be directly responsive to fee-paying parents. Private-school teachers may have less "free" time to become involved in community-based political activities, for instance, because they more typically have pastoral duties in addition to teaching. Where they are poorly paid, they may be busy with one job in a private school and another in a public school or some other setting. They may, for example, do private tutoring, a welcome source of additional income in countries as poor as Bangladesh and as relatively rich as Turkey. None of these situations leaves them much time for sustained political activity outside school hours.

To take Sri Lanka as an example again, private religious schools must teach the secular curriculum in return for state subsidies. This often means that teachers work longer hours than in public schools where religion is a relatively minor curricular element. Teachers have less time for out-of-school activity in general and any political work tends to be tied up with running the schools. Much of this is in response to the lobbying of parents or negotiating fees and mobilizing funds from them. For instance, in the elite private schools of Colombo, much of the principals' time is taken in allocating too few, precious school places to a long line of qualified applicants.

Classroom Pedagogies

The only area where teachers may inevitably remain politically active is in the classroom, through influencing their pupils. Teaching has always played a role in political-value formation or socialization but has had less direct impact on political behavior. The proposition is put forward somewhat cautiously here that specific modern teaching methods may change this, as an unintended outcome of official policies to improve the quality of education. They may stimulate in some teachers and some pupils a heightened political awareness, a sense of political efficacy, and even enhanced political skills. For those who do not have access, resentment and alienation may result.

Now that past pressures for school-system expansion are lessening, many countries have turned their attention to the difficult issue of quality enhancement. An important priority is improving teaching—in order to enhance pupil learning and to equip them with the knowledge, values, and skills demanded by contemporary society and the workplace. Experience has convinced policymakers that how teachers teach is a key ingredient for quality enhancement—just as much as what they teach—and that mere chalk-and-talk is not enough. Recent policies direct teachers to use teaching methods to encourage self-directed learning, stimulating pupils' capacities for problem solving, innovative thinking, and team collaboration—cognitive and personal qualities needed in the modern workplace and society. The important point is that these "active" pedagogies run counter to traditional, passive, authoritarian teaching modes and appear well suited to stimulating activist political values and skills.

These pedagogies are not new. They have been around in industrialized school systems, at least rhetorically, for nearly a century (Fuller 1991). What is new is that most developing country education policies have espoused them over recent years. This does not necessarily mean that they will be effective, any more than they have been a universal success elsewhere. For one thing, governments are constrained by lack of funds to retrain teachers. For another, some governments are conflicted about whether the new teaching methods are politically risky.

They are, therefore, content with superficial change or changes only in a few "model" schools.

There are a number of factors that may prevent the new teaching methods having deep effects. First, as is well recognized, school cultures generally transmit society's culture as much as they serve as change agents. So, authoritarian, patriarchal societies are likely to be mirrored by what goes on in classrooms, while democratic, egalitarian societies are likely to adopt the new pedagogies more easily.

Second, dissonance between the rhetoric of participatory teacher training and passive training methods is a widespread problem (Shaeffer 1993; Dove 1982). In courses for preservice trainees on the moral and social aspects of education and on the role of teachers in society, teacher trainers lecture in a manner which, at best, bores the trainees and, at worst, constitutes political indoctrination.

In 1991, a debate about this issue emerged in Poland as policymakers committed to making schools model more democratic institutions. The authorities were aware that teachers' training did not nurture democratic qualities and that teachers were not trained in participatory methods of institutional decision making. Moreover, the centralized administration of the education system sat uneasily with new representative councils for teachers, pupils, and parents, resulting in few opportunities for schools to fashion their own community life. Niemczynski (1993) concluded that, until teachers decide to take their training into their own hands and until the administration of schools reflects participatory involvement of all stakeholders, teachers are unlikely to be politically active role models for their pupils, as intended by the government.

The third reason why new pedagogies may not work as intended is that poor countries have difficulties in providing the essential funds and technical support to ensure that teacher training is really effective. In order to affect what goes on in classrooms more immediately and more directly, policymakers need to invest more in inservice teacher training, as well as preservice. Through inservice training, the teacher becomes a model, coach, guide, and resource to impart teaching-learning methods that help pupils learn independently, in a self-directed manner. In turn, trainers in inservice training programs need to move away from lecturing toward methods that give teachers experience in the approaches they are intended to use and model for their pupils. Good trainers and good training materials are not easy to find.

Recent experience in the Philippines is an example. There, a chronic problem of unevenness in teacher training standards has existed. In the 1980s, once teacher requirements stabilized, the government decided to improve preservice and inservice teacher training as part of an integrated strategy. Longer, more rigorous training standards and examinations were adopted as part of the 1983 "Policies and Standards for Teacher Education." For inservice professional development a system of localized Learning Action Cells was pioneered to provide serving teachers with regular on-site experience in developing their teaching skills and instructional materials, in a democratic environment and with support from specially trained facilitators and school heads. The scheme is noteworthy for attempting to provide experiential, participatory training. But, school heads and supervisors soon ran out of new ideas and new materials and teacher workshops became less frequent. As in many developing countries, the scheme struggles to survive in a resource starved and bureaucratic environment and risks being reduced to a ritual change in methods.

A final point and an important one. Activist pedagogy may prove counterproductive in encouraging a participatory, democratic, and consensual political culture. This is because it may exacerbate social cleavages. Such innovations tend to be adopted by highly trained and experienced teachers in the more privileged schools that have access to the necessary complementary libraries, reference materials, and science and technology equipment, and where school management is proactive in supporting teacher development. The average schools in developing countries have teachers with inferior opportunities for professional upgrading and classrooms starved of good teaching aids, books, and materials. Such conditions practically dictate chalk-and-talk teaching methods, and, in political terms they model authoritarian, passive cultures. They certainly cannot nurture problem-solving, imaginative, and innovative teaching and learning. Unless, therefore, governments find the will and resources to provide equitable access to the new pedagogy for all the teachers, stratification of schools may deepen. Teachers in an elite few schools will encourage political efficacy of an informed, networking, participatory nature, and a large majority will continue to encourage political passivity and a sense of inefficacy. Where such disparities are deep, they tend to be resented. This could lead to violence as a remedy—the last resort of those whose political skills and influence has failed them.

Conclusion

Three periods, roughly speaking, the 1920s–1950s, the 1960s–1970s, and the 1980s–1990s revealed distinct contexts for teachers' roles in the political life of developing countries. The first period, the days of prominence for the teacher-politician at national level, are over for good, because the colonial conditions that produced such men (not women) were unique and are unlikely to be replicated. Teachers' multiple roles in community development, which reached a peak in the second period, are also on the decline due to teachers' status decline vis-à-vis more literate populations and due to the nationalization and bureaucratization of school systems. By the third period, nationalization and bureaucratization of mass school systems had been completed. These processes helped stem development of politically powerful, autonomous teachers' professional organizations. Where teachers are politically involved, it is usually passively, as members of state-controlled unions or as clients of the bureaucracy.

For the future, some trends and issues were reviewed that might affect the range of teachers' political action. Tighter controls over teacher recruitment, where teacher surpluses exist, may inhibit political activity through more rigorous official screening of new recruits. However, none of the other trends in developing countries—feminization, decentralization, and privatization—suggests whether teachers, as individuals or as an occupational group, will remain a political force in the wider society.

The most interesting developments may well be inside the classroom. Teachers could become powerful political role models, helping to nurture politically informed, participatory, collaborative, and innovative citizens for the future. However, governmental ambivalence and scarcity of funds to invest in teacher training, combined with poor technical support and know-how, may lead to mere superficial change and confine the real benefits to privileged, elite schools. Where the state is fragile, where its political legitimacy is limited, and political capital is hard to retain and funds are scarce, government leaders are unlikely to risk equipping teachers with the new pedagogies. Widespread allegiance to the political regime and a well-funded education system may ultimately be prerequisites for deep changes in teachers' political roles in classroom and society.

NOTES

1. For detailed sources for this section see Dove (1979).

2. Due to the need to supply teachers to outlying communities, teachers without an ally in the education office would often be sent to remote schools, becoming lonely strangers in alien communities. The phenomenon of the "tourist teacher," hurrying home on holidays and frequently absent from school, is commonplace not only in Sri Lanka, but also in most countries where the teaching force is deployed nationally.

3. In the 1960s and 1970s there was an academic debate about whether teaching in the industrialized countries is a professional service. An ideal-type profession, according to the literature, is characterized by advanced training in specialized, theory-based skills, autonomous practice, and peer regulation of qualifications, entry standards, selection and discipline, such as enjoyed by doctors or lawyers in private practice (Etzioni 1969). Professionals, as individuals, have high social status and political influence. Professional groups are well positioned to act as pressure groups, pursuing their members'

interests by limiting entry, defining and protecting their markets, setting fees, and maintaining autonomy (Johnson 1972).

4. Nevertheless, in its 1966 *Recommendations Concerning the Status of Teachers*, UNESCO championed "the teaching profession" in order to advance teachers' welfare and status (Obanya 1993).

5. Teachers may undermine their potential political power as a professional interest group by internal fragmentation and demarcation. Secondary subject specialists dissociate themselves from primary teachers and school principals, and administrators form their own associations to distance themselves from the rank and file. As an occupational group with large numbers widely dispersed at the grassroots, teaching has political potential as a profession, but it generally lacks unity and leadership.

6. Bureaucratization, for example, has probably stifled irreversibly any genuine professional autonomy. As government servants working in bureaucratized school systems, teachers are required to follow official guidelines, including inculcating official patriotic, nationalistic, and civic values alongside basic mathematics, language, and science. Because of inadequate education and minimal training, many do not have the skills to develop their expertise and so keep rigidly to official guidelines. Isolated by classroom walls, they have little opportunity or vision to develop potentially influential peer networks and so miss out on political influence. And they are fearful to teach political values that might be interpreted as going against the official orthodoxy. This behavior reinforces their popular image as technical mouthpieces of the state and does little to endear them to parents and communities—particularly among minorities—who do not support the attempts of the state to use schools for political indoctrination.

7. Most teachers would probably like to be respected as professionals and to wield the political influence such status brings with it. But a contrary view is that teachers should not even try to model themselves on the inappropriate example of doctors and lawyers. Illich et al. (1977) claimed that professional groups are "disabling" rather than "enabling." This is because they try to monopolize knowledge and skills and create artificial "needs" to meet for which clients have to pay fees to "specialists." By these criteria, teachers should not, even in principle, aim to be professionals because they ought to be concerned, not with monopolizing knowledge and skills, but first and foremost, with transferring them to their pupils. This, so the argument goes, is what teaching is all about. While it is hard to counter this point, it does not, of

course, follow that teachers should be paid lowly salaries and work in suboptimal teaching environments.

8. Both curriculum and examination practices reduced teachers' potential professionalism because their training and classroom-based experience, judgement, creativity, and diagnostic skills to adapt the curriculum to meet individual learning needs were discounted.

9. In practice, however, for teachers who do want to exercise their skills flexibly and autonomously, there is still considerable scope. School supervision and classroom inspection are often inefficient because governments cannot afford intensive controls in mass school systems.

10. This initiative stemmed from the Minister of Education's energetic efforts. She personally toured the country, mobilizing communities to demand teachers for their empty classrooms.

11. By then population control policies also began to yield benefits. Fertility rates and then primary enrollment growth rates declined. By 1985 it was clear that the size of the seven-year-old cohort would stabilize for a decade and total enrollments would decline.

12. The primary teaching force in Indonesia in 1990 comprised over one million persons—a heavy burden in terms of salary and administrative costs. Most of the teachers were fairly young (between 25 and 40 years) and had security of tenure in government service. Teacher costs would inevitably rise over the next thirty years as salaries, and later, pensions increased.

13. Teacher training had usually been the last resort of secondary graduates who failed to enter university. The new, upgraded entry policy (after upper-secondary graduation) required all applicants to make teacher training their first choice, over and above university, and to compete in a special examination, separate from university entrance examinations. This was a controversial policy but it did send signals that teaching is a serious job for committed and qualified people.

14. As noted by Ginsburg et al. (1992), part of the reason the level of political activity is seen to be lower for women than men is because *politics* is often defined as a public sphere phenomenon (where women choose or are allowed to be less active) and as a phenomenon of the public and private sphere (where women choose or are allowed to become more active).

15. Much of the effectiveness of any type of decentralization depends on whether budgets or revenue-mobilizing powers are decentralized along with responsibilities for getting the job done. In the poorest countries of Sub-Saharan Africa, recent attempts to decentralize

have grounded on this rock. Central governments have not had the capacity to channel sufficient recurrent funds to school level and schools saddled with new responsibilities have not easily mobilized additional local resources in poor communities.

16. There are many types of private schools. Some are private by virtue of their sources of funding from charities, wealthy benefactors, or communities. Some are private because they are privately managed, even though they may derive at least some of their funds from public sources. Proprietary schools, religious and charitable foundations, and community-sponsored self-help schools are all private, though they may have little in common by way of culture, *modus operandi*, or clientele. Private schools are often supplementary to the public system, delivering a high-cost and high-quality education service to elites or a low-cost, low-quality, but accessible, service to the poor.

REFERENCES

Abernathy, D. B. (1969). *The Political Dilemma of Popular Education: An African Case*. London: Straford.

Abernathy, D. B., and Coombe, T. (1965). "Education and Politics in Developing Countries." *Harvard Educational Review* 35 (3): 287–302.

Batten, T. R. (1953). "The Status and Function of Teachers in Tribal Communities." In *The Economic and Social Status of Teachers*. World Year Book of Education, pp. 68–79. London: Evans.

Bude, U. (1983). "The Adaptation Concept in British Colonial Education." *Comparative Education* 19(3): 341–356.

Cole, P. (1975). *Modern and Traditional Elites in the Politics of Lagos*. London: Cambridge University Press.

Davies, L. (1987). "Research Dilemmas Concerning Gender and the Management of Education in Third World Countries." *Comparative Education* 23(1): 87–96.

Dibona, J. (1983). *One Teacher, One School: The Adams Reports on Indigenous Education in Nineteenth Century India*. New Delhi: Biblia Impex Private.

Dove, L. A. (1979). "Teachers in Politics in Ex-Colonial Countries." *The Journal of Commonwealth and Comparative Politics* 17(2): 176–191.

———. (1980a). "The Role of the Community School in Rural Transformation in Developing Countries." *Comparative Education* 16(1): 67–79.

———. (1980b). "The Teacher and the Rural Community in Developing Countries." *Compare* 10(1): 17–29.

———. (1980c). *Curriculum Reforms in Secondary Schools: A Commonwealth Survey.* London: Commonwealth Secretariat.

———. (1982). *Lifelong Teachers Education and the Community School.* Hamburg: UNESCO Institute for Education.

——— (1983). "Curriculum Development: The New Commonwealth." *International Journal of Educational Development* 3(2): 149–157.

———. (1986). *Teachers and Teacher Education in Developing Countries: Issues in Planning Management and Training.* London: Croom Helm.

Dreeben, R. (1968). *On What is Learned in School.* Reading, MA: Addison-Wesley.

Edwards, A. C. (1993). "Teacher Compensation in Developing Countries." In *Teachers in Developing Countries: Improving Effectiveness and Managing Costs,* edited by J. P. Farrell and J. B. Oliveira, pp. 43–52. Washington, DC: Economic Development Institute, World Bank.

Etzioni, A. (1969). *The Semi-Professionals and Their Organizations.* New York: Free Press.

The Forum for Advancing Basic Education and Literacy 2(3). (1993). "Education, (De) Centralization and the Democratic Wish." Cambridge, MA: Advancing Basic Education and Literacy (ABEL) Project.

Foster, P. J. (1965). "The Vocational School Fallacy in Development Planning." In *Education and Economic Development,* edited by C. A. Anderson and M. J. Bowman, pp. 142–156. Chicago: Aldine.

Foster, P. J., and Sheffield, J. R. (Eds.). (1974). *Education and Rural Development.* World Year Book of Education. London: Evans.

Fuller, B. (1991). *Growing-Up Modern: The Western State Builds Third-World Schools.* New York: Routledge.

Ginsburg, M., Kamat S., Rajeshwari, R., and Weaver, J. (1992). "Educators/Politics." *Comparative Education Review* 36(4):417–445.

Harber, C. (1984). "Schooling for Bureauracy in Nigeria." *International Journal of Educational Development* 4(2): 145–154.

Herz, B., Subbarao, K., Hebb, M., and Raney, L. (1991). *Letting Girls Learn: Promising Approaches in Primary and Secondary Education.* Washington, DC: World Bank Discussion Paper 133.

Hawes, H. (1979). *Curriculum and Reality in African Primary Schools.* London: Longman.

Hodgkin, T. (1961). *African Political Parties: An Introductory Guide.* Harmondsworth, England: Penguin.

Holsinger, D. B., and Theisen, G. L. (1977). "Education, Individual Modernity and National Development: A Critical Appraisal." *The Journal of Developing Area*s 11: 315–334.

Illich, I. D., Zola, K., McKnight, J., Caplan, J., and Sheiker, H. (1977). *Disabling Professions.* London: Boyars.

Inkeles, A. (Ed). (1974). *Education and Individual Modernity in Developing Countries.* Leiden, Netherlands: Brill.

International Labor Organization (ILO/UNESCO). (1977). *Freedom of Association and Procedures for Determining Conditions of Employment: The Public Service.* Report 7(1 and 2), 63rd Session, Geneva.

Johnson, T. (1972). *Professions and Power.* London: Macmillan.

Kelly, G. P. (1978a). "Colonial Schools in Vietnam: Policy and Practice." In *Education and Colonialism*, edited by P. G. Altbach and G. P. Kelly, pp. 96–121. New York: Longman.

———. (1978b). "Schooling and National Integration: The Case of Interwar Vietnam." *Comparative Education* 18(2): 175–196.

Lasswell, H. (1936). *Who Gets What, When and How.* New York: Smith.

Lewis, L. J. (Ed.). (1962). *Phelps-Stokes Report on Education in Africa.* Abridged version. London: Oxford University Press.

Middleton, J., Ziderman, A., and Van Adams, A. (1993). *Skills for Productivity: Vocational Education and Training in Developing Countries.* New York: Oxford University Press for World Bank.

Morris, B. (1977). *Some Aspects of the Professional Freedom of Teachers: An International Pilot Inquiry.* Paris: UNESCO.

Morris-Jones, W. (1957). *Parliament in India.* Philadelphia: University of Philadelphia Press.

Niemczynski, A. (1993). "Between Intellectual Chaos and Emotional Confusion: Hopes for Desirable Schools in Poland." *Newsnotes*

(The International Network of Principals Centers, Harvard University), 7(1): 6–7.

Obanya, P. (1993). "The Concerns of Teachers' Unions for Quality Education in Developing Countries." In *Teachers in Developing Countries*, edited by J. P. Farrell and J. B. Oliveira, pp. 207–217. Washington, DC: Economic Development Institute, World Bank.

Oppenheim, A. (1975). *Civic Education in Ten Countries*. New York: Harper & Row.

Parkins, G. (1993). "Malaysia Improves Sex Quotas on New Intakes of Teachers." *The Times Higher Education Supplement*. 15 October.

Robins, R. S. (1976). *Political Institutionalization and the Integration of Elites*. Beverly Hills: Sage.

Schiefelbein, E. (1992). *Redefining Basic Education for Latin America: Lessons to Be Learned from the Colombian Escuela Nueva*. Paris: International Institute for Educational Planning, UNESCO.

Shaeffer, S. (1993). "Participatory Approaches to Teacher Training." In *Teachers in Developing Countries*, edited by J. P. Farrell and J. B. Oliveira, pp. 187–200. Washington, DC: Economic Development Institute, World Bank.

Shipman, M. (1972). *Education and Modernization*. London: Faber.

Sinclair, M. E., and Lillis, K. (1980). *School and Community in the Third World*. London: Croom Helm with Institute of Development Studies.

Soemardi, S. (1956). "Some Aspects of the Social Origin of Indonesian Decision-Makers." *Transactions of the Third World Congress of Sociology 3*: 13–48.

Tangyong, A. F., Wahyudi, G. R., and Hawes, H. (1989). *Quality Through Support for Teachers: A Case Study from Indonesia*. London: Office of Education Research and Development, Ministry of Education and Culture, Republic of Indonesia with Development of International and Comparative Education, University of London Institute of Education.

Thomas, R. M. (1970). "Who Shall Be Educated? The Indonesian Case." In *The Social Sciences and the Comparative Study of Educational Systems*, edited by J. Fisher, pp. 159–182. Scranton, PA: International Textbook Co.

Thompson, A. R. (1983). "Community Education in the 1980s: What Can We Learn from Experience?" *International Journal of Educational Development 3*(1): 3–17.

Vulliamy, G. (1981). "Combining a Constructive Rural Orientation with Academic Quality High School Outstations in Papua New Guinea." *International Journal of Educational Development* 1(2): 3–19.

Zolberg, A. (1966). *Creating Political Order: The Party-States in West Africa.* Chicago: Rand-McNally.

Zymelman, M. (1993). "Factors Affecting Teachers' Salaries." In *Teachers in Developing Countries: Improving Effectiveness and Managing Costs*, edited by J. P. Farrell and J. B. Oliveira, pp. 43–52. Washington, D.C.: Economic Development Institute, World Bank.

Teachers and Politics in Central Eastern Europe

Peter Darvas and Maria Nagy

Introduction

The social and political conditions of the teaching profession are central subjects in the educational political arena and in the mass media. For politicians and for educational experts they emerge as rather complex and contested issues influenced by internal educational considerations, traditions, and processes, as well as by external economic, cultural, and purely political conflicts. This complexity attracts intensive research; as Broadfoot et al. (1987, p. 287) argue, "teaching is perhaps the largest single focus for educational research activity."

However, although it is a frequent focus of scholars in the North American and West European educational literature, the teaching profession has hardly appeared as a subject of research in the countries of the ex-Soviet bloc. One reason for this lack of research may be the fact that teachers were not typically placed on the central political agenda between 1945 and 1989 in countries such as Bulgaria, East Germany, Hungary, and Poland. Teachers, as actors who may have represented some danger in terms of control, were replaced in the agenda and in the professional literature by the more impersonal issue of pedagogy. Teachers, however, could become important actors in the politics of societies that are contemplating various forms of pluralism.

The revolts in what used to be the Soviet bloc reoriented policy makers' and scholars' attention towards the social and political environment of teaching. Teachers, as the largest single group of intellectuals in these countries, were driven by their own and by others' political ambitions to the center of the upheaval. Teachers' groups were not only active in the political mobilization and in the efforts of reforming society, but they also raised their own issues to the level of the mainstream political agenda. Democratizing schools, redesigning curricula, reforming the economic conditions of education, decentralizing administration, and the emerging new unions became everyday subjects of debates. However, the activism and optimism, regarding these goals soon diminished after conflicts became increasingly visible. It appears now that the limits of more democracy, more decentralization, more professionalism, and more effectiveness may not be explained purely by ideological or geopolitical constraints. Reform proposals, like political programs, often reflected compromised positions at the expense of earlier radicalism. To understand the meaning of compromises, we should consider the changing teaching profession in particular as an integrated part of the traditions and reforms of the educational system in general.

The complexity of the reform dynamics attracted more and more scholars to the region of Central Eastern Europe (CEE), but it also motivated them to limit themselves to descriptive reporting of events that sometimes followed unpredicted patterns. Thus, these reports soon became outdated if not obsolete. This problem suggests that observers should adapt a more structural analysis, although at times this could be more abstract or hypothetical.

This chapter focuses on the effect of the social and political transformation in the CEE countries on educational reforms and on the fate and role of the teaching profession. We consider dynamics of the broader social and political system and those within the teaching profession to be interdependent; each shapes and is shaped by the other.

Alternative Analytical Foci

There are three possible analytical foci that can be useful for studying our subject: changes in the teaching profession in the western[1] world, general social and political transformation in CEE countries, and educational changes in CEE countries. A focus shaped by considering changes in the teaching profession in the western world offers a broad set of terminologies, research questions, and related literature. Comparative studies have, for instance, analyzed variations in institutional forms of teacher training, specific labor issues, teachers' social status, satisfaction and compensation, professionalization, political attitudes, and participation (e.g., Poppleton 1990; Poppleton et al. 1987, Garrett & Jimenez 1992). These studies typically either use public-opinion polls, or gather comparable data directly through questionnaires of target groups.

As rich as this analytic focus is in terms of terminology and research literature, it also reflects some methodological problems when applying it to the CEE region. The main problem we face is what may be called, "terminological imperialism." Research that uses a conceptual framework the way it was developed by Western scholars for the analysis of the Western societies, would, by definition, set *a priori* indicators, focusing on particular aspects of the subject. These indicators, then, would reflect variations without considering differences in the political and social environment or in the educational system. Thus, the studies may be unable to explain the reasons for these variations among the examined indicators. A good example of these difficulties is shown in the study by Garrett and Jimenez (1992), which analyzed teachers' attitudes toward the concept of problem-solving methods. The researchers found "remarkable" similarities in the attitudes of teachers functioning in these two different educational systems of Spain and England, and concluded that these similarities must be explained by broader, unspecified, contextual features shared by the two nations.

When making comparisons between countries with radically diverse political systems—for instance, between Western and Eastern European societies—differences beyond the obviously differing political conditions are rarely found or explained. The most surprising outcomes of such research are usually the discoveries that teachers and their social conditions are not as different in the East from those in the West as may have been expected. Gershunsky and Pullin (1990) argue that the similarities they observed in their comparison of the Soviet and British systems, for example, indicate that the two systems are converging toward each other. However, such findings may simply be distorted by the lack of a systemic analysis. Wisniewski, for example, joined an ambitious research project that quantitatively analyzed job satisfaction of teachers internationally, but did not attempt to offer an explanation that would have taken into consideration the effect of the Polish national setting on his results. He considered the project to be a pilot that needed be followed by later research that would be "adequate to Polish conditions" (Wisniewski 1990).

The second possible analytic focus for examining CEE teachers' work and lives would be directed by the general social and political transformation of CEE societies. This literature is becoming quite rich; however, its analytical quality and orientation are very diverse. This focus typically challenges the researchers to look at the effect of general changes on teachers in issues such as employment and unemployment, changes in the workload of teachers, teachers as agents of change, and teachers' rights and organizations.

There are two separate, although not analytically independent problems with this context. First, the exclusive focus on the effects of outside changes on teachers does not reflect the effects of internal dynamics of education and long-term traditions of education on teachers. Second, we may not understand why and how general issues (e.g., democratization, marketization, pluralism, and decentralization) have a different appearance in policies and political strategies that are initiated by agents representing the interests of teachers or other actors of the educational scene. Educational policies and participatory strategies of educational actors are also determined by rationales that are sometimes independent from the broader social and political conditions.

The third analytic focus for studying CEE teachers is one that is oriented by the educational changes in CEE. This focus allows us to shed new light on issues that the previous two analytical foci may not help to explain: why education had different dynamics than its general social, political, and economic environment. For instance, in international comparisons, education in CEE proved to be successful (in terms of "producing" relatively high levels of student achievement on standardized tests), while the economy or other spheres of social policy did not stand out in a positive light when compared to countries in other regions. It must be noted, though, that in other perspectives, including the efficient use of public resources in education, or in the effectiveness in terms of employment competencies, the performance of education was far less successful. Nevertheless, the question remains regarding why education seems to have preserved some historical traditions and long-held structural features more effectively than other spheres of the political and cultural environment. This approach also helps us to understand the possibilities and limits in building up new forms of professional control and participation, the effects of changes in the administration, structure, and curriculum on the teaching profession and on its self-organization and representation.

Teachers are not to be considered as passive subjects of institutional or structural changes, especially during periods of profound political activism. Instead, we should take Broadfoot's (1990) directive to bring together objective and subjective sources of influence. We need to see how educational reform strategies affect the conditions and roles of teachers and what strategies the teachers themselves use to become active participants in these reforms. The assumption we take in this chapter is that the position of teachers as a professional group in newly formulated societies will mainly depend on: (1) developments within the educational systems and (2) the corporate and individual strategies of teachers as actors within education and within the society more generally.

The main problems we face with this approach are twofold. First, the extant literature available is very limited. Research and communication in CEE mostly ignored the role of the teaching profession within the educational scene. There is a lack of systematic research, information is scattered, and the scholarship that can be located varies considerably in analytical depth. As a special source of information, however, we may rely on some of the recent results of comparative, Eastern and Western German studies of teachers (Schmidt and Schultz 1990). While this type of comparative analysis combines the advantages of our first and third possible analytic foci (employing Western terminology and conceptual frameworks together with broad knowledge of Eastern educational developments), its relevance unfortunately seems to be rather restricted, the case of Germany being very special among post-Soviet bloc countries. A second limitation of this source is that the research was conducted soon after the collapse of the Communist regime, and thus the observations might not represent a new, stable portrait of the role and conditions of the teaching profession.

As a result, we needed to make some compromises in our analysis presented in this chapter. Our findings may be partly hypothetical and too abstract. Consequently, our main purpose is to challenge further communication and research in the subject, which will hopefully follow and improve our suggested framework. Most of our findings and empirically discernible information are from Hungary, for two reasons. First, reform in education here began earlier than in other CEE countries of the region; therefore, the main trends—limits in implementation and contradictions—are more visible and, as a result, more frequent research has been undertaken on the subject than in other countries. Furthermore, our national origin and our ability to read and speak the native language provide us with access to more information about Hungary than for any other countries in the region.

Our suggested approach requires that we analyze recent changes in light of historically developed traditions of educational system, the influence of the previous regimes, changes in the role and conditions of the teaching profession, and the emergence of various forms of political participation. Following this, we identify some important issues in the present dynamics in the educational system, the changes in administration and control, and in the educational structure. We consider these elements to be crucial in influencing the transformation of the role and conditions of teachers in the post-

Communist societies. Finally, we analyze the strategies and forms of participation and changes in the political attitudes of teachers as actors in both the educational policy making and the broader political arena.

Historical Developments

The analysis of the present conditions should take into consideration the effects of the past developments of the teaching profession. These events often represent sources of intrinsic limits of reforms in the midst of high public expectations. The educational systems of CEE countries emerged in relation to continental European traditions. Most directly, the structure, content, and pedagogical values of education were politically and culturally influenced by the Prussian system of education even more perhaps than in other parts of the world.[2] This influence, however, decreased dramatically with the role Germany played in World War II, and with the military defeat of that country. The military and political victory of the Allies brought about changes within the microsystems of Western European societies as well. After World War II, these societies increasingly adopted the values and traditions of the American education system, and modern child-centered pedagogy, based on Deweyan traditions, which had been less influential before in Europe, gradually gained ground over old Herbartian traditions in the Northern and Western societies of Europe. Meanwhile, CEE countries that came under Soviet rule, less able and perhaps less willing to adopt the (less-developed) Soviet model, preserved much of the Herbartian traditions of pedagogy in the dominant methods, school climate, and in the elitist, hierarchical nature of educational structure.

After the Communist takeover the educational policies of the governments had quite profound effects on the profession. First, they mobilized teachers to directly participate in restructuring the society and the economy. Teachers, as the largest group of intellectuals, were to take an active part, for instance, in the nationalization of agriculture and the organization of cultural and political programs designed to socialize the masses. As professionals, they were to serve the values of the official government and party ideology through their pedagogy.

Second, and more important, the Soviet type of control throughout the region uniformly blocked the teaching profession from outside influence. Information from outside of the Eastern bloc about pedagogical innovation and other aspects of professional development was excluded. Thus, although the most aggressive aspects of ideological-political control soon decreased or became ineffective, pedagogical innovation was to be stimulated exclusively by ideas within the region. The possibilities for teachers to innovate—or, in CEE terminology, to carry out school experiments—were not totally excluded from school life; they were even encouraged from time to time. However, the infrastructure for school innovation had not been established. In most Western societies educational development, in the 1960s and 1970s can be exemplified by the emergence of massive educational support systems, centers for innovation, curriculum development evaluation and research, a booming textbook market, and in-service training. In the meantime, CEE teachers badly lacked efficient professional support. Moreover, there were no rewards for efforts to innovate, and teachers' workloads were so tightly regulated that teachers had practically no time or capacity for unscheduled activities.

As for the main goals of education, professional priorities were, on the whole, subordinated to political determination. Above all, education had to serve the direct needs of economy. With the Communist takeover, the structure of programs was reoriented toward the sciences and mathematics, at the expense of humanities and languages, mostly foreign languages at lower levels, and towards vocations at the expense of liberal arts and traditional professions at upper levels. Due to the strange combination of these changes, forced into the system from above, and the ability of the profession to preserve old Herbartian traditions on the bottom, CEE countries, like Poland or Hungary, produced relatively effective educational programs, particularly in terms of promoting pupils' achievement in subjects of mathematics and the sciences. Moreover, an orientation toward specialization and vocationalism raised the formal importance of qualifications, and the number of vocational degrees increased significantly.

These tendencies suggest that the importance of education was great. Yet, we should take into account the formality of this role. The increase of the educational production was administered with low capital investment and was, instead, to be achieved through tightened centralized control. Bureaucratic institutions and professional associations alike were re-established with the assignment that they should serve the politically determined goals. Teachers' associations were unified and centralized; their focus was reoriented toward the members from the contested arena of policy making; and thus they became institutions of control instead of representation.

The growth of educational output had different dynamics in the CEE region than that of the dominant pattern in the West. In Western Europe educational expansion was gradual and can be seen to be more organic. The increase in the enrollments at a given level was generally preceded by a similar or even faster rate of growth in the number of graduates from the previous level of education. The expansion in Western Europe may also be considered organic in the sense that it involved a relatively stable educational administration and a profession that had established corporate structures and identities. In contrast, the rapid increase of educational output in the CEE region greatly inflated the system, subordinated to extraeducational, politically driven administration and needs, and excluded the consideration of educational standards or quality concerns.

Teachers' Work and Lives in Communist Regimes

The centralized control over education also included official versions of acceptable values and uniform patterns in the identity for the teaching body. There was an effort to create a homogenous identity among teachers, adopting the image of the traditional "volk-school" teacher, which many viewed as incompatible with the academic profile of the teachers in the traditional gymnasia. It can be best characterized by some features of the profession, already mentioned earlier: an extended professional role in which direct political activities could be included; the acceptance of centralized and bureaucratic control at the expense of professional autonomy; and the accommodation to poor professional support. In practice, however, some features of the Herbartian academic tradition survived, such as a strong insistence on pupil achievement and strict subject teaching. All this produced a strange mixture of professional identity, an ambiguity that had never been explicit among other ambiguities of the systems of state socialism. As much as the political subordination of education affected the position of teachers, it also made it unnecessary to separate their corporate identity from their state-controlled duties and capacities. No conflicts were manifested, and hardly any professional difficulties were discussed publicly. As Bathory observes (1990, p. 9): "In the centralized system the educator guild found itself in a condition of split personality. [Educators] conceded—as others did—their diminished liberty and professional autonomy. It became clear that no one needed their professional opinion."

Teachers as employees had the status of state civil servants and were forced to yield their educational standards to outside interests. For instance, when labor needs required increased student graduation, it became the teachers' duty to decrease the proportions of failing exams or grades. Research was established to serve the states' educational policies, unlike in most Western countries, where it at least partially provided disciplinary support for the profession in school practice, curriculum development, and evaluation. The labor conditions of teaching meant that teachers were deprived economically and socially as well. Average teachers' salaries were set at the lowest of the intellectual professions, which were already low compared to similar professions elsewhere in Europe. Furthermore, teachers felt denigrated by the amount of paperwork and bureaucratic procedures unbefitting a professional group. These nonteaching roles were reflected in their "professional identity," deemed by some teachers more a "trade" than a profession.[3] As employment, education offered a contradictory career for teachers.

The centralized control maintained high requirements in terms of formal qualifications. For the first time, teachers' training programs for all levels of schooling became formally part of higher education. The quality of training, however, remained unequal.

Teachers had broad responsibilities at individual and school levels, and, therefore, their self-identification was associated with the enormous problems schools were facing. Their duties were defined in a broad way from the beginning of the Communist regime, by having been assigned to a wide range of tasks related to transmitting ideology and participating in other activities inside and outside the schools. Nevertheless, even after the gradual de-Stalinization, their role was complicated by the increasing ambiguity of pedagogic values. Since neither the Communist values nor the ideologically determined educational principles could be operationalized, the educational activities of teachers—below the bureaucratic surface—remained anything but formal. Their pedagogical difficulties had begun to increase as early as the 1960s, when the political regimes of the region were compelled to consolidate their power and make some general social compromises of different scales. Through these compromises the ideological content and control of education coexisted with traditional functions and contents, thus increasing the role of the teachers in both pedagogic and instructional senses.

First, teachers had to cope with increasing gaps between the values of the Communist ideology—which always remained a centrally controlled part of the curriculum—and the ever-changing individual sociological and psychological difficulties of pupils. As an official school opening article commented: "The educator desperately tries to correct what the family and the society ruined. However, he (she) may not count for support and acknowledgment but criticism and adversity for this" (Medvegy 1990, p. 8). These conflicts required immediate pedagogical responses and ever increasing responsibilities from the teachers. Although teachers had a few ideas about how to tackle the increasing problems of socialization, they were hardly ever discussed in the professional media of the countries.

Second, teachers were given greater responsibilities by the increasing competition among students to get into elite forms of schooling. Despite the declared principle of equality, the educational systems in the CEE region reflected manifest and latent effects of tracking, early selection, and unequal schooling. As Bathory (1990, p. 10) puts it: "During the last forty years the educational administration and pedagogy denied the significance of differentiation, and it tried with a voluntaristic theory and practice to create educational equality. The result: the inequality did not decrease but grew." Teachers' responsibilities were greatly increased, especially by the in-school forms of selection, the lack of external examination systems, everyday grading, and the burden of decisions, all of which basically determined the pupils' educational and working career at an early age. Although these tasks are not dissimilar from other educational systems where selection begins at early age, teachers' responsibility in CEE nations was exacerbated by the low proportion of general education at the secondary level, by the competition for admission to better gymnasiums, and by the extremely low proportion of students who were admitted to full-time programs in higher education. Furthermore, these selection processes—with the exception of the entrance exam for higher education—were not controlled by open tests, giving more significance to the grading practices of teachers.

These tasks and responsibilities helped teachers to maintain a curious status, one that appeared in the image of being an overburdened and uncompensated duty—but one which remained crucial in the lives of students. Since teachers did not enjoy particularly high prestige, they needed some professional legitimacy, which was oddly given by the external bureaucratic control. This administative structure was both a burden for teachers and a kind of protection, or assurance of stability from unexpected, uncontrolled forms of evaluation and criticism.

The broad set of expectations that included responsibilities of socialization and selection is similar to what Broadfoot and her colleagues (Broadfoot and Osborne 1988; Broadfoot et al. 1987) defined as broad definition of responsibility or what Hoyle (1980) classifies as extended professionalism. However, they describe this professional attitude as being influenced by endogenous processes in educational systems with predominantly local or community control, whereas in CEE the broad definition exists despite centralized control and external influences.

This curiosity may be explained by the structural ambivalencies of the CEE educational systems. Whereas in the systems, described by Broadfoot and Hoyle, the broad definition of responsibilities is connected to a comprehensive ideal of schooling, in CEE the school structure remained traditionally elitist. Beyond the system that was based on the general education for eight to ten years, there were diverse and conflicting expectations of comprehensive schooling versus academic competition. Whereas the official ideologies praised the values of the "volkschool-educators," parents pressured the teachers for more academic-type provisions.

Recent and Future Developments

What has occurred in education since the fall of the Stalinist-Communist regimes and what are the prospects for the future? The most often quoted and praised element of education is the decreasing role of the state in educational control in general, and the devolution of the centralized educational administration in particular. However, the directions of change are far from clear, as different statutory actions and other legislative measures have various, and sometimes contradictory, effects, and policies aimed at introducing new ways of control have had little time for implementation.

Furthermore, these legislative and policy measures are not directed toward a newborn profession; instead they are aimed at a profession that embodies a composite burden of predetermined skills, identities, and prestige. For teachers the various reforms in administation are not straightforward or clear in their effects, for changing administrative patterns signify changing teachers' interests in administrative control. In fact, several ways are apparent to depart from the monolithic, centralized administration of governance that subordinated both lay and professional interests to those of the state bureaucracy. Some of these departures were not necessarily instigated by the collapse of the Stalinist-Communist regimes, but had been initiated before.

As the process of de-Stalinisation consolidated politics, new reforms were introduced throughout the region that resulted in delegating some administrative tasks to lower and regional levels of the state bureaucracies. Although these processes varied from country to country, they helped, in all cases, the bureaucracies rationalize their activities and get rid of the most rigid ideological constraints. However, regionalization of administration did not modify the basic nature of control, which was still bureaucratic and rigid, with communication and control remaining top-down in nature.

As the societies experiment with various types of autonomies and shared power relations, previous developments would gain new significance. The professionalized and de-ideologized regional educational administrative capacities may be employed by two alternative arrangements of control: (1) An effective administrative system may assist the reestablishment of strong central control, as it seems to do in Poland. In this case, the local government may be employed to implement the reforms of central political forces. (2) A radical decentralization of public administration may also result in increased community control, as it does, for the moment, in Hungary. In this case the strengthened municipalities would inherit some the administrative expertise of the previous regional councils' bureaucracies.

There are several possible scenarios that could increase pluralism in the educational sphere. The removal of centrally determined and imposed curriculum increases the professional influence of teachers. Schools may also gain more autonomy in determining their own programs and schooling strategies. Both schools and local self-governing bodies can have more flexibility if the previously predominant legal restrictions are replaced by various means of financial regulations. Furthermore, lay control may also be by individual choice, in case the educational systems move toward "market" coordination.

For teachers, the direction of decentralization could bring about contradictory results. Increased control in the hands of regional municipalities could mean the loss of job and employment security, which earlier had been guaranteed by the state for the simple reasons that municipalities would become the arena of competing local interests, including health, education, infrastructure, and so on. Municipalities could also try to manipulate the nominations for principals and other positions for local political reasons. Increased professional responsibility may cause fears for teachers who already feel overburdened by extracurricular duties and for whom new professionalism could mean new liabilities. CEE teachers may find it more convenient to comply with the bureaucratic duties they have, since widespread administration and interferences may substitute for professional legitimacy. This assumption follows the logic of Lortie's (1975) analysis, which argues that teachers are socialized into a subordinate position in the system where bureaucratic aspects dominate professional ones.

Finally, decentralization of educational administration may not suit the interests of some central political forces. Since the expectation of reform is brought about by political transformation, the struggle for political control and substantiation of political, ideological claims by certain parties could reinforce their bid for centralized administration. Szebenyi (1992) argues that the main question is whether the new political system constructs a new ideological monism that replaces the old one or allows the establishment of ideological pluralism. Strong candidates favor the first, among them some clerical groups and some nationalist political parties, which would like to control where the new educational system is heading. For teachers, these developments could naturally lead to the reinforcement of strong control over curriculum and teaching.

It is far too early to identify clear trends in change of control and administration in the reforming countries. One reason for this difficulty is the delay in legislative actions that would establish the institutional system of administration. The delay is not only caused by obvious power struggles between emerging political forces, but also by the lack of common codes, political rituals, and consensual communication forms for

negotiations, and conflict resolutions within the parliaments and
in other political forums. The other reason for the lack of clear
trends is the contradictions and opposing trends within the
legislative and statutory actions. New laws and regulations
addressing different but overlapping aspects of education
prescribe contradictory authorities, rights, and responsibilities.

A good example of these contradictions is the competing
concepts of control as they appear in the new Hungarian legal
codes, which were enacted, regulating subsequently the
institutional structure of local government, public employment,
and education. One of the early legislative actions was the local
government act, which was enacted during the euphoria of the
democratic transformation and gave unprecedently large powers
to local governments. It set a high level of local autonomy that is
supported by a lump-sum financing system and is to be
controlled through codes of public accountibility. This model,
usually observed in countries with Anglo–Saxon traditions, is
not totally unknown in Hungary, but it differs from the broader
institutional traditions that are typical in region. The public
administrative system in this region usually follows the German
traditions of state-governmental administration and strong
dependency from the center. These traditions appear more
clearly in the later-issued Public Employment Act, which assigns
strict dependency and protection to the public employees.

Finally, in 1993, the Parliament enacted the new Education
Act, which offers a mixture of centralizing and decentralizing
measures. Although the authority of local governments is being
reinforced, some of the state support is to be earmarked by the
government. In terms of curriculum and other substantial issues,
the Act sets similarly mixed institutional arrangements. New, so-
called "Regional Offices of Inspectors" are to be created, serving
central governmental interests, but a National Framework of
Curriculum could potentially assign a limited range of
standards, allowing some flexibility for the schools and teachers.

This mixed picture suggests that education will most likely
be a shared responsibility of several bureaucratic, political, and
professional actors. The new administrative schemes imply that
the assertive strategies of old actors, like the national
government, have to be modified so that a new balance between

the participants can be set in the long term. At the same time the new administrative schemes depend on the involvement of some actors, notably teachers, who may not yet be ready to expand their capacities of assertion, representation, and control.

Changing Forms and Strategies of Teacher Participation

Since 1989, many analysts have focused almost exclusively on short-term educational reform issues, those imported mostly from the political and economic environment of education, such as the de-ideologization of curriculum and the establishment of private schools. Although analysis of such trends is important, as indicators of the content-oriented trends for change, it is the activities of educational actors through new and revived channels of influence that may prove to be the decisive force in the future.

The previous sections showed that despite the apparent universality of the new ideas—democratization, decentralization, marketization, de-ideologization—they have many contested versions, contradictory effects, and internal limits. Consequently, the effect of political and social changes on education in general, and on teachers in particular, have been received ambiguously by teachers themselves. As Bathory (1990, p. 9) comments: "In the guild of educators one may find the impotency with the innovation, the trust with the doubts, the approval of reforms with the dissapproval of them." Since school has historically been a conservative social institution, it responds to calls for change with considerable inertia. An example of this reaction has been shown by Nagy (1985), who studied the reaction of teachers to the 1985 Act on Education in Hungary. She found that although the Act provided some autonomy for teachers, a great majority of them considered the move unfavorable, because it brought more responsibility, and typically characterized the measure as "A Command for Autonomy."

Another reason why teachers are not always supportive of major changes in education might be found in the diverging professional and political judgement of educational processes and inefficiencies of the system. Earlier, teachers were not part of the official policy making. However, they could informally influence the outcomes of policies through their daily actions in classrooms. No effective control system could regulate these spontaneous processes of compromising between policy and practice. Even institutionalized forms of communication were lacking. Now, these forms are urged by all actors of policy making, and, at least in Hungary, they are being created. However, means and ways of communication among actors are hindered by the lack of experience and skills. Teachers and politicians often fail to understand each other's point or know how to reach common agreements. Despite the short period, the emergence of new forms of negotiation and participation reflects great ambitions and a remarkably rapid improvement in competencies (Nagy, 1993).

At the same time, various administrative and structural reform proposals caused some fears in the profession, and political campaigns resulted in anxieties. Short-term problems caused conflicts, such as the elimination of Russian as mandatory second language for the vast number of Russian-language teachers. There were also long-term conflicts, which originated in the public mistrust toward teachers, accusing them as a whole professional body of collaborating with the previous regime and "miseducating" several generations. Though these sentiments have gradually softened everywhere by now, a similar mistrust by teachers and parents toward political power of any kind seems to prevail more stubbornly.

Another legacy of the former centralized and rather monolithic political system is a tendency of "overpoliticization," which refers to the phenomenon that every issue affecting the working conditions and lives of teachers is expressed in political terms. In the past only those persons who could reach the highest echelons in the political hierarchy had the possibility of having reform agendas considered. This politicization did not necessarily mean that education was always subordinated to external political purposes, but it did mean that local and professional problems could not shape the system unless they were redefined as central political necessities.[4] The new political context means that grassroots movements and actors able to capture public support have the potential to affect educational policy making. Movements and actors have two primary sets of objectives: promoting their objectives and preserving, or even enhancing, their ability to influence the system. Teachers, who fulfill a driving need to mobilize membership or support, remain in a position to govern or affect policy making. As significant as these impulses are in established participatory governments, they are even more profound in a period of political transformation that is characterized by economic crises, a general loss of legitimacy of political institutions, and new and emerging political groups.

Actors attempting to affect educational policy making will have various strategies from which to choose, options depending on where the actors are positioned in the system. That is, they have a choice of (a) pursuing a national versus regional or local focus, (b) playing an insider or outsider role in policy-making arenas (e.g., as a member of a decision-making body or grassroots advocate), and (c) focusing on single or multiple policy spheres (i.e., exclusively educational or many policy areas). In the case of teachers, efforts to influence educational policy have come in three primary forms, each representing a different profile with respect to these three choices: the establishment of unions, direct political representation, and professional associations designed to affect the development of a particular field of education or curriculum.

Teachers' unions usually have a national purview but limited access to policy making, considering the efforts of the government and the political parties to limit the reform at the legislative level. As the first wave of advocacy groups, teachers' unions must forge new ground in designing and developing organizational capabilities in a period of resource shortage. Teachers' unions may represent their constituency in collective bargaining on issues such as wage levels and working conditions, or can become agents of change, asserting a new identity for their constituency, that of representing the interests of the profession in major reforms and advocating for greater access to the field of educational policy making in general.

As mentioned earlier, some of the unions existed in another form under the previous regime and are now struggling to assert a new identity, that of representing the popular interests of the profession. In the interest of survival, the unions are acutely interested in appearing to be big players. This motivation is supported by the increased politicization of education and by the previously mentioned public mistrust that has clearly political origins. As Damjanova (1990, p. 8) describes the situation in Bulgaria: "Sometimes I got the feeling that by practicing democracy we only mean strikes, since only this April there were 700 strikes and most of them were organized by teacher unions."

In Hungary, in contrast, where pluralization of teachers' unions, and the establishment of forums for interest negotiation began to take place somewhat earlier, there has been no teachers' strike on a national level so far. Strike threats, however, are sometimes used in negotiations. New rivals of the old teachers' unions, like the Democratic Union of Pedagogues (DUP), established in 1988 in Hungary, broaden their scales of activities, and learn new techniques of union activities and image making. The DUP is oriented not merely toward workplace issues, but toward promoting the increased role of teachers in affecting directly the spectrum of educational issues. Even before the DUP, and before 1989, the pedagogic branch of the Solidarity Union was in the forefront of the struggle against the Communist regime. Its political strategy, however, was so predominantly focused on this ideological opposition, that it seemed to be even "conservative" in terms of educational reform. The difference between the strategy of the DUP and the Solidarity was that, while the DUP was successfully politicizing the edu-cational agenda, the Solidarity was politicizing the teachers (see Darvas 1991).

In addition to reformulated trade unions, at the national level we find professional educator associations advocating greater access to the field of educational policy making in general. They usually are specialized to specific subjects, school type or school level and try to take on the activity of creating a new expertise for transforming society. They have national focus but single or at least specified policy spheres, and being the representation of newly defined professional identities, have insecure, unestablished access to policy-making arenas. Their principal aim is to increase their influence in determining standards for the profession and to develop new channels for effecting public policies and administrative practice related to teacher training and recruitment.

Educational professionals are also creating permanent local structures as well as transitory opportunities to affect special areas of policy making through the formation of local chambers, or councils, and the organization of conferences, forums, and lobbying organizations. Through alliances with experts and other political actors and representatives of other public or professional interests, educators can attempt to affect curricular issues, procedures for nominating local admin- istrators, and the like. The immediate focus is less on the maintenance of the organizing unit *per se*, than on influencing decisions on a particular issue.

Teachers also appear as individual actors in local and regional or central educational policy spheres, either by running candidates for office or lobbying for the appointment of individuals sympathetic to their views.

Concluding Remarks

The responses and initiatives of teachers to the dramatic political changes are obviously quite complex. To some extent we might understand these metaphorically as part of an unpredictable game between traditional actors, such as the Ministries of Education and experts, and new, emerging actors, such as professional associations and lay participants. The obstacles to real change can be identified as economic conditions, social apathy, historical realities, and the lack of articulated needs and values, as well as other practical considerations.

Furthermore, there are several dimensions of differences between individual countries in the region: the degree of openness for the formation of political parties and associations; the degree to which political platforms are structured along party dimensions; the degree of autonomy practiced by teachers, whether through associations or practices in the schools; the degree of interest of lay people in participating in education; and the extent to which educational reform focuses on direct change in educational policy and practice (e.g., revision of curriculum) versus liberating access to the policy-making process itself.

For CEE teachers this period is not only about democratization and openness. Teachers are, at the same time, trying to find the way back to their own traditions from which they had been separated by direct political and bureaucratic interventions. They also have to reflect upon their experience of the last forty years. Furthermore, they have to adapt themselves to a developed world that, since World War II, went through a process of convergence. They need to do so in the midst of a process of European integration that has somewhat been slowed down, partly by the collapse of the state-socialist regimes in CEE.

NOTES

1. In this chapter we refer to the "Western" and "West" as a simple distinction between the region that is the subject of our analysis, and the countries that belong to the so called "developed world" and are commonly referred to as such in CEE. We understand that there is a serious simplification in these categories, however, and we do not intend to analyze the "West" in depth or to look at its internal differences.

2. This traditional German model of education, of course, had an enormous influence on the development of modern educational systems in general. The influence of the Prussian model of education on the modern urban educational system in the United States at the end of the nineteenth century, for instance, is traced by Tyack (1974) in his book *The One Best System*.

3. Such concerns among teachers have also been documented in non-CEE nations, such as England, India, and the United States (see Ginsburg, Meyenn, and Miller 1980; Ginsburg and Chaturvedi 1988; Ginsburg et al. 1988).

4. As Darvas (1991) has noted, educational institutions and professional associations served as "transmission belts," an expression used by the official communist-controlled press in conveying from the State to the classroom the requirements and expectations of the governing regime. Teachers had to subsume their pedagogical values to state-mandated ones. There was a lack of professional autonomy in a system where ideological criteria, established in central organs, determined the selection and promotion of teachers, curricular content, and classroom practice. There were few rewards and potential penalties for teachers and students who exhibited behavior not officially sanctioned.

REFERENCES

Bathory, Z. (1990). "Negy Tetel a Magyar Pedagogia Megujitasahoz" ("Four Studies to Renew the Hungarian Pedagogy"). *Kozneveles (Public Education)* 19: 9–10.

———. (1993). "A National Core Curriculum and the Democratisation of Public Education in Hungary." *Curriculum Studies* 1 (1): 91–104.

Broadfoot, P. (1990). "Research on Teachers: Toward a Comparative Methodology." *Comparative Education* 26(2/3):165–169.

Broadfoot P., and Osborn, M. (1988). "What Professional Responsibility Means to Teachers." *British Journal of Sociology* 88 (3): 265–289.

Broadfoot, P., Osborn, M., Gilly, M., and Paillet, A. (1987). "Teachers' Conceptions of Their Professional Responsibility: Some International Comparisons. *Comparative Education* 23 (3): 287–301.

Damjanova, K. (1990). "Interview with the Head of Department of the Bulgarian Teachers Union." *Public Education* 21: 8.

Darvas, P. (1991). "Perspectives of Educational Reform in Hungary." In *Understanding Educational Reform in Global Context*, edited by M. Ginsburg, pp. 229–256. New York: Garland.

———. (1992). "Hungary." In *Labor Relations in Education: An International Perspective*, edited by B. S. Cooper, pp. 137–156. Westport, CT: Greenwood Press.

Garrett. R., and Jimenez, M. (1992). "A Comparison of Spanish and English Teachers' Views of Problem Solving." *Comparative Education* 28 (3): 269–279.

Gershunsky, B., and Pullin, T. (1990). "Current Dilemmas for Soviet Secondary Education: An Anglo-Soviet Analysis." *Comparative Education* 23 (3): 307–317.

Ginsburg, M., and Chaturvedi, V. (1988). "Teachers and the Ideology of Professionalism in India and England: A Comparison of Case Studies in Colonial/Peripheral and Metropolitan/Central Societies." *Comparative Education Review* 32:465–477.

Ginsburg, M., Meyenn, R., Khanna, I., Miller, H., and Spatig, L. (1988). "El Concepto de Profesionalismo en el Profesorado: Comparacion de Contextos Entre Inglaterra y Estados Unidos" ("Teachers' Conceptions of Professionalism: A Comparison of Contexts in England and the United States"). *Revista de Educacion* 285(enero–abril): 5–31.

Ginsburg, M., Meyenn, R., and Miller, M. (1980). "Teachers Conceptions of Professionalism and Trades Unionism: An Ideological Analysis." In *Teacher Strategies*, edited by P. Woods, pp. 178–212. London: Croom Helm.

Holye, E. (1980). "Professionalization and Deprofessionalization in Education." In *Professional Development of Teachers*, edited by E. Hoyle and J. Megarry, pp. 42–54. London: Kogan-Paige.

Lortie, D. (1975). *Schoolteacher: A Sociological Analysis*. Chicago: University of Chicago Press.

Medvegy, A. (1990). "Az oktatasugy es a pedagogus-kozvelemeny" ("Education and Teachers Opinion"). *Kozneveles (Public Education)* 17: 8.

Nagy, M. (1985). "Command for Autonomy." Unpublished manuscript. Budapest.

———. (1993). "Szakmai szervezodesek, erdekervenyesites" ("Professional associations and interest-negotiations of teachers"). *Edukacio* 2 (4): 639–650.

Pachocinski, R. (1993). "Current Curriculum Changes in Poland: A National Report." *Curriculum Studies* 1 (2): 215–232.

Poppleton, P. (1990). "Work Perceptions of Secondary School Teachers: International Comparisons" (special double number). *Comparative Education* 26 (2/3).

Poppleton, P., Deas, R., Pullin, R., and Thompson, D. (1987). "The Experience of Teaching in 'Disadvantaged' Areas in the United Kingdom and the USA." *Comparative Education* 23 (3): 303–331.

Schmidt, G., and Schultz, D. (1990). "Zur Situation des Lehrers in Beiden Deutschen Staaten: Stand und Perspektiven." *Bildung und Erziehung* 43 (l): 57–78.

Szebenyi, P. (1992). "Change in the Systems of Public Education in East Central Europe." *Comparative Education* 28 (1): 19–31.

Tyack, D. (1974). *The One Best System: A History of American Urban Education.* Cambridge, MA: Harvard University Press.

Wisniewski, C. (1990). "The Job Satisfaction of Teachers in Poland." *Comparative Education* 26 (2/3): 299–305.

Professors and Politics: An International Perspective

Philip G. Altbach

Colleges and universities are seen to be bastions of truth and knowledge, seemingly immune to politics and contention. This is the idealized fiction of higher education. The fact is that universities are highly politicized institutions, full of dispute and contention. Further, key components of the academy—faculty and students—are frequently involved in politics, on campus and off. Indeed, politics is an integral part not only of the governance of academic institutions but of the creation and dissemination of knowledge. This chapter is about one element in the politics of higher education, the activism and political involvement of the academic profession.

Professors as Political Activists

Professors are an extraordinarily important group in every society. Through their work they shape one of the most important institutions in modern societies—the university. They determine, for the most part, the curriculum, degree requirements, admissions standards, and the like. The academic profession also constitutes probably the largest single group of highly educated people in the society, and many intellectuals gravitate to university faculties. While the professoriate is seldom in the economic elite of a country, it is in the social and prestigious elite. Professors are influential through their teaching and through their academic research and writing. They may also be more directly involved in politics and in the intellectual life of the nation. It is this extra-academic activity with which this chapter is concerned.

The politics of the academic community has had a remarkable impact on society. Student activism on occasion has toppled governments and has frequently caused disruption and focused attention on political matters of concern to the students (Altbach 1989). Faculty activism has in general been more indirect, expressing itself through professorial writings and utterances. At times, however, professors have organized themselves for political purposes as well, but these have been fairly unusual occasions. The academic profession has been politically involved through a wide range of activities, including running for public office, serving in advisory capacities to political leaders, providing expertise on issues of political importance, involvement in oppositional movements and organizations, writing for newspapers and magazines, appearing on television, and a variety of other activities. Professors are also sometimes involved in politics at the local or regional levels as well as nationally. This activity goes back many centuries. Students and faculty are uniquely able to express ideas, and the activism of the academic community is very often the activism of ideas and ideologies. Ideas are at the center of the academic enterprise, and are very often characteristics of academic activism. For the most part, the academic community deals with ideas and concepts within the confines of the academic disciplines, relating them to teaching and research. On occasion, however, these concerns spill over into the realm of society and politics. Academic activism frequently takes the direction of expressing ideas and shaping debate on a topic. This is often done through publication, both in scholarly journals and books, and sometimes to a broader audience. It can also be achieved through speaking and increasingly through the mass media. Activism sometimes expresses itself through demonstrations and agitation.

The impact on society of academic activism can be considerable. University-based intellectuals very often frame the discussion on topics of public importance, from the environment to medical ethics. The role of campus activists in framing the debate on issues in the early stage of debate is of special importance. The opinion pages of major newspapers in many countries are filled with articles by professors on topics of emerging societal importance and debate.

Direct action can be of special importance in focusing public attention on societal issues. In the United States, debate and then activism concerning the Vietnam war emerged from the campuses, and later became a matter of public concern, eventually convincing a President not to seek another term (Gitlin 1988). Students were most directly involved, but many professors were also engaged in writing, teaching, and providing moral support to student activists. Concerned professors were a key cadre in the antiwar movement, not often on the barricades but nonetheless involved. It should be noted that even on campuses with the most ferment, only a minority of the community is generally politically engaged, but this minority is of special importance, not only because of its involvement but because it frequently represents a wider section of the campus community, and it sometimes also reflects wider social concern.

The university, in almost every society, is a kind of sanctuary where individuals have more freedom (and usually more leisure) to reflect on ideas—including political ideas. Even in societies that are repressive and authoritarian, the campus still offers somewhat more freedom. Governmental authorities sometimes shut academic institutions entirely to root out. political activism. Because of their tradition of freedom of teaching and expression, universities are able to harbor dissident ideas and people more easily than other institutions. The tradition of academic freedom and autonomy, however vitiated in practice, is nonetheless a powerful idea that has an impact on both society and the academic community.

It would be a mistake, of course, to assume the campuses are seething with agitation and political concern. This is not the case, except in very unusual circumstances. In general, the academic community is engaged in the normal pattern of teaching and research, which as noted, can be analyzed as forms of political activity. Nonetheless, ideas of social importance are

constantly percolating in the universities and from time to time
these take on a broader societal importance. It is at this
intersection of ideas and political debate and practice that
campus activism enters.

The Impact of Activism

Campus-based activism may affect society as well as the
university itself. The societal impact, particularly of the academic
profession, is often subtle and indirect. It has most to do with
ideas and expertise. The role of the "academic as expert" and the
political sphere are sometimes related. Publications with
significant participation from academics frequently have an
impact on society. In the United States, journals like *Foreign
Affairs*, the *Bulletin of the Atomic Scientists*, *Commentary*, and *The
Public Interest* are examples of publications that focus on public
policy issues, which have limited circulations, but which are
taken seriously by elites and have had an impact on policy and
politics. In Britain, *New Statesman and Society* and *Granta* play a
similar role. Japan's *Sekai* and *Bungei Shingu* and the (former)
Soviet Union's *Literary Gazette* are other examples. *Science* in the
United States and *Nature* in Britain not only provide analysis of
scientific developments, but are influential in debates about
scientific policy. In these publications, new ideas, stemming
frequently from the universities, are expressed. They sometimes
receive wider attention and sometimes do not.

Academics also write for wider circulation publications. In
some countries, Britain and Japan among the more prominent,
academics frequently appear on television to discuss their ideas
and interpret events. Op-ed pages of newspapers worldwide are
filled with the writings of professors—analyses of contemporary
issues, often based on research findings. Academics, because of
their access to data and often their connections with the media,
are able to place their ideas before both the public and policy
makers. The ideas and interpretations from the campuses may
quickly be brought into the mainstream of societal thinking. It is
also sometimes the case that publication in scholarly journals
may have an impact on society. In the United States, the *New*

England Journal of Medicine has an impact not only on medical research and practice but also on policy discussions relating to health. Professorial publication of this kind represents a link between the role of "professor as expert" and "professor as politician." In virtually every society, regardless of the level of freedom of expression or complexity of the media system, the academic community is expected to play a role in the generation of ideas and in reflecting on public issues. It is clear that the ideas expressed by professors have consequences that go far beyond the classroom. The professor, even serving as an "expert," may have significant influence on policy and politics.

The academic community is also indirectly involved in government. This involvement takes place in a variety of contexts, and again reflects the linked roles of expert and politician. Most professors, even when relating to controversial matters of public policy, see themselves as experts, providing information and research-based analysis rather than directly participating in political disputations. The role of "professor as expert/politician" has a very long history. Professors at the University of Paris, in the medieval period, provided the expertise that solved one of the most volatile political disputes of the day—the division of the Papacy between Avignon and Rome (Haskins 1965). The theological ideas coming from the academic community during the Reformation had a profound influence on religious thinking—and had direct influence on the politics of Europe, on the rift between Roman Catholics and Protestants, and on the bitter conflicts that this split engendered. Martin Luther, it should be remembered, was a professor of Scripture and theology.

German scholars in the nineteenth century not only assisted the development of Germany through their scientific research but also through their advice to the government on a range of subjects (Ben-David and Zloczower 1962). It was in newly unified Germany after 1872 that the idea of the "professor as expert" became an important part of the academy. Two other rapidly developing countries, the United States and Japan, found the German academic model appealing and the idea of linking the universities to national development was adopted in both countries (Nakayama 1989). In the United States, professors have a long tradition of providing expertise to governmental agencies. For example, the faculty at the University of Wisconsin played a key role in framing the progressive social legislation that shaped the state's social policies early in the twentieth century (Curti and Carstensen 1949). From the late nineteenth century to the present, academics have been providing their expertise to the government on many issues and in different contexts (Veysey 1965). Indeed, the emergence of professional associations in the social sciences was stimulated in part by a desire of the professors to play a prominent role as experts in public policy making (Silva and Slaughter 1984).

Professors are not only experts, they are sometimes direct participants in government. At the least important, but probably the most common level, professors are frequently appointed to commissions and committees set up to advise governments or to solve specific problems. These appointments are made to take advantage of professorial expertise and to utilize the skills of qualified individuals who are not directly involved in an issue. The professor, in his or her role as "expert," is also often appointed to government posts that require high levels of expertise. For example, in the United States, the President's science advisor, the chair of the Council of Economic Advisors, and other senior posts of this sort, are typically filled by professors. The architect of the deregulation of America's airlines was a professor who served as head of the Federal Aviation Administration. Henry Kissinger, foreign policy advisor and later Secretary of State, and William Bennett, Secretary of Education in the Reagan Administration, were appointed in part because of their specific expertise but gained wider political influence. Many Western European countries frequently use professors for policy-making positions in government.

Other countries make similar use of academics in policy-making positions. The Indonesian economy, for example, was restructured by a group of U.S.-trained academics, commonly referred to as the "Berkeley Mafia," who were appointed to policy positions in the government. Nicaragua's Sandinista government had a former professor as Minister of Foreign Affairs, and other academics also served in powerful positions. It is common in Third World countries for professors to serve in government positions, even as presidents or prime ministers, in part because the pool of highly educated people is small, and many of the intellectual elite naturally find jobs in higher education, and find that their careers take them in and out of the government.

Professors sometimes take a direct role in electoral politics. In a relatively small number of cases, professors have become presidents or prime ministers. Several of Italy's postwar premiers have been professors, and academics have served in many senior ministerial positions. Professors have also served as presidents or prime ministers in other countries, including the United States, Thailand, Benin, Greece, Czechoslovakia, Portugal, Taiwan, Britain, and Canada. Academics serve in significant numbers in many legislatures or parliaments. Several U.S. senators and representatives have been academics and a large number of parliamentarians in France and Italy are professors. In some instances, faculty members must resign their academic positions when they enter politics, while in others they can fulfill both roles.

Professors can also provide political leadership locally. It is generally the case that the academic profession has a high level of social prestige—academics are respected and admired in their societies. Most sociological studies of prestige place professors near the top of the rankings. They often have influence on local affairs. In developing countries, professors are often asked their opinions on a variety of issues. In most societies, their involvement in a range of civic functions is welcome and their views are taken seriously. Local involvement may directly concern electoral politics, but more often it consists of providing expertise and judgement on a variety of issues. In this respect, social prestige and respect are combined with expertise.

It has been said that intellectuals are permanently in opposition to any established authority, and the academic profession is, for the most part, part of the intelligentsia (Shils 1972). There is an interesting contradiction here. It is true that many professors have positioned themselves in general opposition to established authority, but overt professorial political activism is rare. Many professors feel themselves to be part of an oppositional intelligentsia, but these scholars are concentrated in the humanities and social sciences (Ladd and Lipset 1975). Faculty members in such fields as management studies, agriculture, and to some extent in the natural and biomedical sciences do not, generally, share this oppositional mentality. There are also significant national variations (Basu 1981). While an important minority of professors see themselves as an oppositional intelligentsia, most faculty are politically uninvolved. It is quite unusual, although by no means unprecedented, for professors to become active in radical or revolutionary politics.

Professors, on some occasions, have been involved in direct oppositional political activism. Professors are more often involved in oppositional politics through their writings and teaching rather than through direct action. There are, nonetheless, examples of direct professorial involvement in oppositional politics. Professors were instrumental in the nationalist movements of 1848 in Europe and they formed a significant number of the members of the nationalist parliament that was dubbed the "Professors' Parliament" (Namier 1964). They not only stimulated students (who were also deeply involved in the movement) through their teachings but also became directly engaged in politics. Significant numbers of academics were involved in antiwar movements on several occasions—in England prior to World War II and later in the United States during the period of opposition to the Vietnam War in the 1960s and early 1970s.

In a few instances, professors have been involved in revolutionary movements in the Third World. In Peru, for example, the now-imprisoned top leader of the of the ultraradical revolutionary group, *Sendero Luminiso*, was a professor. More often, professors have been involved in more moderate movements for civil liberties and social reforms. American professors were instrumental in the early oppositional movements to the Vietnam War—they organized teach-ins and other intellectual activities. When the antiwar movement turned more militant in a later stage, many academics withdrew. A significant number of the architects of the "velvet revolutions" in Central and Eastern Europe were academics. In such countries as Poland, Czechoslovakia (where a number of the liberal Charter of 77 signatories were academics), Hungary, and Rumania, professors provided intellectual leadership and were then prominent in the new post-Communist governments. In China, Fang Lizhi, a professor of astrophysics, is one of the most prominent spokespersons for democratization.

Occasionally, when professors are involved in political activism, they lose their jobs or are jailed. This has happened, for example, in Burma in 1988, in Argentina and Chile (where a significant number of academics were imprisoned and many others were forced into exile in the aftermath of the military takeovers of the 1960s) and at different times in Eastern Europe. Governments, particularly in the Third World, take professorial activism very seriously because they feel that the academics have the potential to provide leadership to broader-based oppositional movements.

The professoriate has also had an impact on the university through its activism. This opposition can take place within the established processes of governance, through, for example, organizing groups within the professoriate in order to influence votes in academic bodies. Such internal organization efforts can significantly bring conflict out in the open in the academic community. On rare occasions, activist professors may go outside of the governance structures altogether in order to influence policy. They may go on strike, for example, to enforce their views. They may organize professorial labor unions. They may directly appeal to the public or to governmental bodies. On very rare occasions, political parties may become involved in campus affairs among the academic staff—this has been the case in India in recent years (Chitnis and Altbach 1979). In the aftermath of the 1960s, reforms in the West German universities, elections to faculty and administrative posts became highly politicized, with groups of professors, academic staff, and students supporting political factions (Hennis 1982). The debate in the United States concerning "political correctness" and multiculturalism in the curriculum is, in considerable degree, an intellectual conflict among sections of an ideologically divided academic profession (Berman 1992).

The concerns of academic activists vary quite a bit. In some contexts, they have sought to form academic labor unions for ideological reasons or to ensure higher professorial salaries or better conditions. Academic activists may wish to change university policies—to provide better assurance of tenure or to force the university out of certain kind of research. They may wish to protect academic freedom from either external threat or sometimes internal violations. Academic activists have on occasion pressed the university to change its orientation—to focus more attention on research or to reform the curriculum.

Perspectives on Faculty Activism

Professorial activism is more subtle and less dramatic than student activism. It includes involvement in political affairs from many different perspectives—from providing expertise to the government and commentary on current affairs in the mass media to direct involvement in oppositional politics on and off of the campus. The vast majority of professors are not involved in public forms of political activism of any sort; instead they limit their political involvement to what they do as teachers and researchers. While research on professorial activism in particular and on the academic profession generally is very limited, it is possible to provide some generalizations concerning the phenomenon (Altbach 1991).

Gouldner (1957) divided the academic profession into *cosmopolitans*, those who look mainly to their disciplines and to the wider world of scholarship, and the *locals*, whose links are mostly to their home academic institution. It is useful to examine professorial activism from this perspective as well. The most visible professorial activists are cosmopolitans. These professors tend to be at the top of their disciplines, on the staff of the prestigious universities, and most involved in research. They have reputations and visibility that permit them to function outside of their home institutions. They are called on to provide expertise and they have the contacts in the media and elsewhere to project their voices to a wider audience. Faculty members with a local orientation seldom are engaged in activism outside of their own institutions, and their reputations seldom spread beyond their campus. Local academics probably have less propensity to be involved with societal activism, regardless of academic discipline, although as Gouldner (1957) pointed out, these individuals provide the backbone of the campus governance process and serve on university committees and the like. Local academics constitute a majority in their universities, and some of them are heavily engaged in campus-based activism, serving not only on academic committees but also providing the leadership for campus unions and other faculty pressure groups. During periods of campus turmoil and crisis, however, cosmopolitan academics may also become involved with local issues.

Activist "experts" can be found in most disciplines but predominate in fields that have relevance to public policy, such as, in recent years, environmental science, nuclear physics, and many others. Crises in China will bring relevant professorial experts to the mass media and to the attention of governmental leaders. A nuclear accident will also require relevant professorial expertise and commentary. Professors of classics or analytic philosophy are less likely to be called on for their expertise, although even in these cases there are examples of "public expertise." Philosophers Sidney Hook and Paul Kurtz in the United States have been frequent participants in public debates, bringing their philosophical perspectives to debates on public policy issues. Recently, issues in medical ethics have involved experts from philosophy, law and other fields, as well as from the medical sciences. With the growing concern about educational quality and standards, professors of education have again become embroiled in public debates concerning the future of the schools, and have been joined by sociologists and political scientists. At their best, academic experts focus both research data and analytic insights on issues of public concern.

Academic activists who are involved in "unofficial" activism or even in criticism of established institutions or policies are more controversial. They, too, are mostly cosmopolitans who have access to the media and have a claim to expertise in their fields. They are generally senior scholars at key universities. They have the self-confidence to speak out on issues and security of tenure and reputation. Such "critical academics" disproportionately come from the social sciences and, to some extent, from other policy-relevant disciplines. They often have some political experience as well, frequently as alumni of student political movements. Critical academics are often more ideologically oriented than their compeers and tend to have a broader political perspective on society and government. They are often to the left of the political spectrum in their societies. Few seem to be directly involved with political parties in any activist sense. Critical academics are a small proportion of the professoriate but they are often among the most visible. They speak out in the mass media, sign letters of protest in newspapers, and are occasionally arrested for their activities. Generally, however, critical academics, unlike student activists, work within the confines of accepted political discourse in their countries. They are seldom willing to expose themselves to possible political sanctions.

Professorial activism, like its student counterpart, is very much a minority phenomenon. The socialization process of academics in most countries emphasizes detached scholarship and teaching, not public forms of political activism. For junior staff, there are frequently sanctions against involvement in politics, particularly critical activism. In some countries, the professoriate is seen as a very important group and is watched closely. Yet, academics, particularly in the senior ranks, have high prestige and job security. The tradition of academic freedom also provides some procedural protections and also an ideology that supports speaking out on issues. The traditions and structures of the academic profession and of contemporary universities present some contradictory pulls and pushes in terms of professorial activism. Cosmopolitan academics, however, are increasingly pulled into the mainstream of debate on important societal issues because of their expertise. The universities are increasingly the repositories of knowledge and expertise on most topics affecting society, and the professoriate, especially those senior academics at the major universities, have become a kind of mandarin of expertise.

Conclusion

Campus activism has a long tradition. It has also become an even more important phenomenon in the post World War II period, as universities have expanded and become more central institutions in their societies. Campus-based activism has had significant effects on society and on the university, and it will continue to do so. Student political movements have toppled regimes, created political crises, and have pointed to major social issues. Student activists have frequently been the "conscience of their generation," speaking for significant segments of the population.

Professorial activism is a more complex phenomenon. The role of the academic as expert has grown increasingly important. Academics also play a key role as social commentators and critics, helping to shape discourse on important topics. Academics occasionally play a direct role in politics, sometimes serving in government and sometimes in oppositional roles.

Because of the nature of the academic community, activism will continue to be an important phenomenon. As knowledge and expertise become increasingly central to contemporary societies, those involved in its creation and transmission, largely students and faculty in universities, will inevitably play a key societal role. For the most part, that role is limited to the direct concerns of higher education, but in important ways the academic community is affected by and sometimes influences the wider society. Activism, by both students and professors, is inherent in the nature of the academic community. The combination of academic freedom and relative autonomy in universities, the role of ideas (and sometimes of idealism) in higher education, the power of the expertise of the universities, the relative ease of organizing campus-based activism, and the increasingly central role of the academic community means that academic activism will continue to be a powerful force.

REFERENCES

Altbach, P. G. (Ed.). (1977). *Comparative Perspectives on the Academic Profession*. New York: Praeger.

———. (Ed.). (1989). *Student Political Activism: An International Reference Handbook*. Westport, CT: Greenwood.

———. (1991). "The Academic Profession." In *International Higher Education: An Encyclopedia*, edited by P. G. Altbach, pp. 23–46. New York: Garland.

Baldwin, J. W., and Goldthwaite, R. A. (Eds.). (1972). *Universities in Politics: Case Studies from the Late Middle Ages and Early Modern Period*. Baltimore, MD: Johns Hopkins University Press.

Basu, A. (1981). *Culture, Politics and Critical Academics*. Meerut, India: Archana.

Ben-David, J., and Zloczower, A. (1962). "Universities and Academic Systems in Modern Societies." *European Journal of Sociology* 3:45–84.

Berman, P. (Ed.). (1992). *Debating PC: The Controversy Over Political Correctness on College Campuses*. New York: Dell.

Chitnis, S., and Altbach, P. G. (Eds.). (1979). *The Indian Academic Profession*. New Delhi: Macmillan.

Clark, B. R. (Ed.). (1987). *The Academic Profession: National, Disciplinary, and Institutional Settings*. Berkeley: University of California Press.

Curti, M., and Carstensen, V. (1949). *The University of Wisconsin: A History, 1848–1925*. Madison: University of Wisconsin Press.

Gitlin, T. (1988). *The Sixties: Years of Struggle, Days of Rage*. New York: Bantam.

Gouldner, A. (1957). "Cosmopolitans and Locals—I." *Administrative Science Quarterly* 2: 281–306.

Halsey, A. H. (1992). *The Decline of Donnish Dominion: The British Academic Profession in the Twentieth Century*. Oxford: Clarendon Press.

Haskins, C. (1965). *The Rise of Universities*. Ithaca, NY: Cornell University Press,

Hennis, W. (1982). "Germany: Legislators and the Universities." In *Universities, Politicians and Bureaucrats: Europe and the United States*, edited by H. Daalder and E. Shils, pp. 1–30. Cambridge: Cambridge University Press.

Horowitz, H. L. (1987). *Campus Life: Undergraduate Cultures from the End of the Eighteenth Century to the Present.* Chicago: University of Chicago Press.

Ladd, E. C., Jr., and Lipset, S. M. (1975). *The Divided Academy: Professors and Politics.* New York: McGraw-Hill.

Namier, Louis. (1964). *1848: The Revolution of the Intellectuals.* New York: Oxford University Press.

Nakayama, S. (1989). "Independence and Choice: Western Impacts on Japanese Higher Education." In *From Dependence to Autonomy: The Development of Asian Universities,* edited by P. G. Altbach and V. Selvaratnam, pp. 97–116. Dordrecht, Netherlands: Kluwer.

Shils, E. (1972). *The Intellectuals and the Powers and Other Essays.* Chicago: University of Chicago Press.

Silva, E., and Slaughter, S. (1984). *Serving Power: The Making of the Academic Social Science Expert.* Westport, CT: Greenwood.

Veysey, L. (1965). *The Emergence of the American University.* Chicago: University of Chicago Press.

Walter, R. (1968). *Student Politics in Argentina: The University Reform and Its Effects, 1918–1964.* New York: Basic Books.

Contributors

Philip G. Altbach is professor and director of the Comparative Education Center, State University of New York at Buffalo and Senior Associate of the Carnegie Foundation for the Advancement of Teaching. He is editor of *International Higher Education: An Encyclopedia* and *Perspectives on the Academic Profession*, and author of *The Knowledge Context, Higher Education in the Third World*, and other books.

Richard J. Altenbaugh, a faculty member at Slippery Rock University (Pennsylvania), has taught American Educational History and U.S. Social History at Indiana University, the University of Louisville, the University of Pittsburgh, and Northern Illinois University. He has written *Education for Struggle: The American Labor Colleges of the 1920s and 1930s* (1990) and edited *The Teacher's Voice: A Social History of Teaching in Twentieth-Century America* (1992). He is currently editing the *Historical Dictionary of American Education.*

Robert W. Connell is professor of sociology at the University of California at Santa Cruz. Books he has authored or coauthored include: *Making the Difference: Schools, Families and Social Division* (1982), *Teachers' Work* (1985), *Gender and Power: Society, the Person and Sexual Politics* (1987), *Staking a Claim: Feminism, Bureaucracy and the State* (1989), *Running Twice as Hard: Disadvantaged Schools Programs in Australia* (1991), and *Schools and Social Justice* (1993).

Peter Darvas is a Spencer Fellow at New York University, doing research on the state and higher education in Hungary. He is on leave from the Hungarian Institute for Educational Research. His scholarship in the fields of comparative education and higher education focuses primarily on dynamics of educational reform in Central and Eastern Europe.

Linda A. Dove is a Senior Evaluation Officer in the Operations Evaluation Department of the World Bank. Until recently she worked in the World Bank's operational department in education project design and supervision in Asia, the Middle East, North Africa, and Europe. Books she has authored include *Lifelong Teachers Education and the Community School* (1982) and *Teachers and Teacher Education in Developing Countries: Issues in Planning, Management and Training* (1986).

Mark B. Ginsburg is professor in the departments of Administrative and Policy Studies and Sociology at the University of Pittsburgh (Pennsylvania). His research and teaching focus on the relationships between education and class, gender, racial, and international inequalities; the work and political action of educators; and the occupational and political socialization of teachers. He authored *Contradictions in Teacher Education and Society* (1988) and edited *Understanding Educational Reform in Global Context: Economy, Ideology, and the State* (1991). He is currently collaborating with Beverly Lindsay in editing *The Political Dimension in Teacher Education: Policy Formation, Political Socialization, and Society*.

Madeleine R. Grumet is professor and dean of the School of Education at Brooklyn College of the City University of New York. She is editor of the series on feminist theory and education for SUNY Press and author of the book, *Bitter Milk: Women and Teaching* (1988).

Sangeeta Kamat is a doctoral student in the Social and Comparative Analysis in Education program area at the University of Pittsburgh. Her dissertation, *(Re)presenting Development: Histories of Domination and Struggle in Tribal Development Work*, examines issues of power, knowledge, and discourse in the relations between professionals/intellectuals and subaltern groups in educational and other social change processes.

Martin Lawn is a reader in education at Westhill College in Birmingham, England. His research is focused on the oral history of teachers' work, the sociology of the labor process, and the politics of curriculum change. He is the author or coauthor of the following books: *Teachers, Professionalism and Class* (1981) and *Servants of the State—the Contested Control of Teaching 1900–1930* (1988). Edited or coedited volumes include: *Politics of Teacher Unionism: International Perspectives* (1985) and *Teachers: The Culture and Politics of Work* (1987).

Maria Nagy is a research fellow at the National Institute of Public Education. Her publications focus on educational policy, administration, teachers, and curriculum.

Rajeshwari Raghu completed her doctorate in the Social and Comparative Analysis in Education program area at the University of Pittsburgh. Her dissertation, *Development of Teachers as Political Actors in a Private German University: How Teachers Anticipate Their Contribution to Preserving/Transforming Gender Relations*, explores the political socialization experiences of prospective teachers.

Carlos Alberto Torres is an associate professor and assistant dean for student affairs in the Graduate School of Education and Coordinator of Comparative and Topical Programs in the Center for Latin American Studies at the University of California-Los Angeles. His research interest is on Latin American education policy and planning, political sociology of education, theories of the state and education, and the works of Paulo Freire and liberation pedagogy. He is editor, author, and coauthor of nineteen books, including *The Church, Society and Hegemony* (1992) and *Social Theory and Education: A Critique of Theories of Social and Cultural Reproduction* (in press).

John Weaver is a doctoral student in the Social and Comparative Analysis in Education program area at the University of

Pittsburgh. His dissertation, *Academic Politics: The Case of Former East German Historians and the Restructuring of the University System in Reunited Germany*, examines knowledge/power in the processes of evaluating faculty "competence" in higher education institutions in the German Democratic Republic and, subsequently, during the transition to a (re)unified Germany.

Subject Index

Author Index